CASES IN MANAGEMENT ACCOUNTING AND BUSINESS FINANCE

Second Edition

Cases in Management Accounting and Business Finance

Second Edition

Edited by Noel Hyndman and Donal McKillop

Published by
Chartered Accountants Ireland
Chartered Accountants House
47–49 Pearse Street
Dublin 2
www.charteredaccountants.ie

© Chartered Accountants Ireland, 2009

Copyright of publication rests in entirety with Chartered Accountants Ireland. All rights reserved. No part of this text may be reproduced or transmitted in any form or by any means, including photocopying, Internet or e-mail dissemination, without the written permission of Chartered Accountants Ireland. Such written permission must also be obtained before any part of this document is stored in a retrieval system of any nature.

The opinions expressed in this publication are those of the author and do not necessarily represent the views of Chartered Accountants Ireland. The text is designed to provide accurate and authoritative information in regard to the subject matter covered. It is sold on the understanding that Chartered Accountants Ireland is not engaged in rendering professional services. If professional advice or other expert assistance is required, the services of a competent professional should be sought.

ISBN: 978-0-903854-74-0

First published 2006
Second edition 2009

Typeset by: Datapage
Printed by ColourBooks, Dublin, Ireland

Contents

The management accounting/ cases are presented first (Section A), followed by the cases in business finance (section B) and then by integrated management accounting/business finance cases (section C). With each case, the main topics covered are listed, with a maximum of four topic descriptors. In some instances more than four topics are covered in a case, and in these situations the four main topics are indicated. Those cases which have the solution in *Solutions to Cases in Management Accounting and Business Finance* (Second Edition) are indicated with an asterisk.

Section A: Cases in Management Accounting

No.	Case name (* indicates solution is in *Student Solutions* book)	Main topics	Author(s)	Page
1.	Beara Bay Cheese*	CVP analysis; decision making; activity-based costing	Margaret Healy, University College Cork	3
2.	Terra Inc.*	CVP analysis; decision making; balanced scorecard; kaizen costing	Tony O'Dea and Tony Brabazon, University College Dublin	11
3.	Mississippi Inc.	CVP analysis; decision making; balanced scorecard	Tony Brabazon and Tony O'Dea, University College Dublin	19
4.	EasyONline*	CVP analysis; sensitivity analysis; optimal pricing strategies	Tony Brabazon and Tony O'Dea, University College Dublin	23
5.	Varsity plc	CVP analysis; life-cycle costing; return on investment; investment appraisal	Joan Ballantine, University of Ulster	27
6.	Castlegrove Enterprises*	Absorption and variable costing income statements; decision making	Tom Kennedy, University of Limerick	33
7.	Spektrik plc	Target costing	Falconer Mitchell, University of Edinburgh	41

8.	Chicken Pieces*	Non-financial performance measures; cost allocation; CVP analysis; decision making	Peter Clarke, University College Dublin	45
9.	Horizons Group	Decision making; activity-based costing; target costing; balanced scorecard	Tony O'Dea and Tony Brabazon, University College Dublin	51
10.	Newtown Manufacturing Limited*	Activity-based costing; decision making	Tom Kennedy, University of Limerick	59
11.	Lennon Department Store Limited*	Budgeting; decision making; risk and uncertainty	Bernard Pierce and Barbara Flood, Dublin City University	67
12.	Genting Theme Park*	Performance measurement; budgeting; strategic management accounting; decision making under uncertainty	Iqbal Khadaroo, Queen's University Belfast	75
13.	Autoparts SA*	Divisional performance; compensation schemes	Tony Brabazon and Tony O'Dea, University College Dublin	79
14.	IXL Limited*	Return on investment; capital investment decisions; decision making	Joan Ballantine, University of Ulster	83
15.	Top Flite plc	Return on investment and residual income; balanced scorecard	Joan Ballantine, University of Ulster	89
16.	Choco Group*	Divisional performance measurement; transfer pricing; life-cycle costing	Iqbal Khadaroo, Queen's University Belfast	93
17.	Elveron Limited	Divisional performance; variance analysis; budgeting	Barbara Flood and Bernard Pierce, Dublin City University	97

Section B: Cases in Business Finance

No.	Case name (* indicates solution is in *Student Solutions* book)	Main topics	Author(s)	Page
18.	The Pottery Company Limited 1	Working capital management; financial evaluation of strategy	Anne Marie Ward, University of Ulster	107
19.	The Pottery Company Limited 2	Cash and profit budgets; working capital management	Anne Marie Ward, University of Ulster	115
20.	The Corner Café*	Sources of finance; cash and profit budgets; working capital management	Jill Lyttle, Queen's University Belfast	123
21.	Calvin plc*	Investment appraisal; capital structure; dividend policy	Peter Green, University of Ulster at Jordanstown	131
22.	Darling & Company: Facing Future Challenges	Investment appraisal; company valuation; takeovers	Maeve McCutcheon, University College Cork	135
23.	Sun Shine Limited*	Investment appraisal; foreign exchange risk	John Cotter, University College Dublin	141
24.	Blackwater Hotel Group plc*	Investment appraisal; cost of capital; sensitivity analysis	Peter Green, University of Ulster at Jordanstown	149
25.	Tannam plc*	Investment appraisal; cost of capital; financing decisions; diversification	Louis Murray, University College Dublin	153
26.	Salmon Spray*	Investment appraisal; cost of capital; accounting profit and DCF; sensitivity analysis	Ray Donnelly, University College Cork	163
27.	Waterlife plc*	Cost of capital; capital structure; financing decisions	Evarist Stoja, University of Bristol	169
28.	Mega Meals Limited	Risk management; interest rate swaps; foreign currency swaps	Donal McKillop, Queen's University Belfast	175

No.	Case name	Main topics	Author(s)	Page
29.	First Financial	Interest rate risk	Ronan Gallagher and Donal McKillop, Queen's University Belfast	179
30.	First National	Pensions; credit risk	Ronan Gallagher and Donal McKillop, Queen's University Belfast	183
31.	Good Eating Company plc*	Valuation of pension funds; CAPM; defined contribution and defined benefit pension schemes	John Cotter, University College Dublin	187
32.	Personal Financial Planning: Tom Smith*	Personal financial plans; personal financial objectives; net worth and net income; risk and return	Anne Marie Ward, University of Ulster	193

Section C: Integrated Cases in Management Accounting/Business Finance

No.	Case name (* indicates solution is in *Student Solutions* book)	Main topics	Author(s)	Page
33.	Bolo's Food Company	CVP analysis; sources of finance; venture capital	Maeve McCutcheon, University College Cork	201
34.	Toffer Group plc*	Absorption and marginal costing; budgeting; company valuation; dividend policy	Ciaran Connolly and Martin Kelly, Queen's University Belfast	207
35.	Glenview House Hotel*	Decision making; leasing	Margaret Healy and John Doran, University College Cork	217

36.	Delaney's Bakehouse Breads*	Decision making; activity-based costing; investment appraisal; working capital management	John Doran and Margaret Healy, University College Cork	223
37.	Jenson Car Components	Activity-based costing; target costing; company valuation	Noel Hyndman and Danielle McMahon, Queen's University Belfast	229
38.	Malvern Limited*	Budgeting; investment appraisal; working capital management	Ciaran Connolly and Martin Kelly, Queen's University Belfast	239
39.	Bolt Industries	Budgeting and standard costing; decision making under uncertainty; foreign exchange risk	Noel Hyndman and Danielle McMahon, Queen's University Belfast	247
40.	Drumview Limited*	Variance analysis; budgeting; foreign exchange risk; cost of capital	Ciaran Connolly and Martin Kelly, Queen's University Belfast	255
41.	Ravenhill Group Limited	Return on investment; residual income (EVA); investment appraisal; non-financial performance measures	Noel Hyndman, Queen's University Belfast	263
42.	The Killyleagh Cycle Company	Transfer pricing; variance analysis; cost of capital; non-financial performance measures	Noel Hyndman and Danielle McMahon, Queen's University Belfast	269
43.	AerThomond plc	Investment appraisal; multidimensional performance measurement systems; sources of finance; dividend policy	Antoinette Flynn and Mairead Tracey, University of Limerick	277

44. Plastic Products*	Investment appraisal and cost of capital; company valuation; JIT and optimal pricing policy; activity-based costing	Michelle Carr and Derry Cotter, University College Cork	285
45. Stationery Products	Investment appraisal and cost of capital; company valuation; foreign exchange risk; divisional performance and the balanced scorecard	Michelle Carr and Derry Cotter, University College Cork	295
Index			301

* Solutions included in *Solutions to Cases in Management Accounting and Business Finance* (Second Edition).

Introduction

The Increasing Use of Case Studies

At a university level, cases have become an invaluable resource to extend and improve a student's learning experience; and increasingly they have been used in advanced level courses in accounting, finance and business management once the basics of a subject have been explored. In addition, in professional accountancy programmes, case studies have similarly been used in capstone courses which students undertake near the completion of the professional programme. These courses build on skills and knowledge acquired in earlier studies and emphasise 'real world' situations. In addition, they often provide an opportunity for students to demonstrate competencies and communication skills.

However, the availability of 'good' new cases in both management accounting and business finance that are appropriate to a UK and Irish environment is limited. Many North American cases, while having great merit, are presented using scenarios and styles that are often not the most useful in a UK and Irish academic and professional examination setting. Other excellent cases that are widely used have become 'dated'. This book attempts to fill this gap.

There are two main reasons why case studies are a valuable means of practice. First, knowledge grows and is better remembered when it is worked over and applied. Traditional textbooks are a necessary aid in the delivery of a course, but case studies are valuable in the application of the information presented. Secondly, a case study can help garner the whole picture for the student. While worked examples at the end of a chapter may develop understanding of a particular topic, case studies go further to incorporate many issues in one integrated scenario.

The Aim of the Book

Cases in Management Accounting and Business Finance offers a range of case study material specific to the core areas of management accounting and business finance. It is targeted at postgraduate and final year undergraduate accounting and business students, as well those preparing for case examinations and assessments of the professional accountancy bodies. This unique text, which particularly reflects the development of the ICAI syllabus, contains contributions from leading accounting and finance academics in Ireland and the UK (many of whom have contributed cases that were developed for use in university programmes). It is with considerable thanks that we acknowledge the many leading academics, with very busy schedules, who agreed to contribute to this text. The book is broad in scope and considers areas as diverse as budgeting, divisionalisation and transfer pricing, cost allocation, investment appraisal, risk management, takeovers, mergers, share valuations and interest rate swaps. The hope is that the use of this text will support an enriched contextual study of both management accounting and business finance.

Aspects of the Book

These principles were followed in the preparation of the book.

- The cases are arranged in three sections: those primarily focused on management accounting; those primarily focused on business finance; and cases that are a mixture of management accounting and business finance. This third section is an innovation in the second edition and has been developed as a result of feedback from lecturers. Even where cases are specifically located as 'management accounting' or 'business finance', there is a slight degree of overlap in some of these cases (given the related and, at times, fuzzy dividing line between course material contained in management accounting and business finance courses, this is perhaps inevitable and desirable).
- The cases are prepared on the basis that students will have already studied at least one introductory course and one intermediate course in both management accounting and business finance.
- The cases are written so that they can be utilised in an 'open-book' environment if desired (that is, students will be able to consult their own material, including books and previously prepared notes, when answering).
- Many of the cases, although perhaps focusing on one main topic, contain a variety of management accounting and/or business finance topics.
- A variety of lengths of case are included, allowing a degree of flexibility in how they are used to support teaching and learning objectives.
- Many of the cases require an answer using report or memorandum format, thus helping students develop communication skills that will be particularly valuable in their career development.
- All cases require students to provide a mixture of quantitative and discursive answers.
- To aid independent learning, a substantial selection of full solutions is available in a companion book (*Solutions to Cases in Management Accounting and Business Finance* (Second Edition)). The solutions to the remainder of the cases are available to lecturers on adoption of the book (to facilitate use in a classroom situation).

Acknowledgements

This is the second edition of this book, the first having been published in 2006. The original idea of the book was conceived in discussions at Queen's University Belfast between Noel Hyndman, Professor of Management Accounting, and Donal McKillop, Professor of Financial Services, and developed in talks with Chartered Accountants Ireland (involving Ronan O'Loughlin and the late Kieran Lyons). In planning the second edition valuable input and 'steering' was received from Michael Diviney (Director of Publishing, Chartered Accountants Ireland) and Joanne Powell (Syllabus Development Manager, Chartered Accountants Ireland). Their very useful comments were much appreciated and are particularly reflected in the changed structure of the second edition of the book. Special thanks also go to Denise Savage from Queen's University Belfast, who provided administrative and clerical support in completing the second edition.

Section A

Cases in Management Accounting

Case 1
Beara Bay Cheese
Margaret Healy, University College Cork

Introduction

Jana Williams established Beara Bay Cheese, located 3 miles outside a small village in West Cork, as a commercial vehicle through which to market her highly popular farmhouse cheeses. Initial research and test marketing was highly favourable. Based on this favourable response, Jana expanded production beyond that anticipated in her business plan. This was not without some difficulty given the long lead times required for maturing and ripening the cheeses. However, the annual results for the current year are disappointing and far below Jana's expectations (see Appendices 1 and 2). She stated:

> "Somehow things never seem to work out like the business plan says – I know the basic product works; this year, I even made more cheese than planned – and managed to sell it all and could have sold even more – but I never seem to hit the profit numbers that I expect."

Beara Bay Cheese

Beara Bay produces two products: CaiseBui and BearaBeag. CaiseBui is a gouda-style hard cheese with a rich milky flavour. It is made from cows' milk and takes six months to mature. BearaBeag is a semi-soft table cheese, also made from cows' milk, and it matures in one month. Both products are extremely popular, with demand outstripping supply in the marketplace. Jana currently assumes full responsibility for managing the production facility, as well as marketing and distributing the final product.

Linking production to anticipated future sales demand is a tricky balancing act for Beara Bay Cheese. Given the length of time required for maturing the cheeses and the amount of storage space needed for this stage of the process, Jana is anxious to expand the production volumes of each product. Currently, there is excess physical capacity at her premises. However, her 'feel' for the potential of such expansion does not seem to be reflected in the financial results and she is at a loss to explain why:

> "I just don't get it…the process is simple enough…the cheeses virtually sell themselves…All I have to do is get them to the marketplace – this year I made many more kilos of cheese than I needed just to simply breakeven. Where has all this extra revenue gone from the profits figure?"

Days spent delivering and selling the cheeses are also taking Jana away from the production process, and she is thinking of focusing solely on supplying the catering trade:

> "I know I could easily sell a lot more cheese…I just don't seem to have the time to make it, what with all of the time and effort that goes into getting the product to the customers…Don't get me wrong – I love the customer interaction and the banter of the farmers' markets – I just don't seem to have time to do everything I want to do."

The Sales Process

Beara Bay cheeses are packaged in 2 kg blocks. The waxed cheese is first placed in a protective plastic sleeve and is then boxed into distinctive, pre-printed, rectangular-shaped wooden boxes. The cheese is sold through two distribution channels: to the catering trade, via fortnightly deliveries; and direct to the consumer via weekly farmers' markets in Midleton (150-mile round trip) and Bantry (20-mile round trip). Because deliveries to the catering trade are only scheduled once a fortnight, Jana frequently has to make unexpected trips to catering trade customers who have requested extra cheese. Despite the disruption this causes, Jana is slow to change the current practice of not charging extra for such deliveries:

> "The catering trade is my 'bread-and-butter'…they have always wanted more cheese than I could supply and I no longer even need to go out looking for business. The farmers' markets may be just a passing fad, so why change the way I do business in the one marketplace I can rely on?"

During the past year, Jana has invested heavily in consolidating her presence as a supplier of high quality cheeses. She spent €10,000 to employ a marketing consultant to develop an advertising campaign for the Beara Bay Cheese brand in the catering sector. As part of this process, a company website was developed and is due to go online shortly.

The Management Accounting System

The accounting system at Beara Bay Cheese is, at best, rudimentary. The basic unit of analysis is 'per kilogram of cheese'. Overheads, consisting of all expenses other than direct materials and direct labour used in the cheese-making process, are allocated to each of the products based on the kilograms of cheese produced. In the current year, for example, overheads were expected to amount to €67,200; planned sales level was 12,000 kg of cheese; thus the overhead rate used by Jana in drawing up the business plan was €5.60 per kg. Retail price per kilogram of cheese was then calculated based on a required mark-up of 20% for CaiseBui and 40% for BearaBeag. Using this information, Jana calculated the budgeted breakeven level of sales to be just over 7,000 kg of cheese, as shown below.

Contribution per kilogram of cheese sold	=	€113,960 / 12,000 kg
	=	€9.50 per kg
Break-even sales level	=	€67,200 / €9.50 per kg
	=	7,076 kg of cheese

The overhead allocation process at Beara Bay Cheese is very simple: the accountant explained the objective as being that of apportioning overheads to units of product – so Jana has done just that. Closer investigation has yielded further information. Production-related overheads (30% of total overheads) consist largely of those costs related to storing the cheeses during the maturation phase. The greater the amount of time taken for this process, the higher the cost. Details relating to marketing-related overheads are in Appendices 3 and 4. It has been suggested to Jana that she use this additional information to install a more sophisticated, activity-based costing system.

Thom's proposal

Jana's son Thom is interested in getting involved in the business on a part-time basis and has approached her with a proposal. He is aware of his mother's growing frustration with the 'accounting numbers' and has begun to research the area in an effort to gain her confidence in his ability. Thom has come to the conclusion that focusing on the contribution margin and breakeven level of sales is simply focusing on maximising short-term profits from the marketplace:

> "I believe the business should ignore the short term in favour of a longer-term view: we need to increase our market penetration and profits will follow…that breakeven calculation is useless anyway…all it does is give an estimate of how much cheese to produce – but then provides no clue as to how much of each *type* of cheese."

Thom is interested in acting as an agent for the Beara Bay Cheese brand, initially on a part-time trial basis. Under the terms of his proposal, Thom would purchase BearaBeag cheese from Jana, at a pre-agreed price, for re-sale at a new, Cork

City-based farmers' market held in the car park of a major shopping complex where Thom is convinced that there is a clear demand. Thom intends to purchase the cheese direct from the Beara Bay ripening sheds. He does not require the cheese to be placed into wooden boxes. Instead, it will simply be double-wrapped in protective plastic, thus reducing the packaging costs to 10% of current levels. All subsequent sales expenses are Thom's responsibility; however Jana, as producer, remains liable for any customer complaints and product returns. Revenue foregone resulting from unsold stock is Thom's responsibility. Jana is unsure about the proposal, both in light of the current profitability levels of the company and her removal from direct contact with the customer.

Thom has identified a number of costs involved in his proposal. He will need to pay an annual registration fee of €300 to join the market and an annual levy, currently €100, to cover the public liability insurance premiums for the market. The round trip from Durrus to the market is 130 miles. Thom intends expensing this mileage at the same rate as that used by Beara Bay Cheese (€0.40 per mile). The market is run once a week, every week of the year. The purchase of a display stand and weighing scales for selling the cheese will cost Thom €520. Thom intends to sell the cheese on a per weight basis, charging €19 per kilogram. He estimates the annual cost of packaging supplies to be €800. Jana has indicated that if the proposal goes ahead, the maximum amount of product she could make available to Thom for the coming year would be 1,200 kg of BearaBeag. Doing so, however, would mean there would not be enough production in the short term to service the current levels of demand for all existing customers. Thom anticipates earning €2,500 from this project. Jana is not willing to sell the cheese for less than €14 per kilogram.

Required

Jana and Thom have yet to make a decision regarding the future development of Beara Bay Cheese. They have identified two issues to be addressed. There are concerns regarding the adequacy of the current management accounting system. Jana is also unsure as to whether Thom's proposal is viable for either Thom or Beara Bay Cheese. They have approached you as an independent financial consultant and, having made all of the above information available to you, they now await your advice and recommendations.

Your report to Jana and Thom should include consideration of the following matters.

Question 1

With respect to the existing management accounting system:

(a) using the figures in the business plan, review the budgeted breakeven level of sales calculated for Beara Bay Cheese. In your answer, include a commentary on the figures previously provided by Jana.

(10 marks)

(b) Discuss the relevance and limitations of breakeven analysis to business decisions at Beara Bay Cheese.

(15 marks)

(c) Determine the profitability of each of the customer groupings identified by Jana, based on the actual costs provided for the year and using principles of activity-based costing. Comment on these figures.

(20 marks)

(d) Advise regarding the suitability of an activity-based costing system for Beara Bay Cheese. Comment on how such systems assign indirect costs to cost objectives. Should Jana continue using the existing simple cost system or should Beara Bay Cheese install a more sophisticated, activity-based costing approach?

(25 marks)

Question 2

With regard to Thom's proposal:

(a) determine the maximum price Thom should pay for the BearaBeag cheese, and the breakeven sales revenue and units, if his agency proposal is to earn its target profit. Comment on the implications of accepting Thom's proposal. Include in your answer an estimated calculation of the financial consequences for Beara Bay Cheese.

(15 marks)

(b) Advise Beara Bay Cheese on the feasibility of expanding the business via the agency proposal. Include specific suggestions as to any other options that may be available, or that should be considered.

(15 marks)

Total 100 marks

Appendix 1: Extract from Business Plan: Beara Bay Cheese

Budgeted Profit and Loss Account for the year ending x/x/xxxx

	CaiseBui	BearaBeag	Total
Turnover	€75,600	€119,560	€195,160
Direct materials	15,000	21,000	36,000
Direct labour	20,000	25,200	45,200
Contribution	40,600	73,360	113,960
Net Profit	12,600	34,160	46,760

Appendix 2: Actual Figures: Beara Bay Cheese

Profit and Loss Account for the year ending x/x/xxxx

	CaiseBui	BearaBeag	Total
Turnover	€89,400	€144,500	€233,900
Direct materials	18,600	34,000	52,600
Direct labour	22,980	28,050	51,030
Contribution	47,820	82,450	130,270
Net Profit	3,420	19,550	22,970

Appendix 3: Market-related Overhead Costs

Activity	% of total
Packaging[1]	10
Travel	35
Advertising[2]	15
Product Promotions[3]	3
Cost of late orders	5
Administration[4]	32

Notes

1. There was no opening stock of boxes and there were 261 boxes in stock at the end of the current period.
2. Advertising costs largely relate to the marketing campaign aimed at the catering trade, although the additional cost of recipe sheets for distribution to customers at the farmers' markets is also included here. The recipe sheet cost is split evenly between the two farmers' markets.
3. Costs recorded here relate to 'taster' cheese samples provided free to customers at the farmers' markets and are allocated based on the percentage of cheese sold at each market. 75% of the cost related to BearaBeag product.
4. Administration overheads include market registration charges as follows:
    (a) Midleton market €250 per annum;
    (b) Bantry market €100 per annum.

Beara Bay Cheese employs a part-time bookkeeper (Sandra Cronin). She has recommended that her salary of €15,000 per annum, currently included in the Administration cost pool, is best spread across product or customer profitability calculations proportional to turnover. The remainder of the administration overheads relate to the costs of sales dockets and are allocated based on the number of transactions in each marketplace.

Appendix 4: Customer Transaction Details

	Midleton Market	Bantry Market	Catering Trade
Sales in kgs:	(kg)	(kg)	(kg)
CaiseBui cheese	1,700	300	4,000
BearaBeag cheese	2,000	1,000	5,500
Average size of transaction	0.25	0.20	20

Case 2
Terra Inc.
Tony O'Dea and Tony Brabazon, University College Dublin

Terra Inc. is one of the largest manufacturers of generic pharmaceuticals in the US. Generic pharmaceuticals are the chemical and therapeutic equivalents of brand-name drugs. The sales of generics have grown rapidly in recent years due to the cost advantages they offer, with generics being typically 30% cheaper than the corresponding brand-name drug. It is anticipated that the total market for generics will grow by 20% per annum for the foreseeable future. Terra currently sells approximately 400 distinct products, representing 140 generic drugs in a variety of dosage strengths and packaging sizes. These products include generic versions of well-known drugs such as Glucophage, Prozac, Zanaflex, Augmentin and Permax. Terra has been particularly successful in being the first-to-market with a generic competitor to branded drugs coming off-patent, often adopting an aggressive legal strategy to force open a drug market to generic competition. Currently the FDA awards 180 days exclusivity to generic manufacturers who successfully challenge a drug patent. Hence, a successful legal challenge to a patent confers a window of opportunity to launch a generic product. Price competition from other generic manufacturers increases rapidly once a new market is established, so there is a substantial profit benefit to being the first entrant into the generic market for a top-selling branded drug.

Moninicol Generic

Moninicol is an injectable neurological drug whose patent is due to expire next year. Moninicol generates sales of $50 million per annum in the US market and, based on current knowledge, no break-through competing product is anticipated in the next five years. Expert opinion estimates that the market demand for Moninicol and any competing generics will remain at $50 million per annum for the next five years.

Roberta Cullon, the CEO of Terra, is considering whether to target this market for the launch of a generic competitor. If the initial numbers look good, Roberta intends to present a full financial analysis of the proposal to the Board of Directors at its next meeting, in order to get approval for the project. After discussions with the marketing and production directors and with the chief scientific officer of Terra, Roberta thinks she has sufficient information to undertake a preliminary financial analysis of the market opportunity. The main costs which are anticipated if a generic competitor to Moninicol is launched are as follows.

Marketing Costs

Initial marketing costs of $500,000 would be required at the launch of the product to cover the costs of advertisements in medical journals and inducements to wholesalers to stock the generic. Post-launch marketing and selling costs would be 5% of sales revenues, plus a fixed amount of $250,000 per annum.

Product Development

Several major steps are required before a new generic can be launched. The manufacturer of the generic must reverse-engineer the branded drug and then develop a production process which is capable of producing the generic reliably. The manufacturer of the generic also requires FDA approval to sell the generic. To obtain this, the manufacturer must establish the bio-equivalency of the generic and the branded drug. The FDA must then be satisfied that the manufacturing processes for the generic are stable and of high quality. Based on previous experience, the chief scientific officer estimates that these steps will cost a total of $2 million.

Costs

The manufacture of the generic would take place in a new production facility. This facility would not produce any other products. Following consultation between the chief scientific officer and the production director, the direct variable material and labour costs associated with the production of each batch of output (a batch consists of 1,000 injectable doses of the generic) were estimated as follows:

	$
Materials	2,000
Packaging	1,000
Labelling	500
Labour	5,000
	8,500

Due to the requirement to ensure that the production process is high quality, substantial use is made of automated machinery during manufacturing. Each batch produced is also subject to a rigorous quality control inspection.

There are notable overhead costs associated with these processes. For the preliminary analysis of the financial viability of the generic project, Roberta has asked the production director to estimate the costs of the manufacturing process, but does not require an in-depth investigation of them until it appears likely that the project will be viable. The director knows that the production processes and the related overheads are similar to those for another generic product which Terra already produces. The manufacturing overhead costs for that product for the last two years are as follows:

Manufacturing Process	50 batches ($)	100 batches ($)
Heating	375,000	750,000
Blending	500,000	750,000
Reducing	250,000	300,000

The batch size for this generic is also 1,000 injectable doses. It is known that any fixed costs in the above overheads remain unchanged across a wide range of output.

The production director considers that the cost of the quality inspection process is a mixed cost, and that the driver of the cost is the number of batches produced and inspected. The inspection process for the generic will be identical in nature and cost structure to that for the other generic that is produced by Terra. The production director collected historic cost and volume data on this process for the other generic and performed a regression analysis on these data. The results were as follows:

R^2	0.98
Intercept coefficient (b_0)	25,000
Slope coefficient (b_1)	750
Standard error of the estimate (SEE)	8,500
Standard error of b_1	25.0

This analysis was undertaken using annual costs and annual levels of inspection activity (batches inspected). There have been no changes in the costs of this process (or the technology used in the inspection process) for several years, and none is anticipated in the near future.

Revenue

Generic products can capture a substantial portion of the market for the branded drug if they are well marketed and if their price is competitive. It is estimated by the marketing director that Terra could capture 20% of the market sales volume if a selling price was set that was 30% lower than the branded drug's current price of $50 per injection. The drug is sold in batches of 1,000 to wholesalers and other customers. Therefore the selling price per batch for the branded drug is currently $50,000.

There is uncertainty as to the reaction of competitors to the launch of the generic. Typically, major pharmaceutical companies employ a range of tactics to reduce the impact on their profitability when one of their branded products comes off-patent. These tactics include launching variants of the branded product and the launch of their own generic version of the drug. It is also possible that other generic manufacturers will target this market for their own launch of a generic product. However, Roberta is confident that the major pharmaceutical company will adopt a profit-harvesting strategy by keeping the price of the branded drug high and giving up some market share. Roberta is also confident that Terra would be first-to-market with a generic, and would be free of competition from other generic manufacturers for at least one year after product launch. If other generic manufacturers do enter the market at that point (after the first year), Roberta anticipates that Terra would need to reduce its selling prices for the generic to $30 at the start of year two and to $28 from the start of year three in order to maintain 20% of market sales volume. Selling prices would then stabilise at the year three level.

Active Ingredients Division

In addition to Terra's activities of manufacturing and selling generic drugs, it manufactures and sells active pharmaceutical ingredients to third parties (non-group companies). This division sells in excess of 80 different active pharmaceutical ingredients. Terra's ability to produce active pharmaceutical ingredients cost effectively in-house is considered to be a major strategic advantage as it ensures continuity of supply of raw ingredients for the manufacture of its generic drugs.

In the last week, an external customer has approached the division seeking a supply of 1,000 kg of a specific active ingredient which is used in the manufacture of generic painkillers. The customer has offered $170,000 for a once-off delivery of this ingredient, if it can be delivered within 60 days. The division accountant has undertaken a preliminary costing of the order and has recommended that the order be rejected. To support this recommendation the accountant has supplied the following information to the general manager of the division:

	$
Raw Materials	
Material A (500 kg @ $40 per kg)	20,000
Material B (1,000 kg @ $80 per kg)	80,000
Material C (500 kg @ $30 per kg)	15,000
Labour (100 hours @ $100 per hour)	10,000
Overheads (100 hours @ $500 per hour)	50,000
	175,000

The general manager requests further information from the accountant and the plant manager and learns the following.

1. The plant manager confirms that the process of manufacturing the active ingredient requires a 'reduction' process, whereby there is a 50% loss of weight during production. Therefore 200 kg of raw material inputs produces 100 kg of output ingredient before final quality inspection.
2. Based on past experience, 20% of the output of active ingredient is rejected at the final quality inspection.

3. The expected ratio in which the raw materials are used is 1:2:1 (Material A: Material B: Material C).
4. The division has 10,000 kg of raw Material A in stock. This raw material originally cost $40 per kg but its current price, and future expected price, is $50 per kg. Raw Material A is used constantly in the manufacture of different active ingredients.
5. The division has 4,000 kg of raw Material B in stock. This raw material originally cost $80 per kg but its current price, and future expected price, is $70 per kg. Raw Material B is used constantly in the manufacture of different active ingredients.
6. The division has 1,000 kg of raw Material C in stock. This raw material originally cost $30 per kg but its current price, and future expected price, is $20 per kg. Raw Material C is no longer used by the division in the manufacture of active ingredients. If not used on this order, it will be disposed of for $10 per kg.
7. Normal labour costs are $100 per hour. At present, the division is operating at full capacity and if this order were accepted, the workforce would need to work the required 100 hours as overtime. An overtime premium of 25% is paid.
8. Overheads are recovered at a rate of $500 per labour hour. Seventy-five percent of overheads are fixed and these will not alter if the order is accepted.
9. If the order is accepted, an additional batch quality inspection will be required. These inspections cost $2,500.

Diagnostic Tests Division

Diagnosta Inc. is a subsidiary of Terra. It manufactures a single product that is used in research laboratories in universities and commercial pharmaceutical companies. The product is supplied by several companies and the market for the product is very competitive.

Following the departure of the previous CEO of Diagnosta, Peter Aston was hired at the beginning of December 2XX0. Peter immediately requested a projected income statement for 2XX0. In response, the financial controller of Diagnosta provided the following statement:

	$
Sales	25,000,000
Variable expenses	20,000,000
Contribution margin	5,000,000
Fixed expenses	6,000,000
Projected loss	(1,000,000)

After some investigation, Peter soon realised that the division's product had a serious problem with quality. Peter requested a special study by the financial controller in order to obtain a report on the level of quality costs. By the end of December 2XX0, he received the following report from the controller:

	$
Inspection costs, finished product	400,000
Re-work costs	2,000,000
Scrapped units	600,000
Warranty costs	3,000,000
Sales returns (quality-related)	1,000,000
Customer complaints department	500,000
Total estimated quality costs	7,500,000

Peter was surprised at the level of quality costs: they represented 30% of sales, which appeared excessive. He knew that to survive, Diagnosta had to improve quality. Thus, Peter decided to pursue a quality-driven turnaround strategy. Revenue growth and cost reduction could both be achieved if quality could be improved.

After meeting with the managers of production, marketing, purchasing and human resources, the following decisions were made, effective immediately (end of December 2XX0).

1. More will be invested in employee training. Workers will be trained to detect quality problems and empowered to make improvements.
2. Two design engineers will be hired immediately, with expectations of hiring one or two more within a year. These engineers will be in charge of redesigning processes and the product, with the objective of improving quality. They will also be given the responsibility of working with selected suppliers to help improve the quality of their products and processes.
3. A new process for evaluating and selecting suppliers will be implemented to ensure the provision of non-defective components.
4. Effective immediately, Diagnosta will begin inspecting purchased components. According to production, many of the quality problems are caused by defective components purchased from outside suppliers.
5. Within three years, the goal is to produce products with a defect rate less than 0.10%. By reducing the defect rate to this level, marketing is confident that market share will increase by at least 50% as a consequence of increased customer satisfaction.
6. To help direct the improvements in quality activities, kaizen costing is to be implemented. For example, for the year 2XX1 re-work costs, a kaizen standard of 6% of the selling price per unit was set – a 25% reduction from the current actual cost.

To ensure that the quality improvements were directed and translated into concrete financial outcomes, Peter also began to implement a Balanced Scorecard for Diagnosta. By the end of 2XX1 progress was being made. Sales had increased to $26,000,000, and the kaizen improvements were meeting or beating expectations. For example, re-work costs had dropped to $1,500,000.

At the end of 2XX2, two years after the turnaround quality strategy was implemented, Peter received the following quality cost report:

	$
Quality training	500,000
Supplier evaluation	230,000
Incoming inspection costs	400,000
Inspection costs, finished product	300,000
Re-work costs	1,000,000
Scrapped units	200,000
Warranty costs	750,000
Sales returns (quality-related)	435,000
Customer complaints department	325,000
Total estimated quality costs	4,140,000

Peter also received an income statement for 2XX2:

	$
Sales	30,000,000
Variable expenses	22,000,000
Contribution margin	8,000,000
Fixed expenses	5,800,000
Income	2,200,000

Required

Question 1

Moninicol Generic

(a) Calculate the number of units of the Moninicol generic that Terra must sell in the first year of sales in order to:
   (i) breakeven;
   (ii) make a profit of $1 million.

Note: in answering this part of the question, ignore all the initial one-off costs of developing the product and the initial market launch costs.

(**15 marks**)

(b) Comment on your answer to requirement (a), bearing in mind the expected sales level of the product.

(**4 marks**)

(c) Calculate the length of time after production commences before Terra will breakeven on the new product launch:

   (i) if no competitors enter the market;
   (ii) if competitors do enter the market.

Note: in answering this requirement, you must include all the initial costs of developing the product and the initial marketing costs. You can ignore the 'time-value-of-money' in answering this part of the question and you may assume that there is no cost inflation.

(15 marks)

(d) Calculate the profit that Terra would make in the first year of sales of the generic if all costs were 10% higher than anticipated, the selling price was 5% lower than anticipated and if Terra captured 25% of the market sales volume.

Note: in answering this requirement, ignore all the initial one-off costs of developing the product and the initial market launch costs.

(12 marks)

Question 2

Active Ingredients Division

Financially evaluate the one-off order for the supply of 1,000 kg of active ingredient.

(15 marks)

Question 3

Diagnostic Tests Division

(a) Evaluate the success of the quality-driven turnaround strategy.

(10 marks)

(b) What additional information would you like to have for the evaluation in (a) above?

(4 marks)

(c) The kaizen standard for re-work was 6% of sales for the year 2XX1. To what extent was the standard met? Describe the role for kaizen costing in Peter Aston's strategy.

(5 marks)

(d) Explain briefly why Peter Aston may feel that a Balanced Scorecard can contribute towards the achievement of the quality improvement strategy.

(5 marks)

(e) Identify the perspectives which could be included in Diagnosta's Balanced Scorecard and suggest two strategic objectives for each perspective. In addition, provide a supporting performance measure for each strategic objective.

(15 marks)

Total 100 marks

Case 3
Mississippi Inc.
Tony Brabazon and Tony O'Dea, University College Dublin

With a weary sigh, Jeff Essos sat back in his chair. It was 6.00 pm on a sunny Saturday evening, but he reckoned that he'd be lucky if he got home before 11.00 pm Ever since he had co-founded Mississippi Inc. with his ex-classmate, Rachel Rosenthal, two years earlier, the work had been hard and the hours long, but generally Jeff had enjoyed the challenge. As Rachel had remarked when they founded the firm, with Jeff's accounting and finance skills and her marketing skills, they were bound to succeed!

Mississippi Inc. is a fast-growing e-business, specialising in direct sales to consumers of both books and CDs. The firm makes all its sales to customers over the Internet and follows a marketing strategy of offering low prices, a wide product range and a nationwide three-day delivery promise. The customer places an order on the firm's website, paying for the goods purchased with his/her credit card. The order is then sent to the firm's distribution centre, where all stocks were kept, and the items are picked from stock, packed in a cardboard box and shipped directly to the customer.

The day before, Jeff had received the latest financial report from his assistant, Barney Shuter. Sales were continuing to grow rapidly and while the firm was far from profitable as yet, Jeff consoled himself with the thought that Mississippi Inc. was the dominant e-retailer in the market and that the current losses were partially arising because of the firm's heavy expenditure on advertising, which was considered necessary in order to build a strong customer base. A more immediate problem that concerned Jeff was the high costs arising in the distribution depot. In earlier months, the rapid growth in sales had placed severe demands on the firm's distribution depot, and delivery times to customers had started to slip. Consequently, the depot had been significantly expanded last month and many of its activities automated. The good news was that the new depot was working smoothly and had sufficient capacity for at least the next six months, even taking into account the expected rapid sales growth. The bad news was that the costs of the distribution depot had increased substantially as a result of the expansion, which was somewhat surprising given that the efficiency of the warehouse had improved due to the increased level of automation.

In the past week, Jeff had been contacted by a major freight carrier (USP Inc.), which had offered to undertake the entire distribution function for Mississippi. USP's proposal was that Mississippi would pass the customer order directly to USP Inc., which in turn would provide its own warehouse facilities (stocked with Mississippi inventory) and staff, and would be fully responsible for picking, packing and shipping the order to the customer. In return for this service, USP would charge Mississippi a flat 8% commission on gross sales revenue (for example, if the value of goods shipped to customers in a given month was €10 million, USP would receive a commission of €800,000).

Jeff was considering this proposal, but was uncertain as to whether the activities of the distribution depot should be outsourced to USP. Although the decision was a complex one, Jeff thought that it would be useful to start by comparing the financial implications of each alternative. Luckily, Mississippi had implemented an activity-based costing system in its distribution depot the previous year, so Jeff thought that much of the necessary information would be readily available.

Last month, sales to customers were €10 million, with an average sales order value of €50 (200,000 individual sales orders last month). On average last month, each order contained two items; so an order could be for two books or perhaps one book and one CD. The key costs associated with the activities of the distribution depot were as follows:

Activities	Activity Cost Driver	Activity Cost Driver Rate
Picking	Number of individual items	€1.25 per item
Packing	Number of individual items	€0.25 per item
Preparation of shipping documents	Number of orders	€0.75 per order
Transfer to shipping area	Number of orders	€0.50 per order

Jeff knew that an activity cost driver rate was not a 'true' variable cost but rather contained both a fixed and a variable component. The fixed component of each of the above activities was as follows:

Activities	Fixed Cost Component (€) Per Month
Picking	400,000
Packing	80,000
Preparation of shipping documents	100,000
Transfer to shipping area	80,000

Based on sales projections developed by the marketing department, it was expected that sales would increase by 30% in euro terms in each of the next two months. Customer loyalty to Mississippi was known to be strong and because a high number of customers would be 'repeat' customers, it was expected that for the next two months the average order value would be €65 and that the number of items would increase to an average of three per order. Fixed costs are not expected to increase next month, but are expected to increase by 10% at the start of the following month.

Note: in answering the following requirements, the following simplifying assumptions can be made.

(i) If the decision is taken to outsource the operations of the distribution centre, the centre can be closed down immediately and all costs associated with the activities of the distribution centre can be immediately avoided by Mississippi.
(ii) Stock-holding costs will not change if the operations of the distribution centre are outsourced.
(iii) Presently, customers pay the shipping charges of their orders and these charges are not included in the sales figures above. This practice will not change if the operations of the distribution centre are outsourced.

Required

Question 1

Calculate the estimated cost of operating the distribution centre for each of the next two months. Clearly show your workings and clearly highlight (and defend) any assumptions you make in your calculations.

(20 marks)

Question 2

Calculate the estimated cost, for the next two months of outsourcing the activities of the distribution centre to USP.

(15 marks)

Question 3

Assuming that the fixed costs of all the non-distribution activities of Mississippi are €4,000,000 per month and that the average total variable costs per order (excluding variable distribution depot costs) are 80% of the selling price of the order, calculate the level of sales required to break even next month if the distribution depot activities are outsourced to USP.

(20 marks)

Question 4

Critically evaluate the proposal to outsource the activities of the distribution centre to USP. Your answer should consider both the financial and non-financial implications of the proposal.

(20 marks)

Question 5

Jeff Essos is concerned that the current budgetary control system of the firm may be providing inadequate information to senior managers. He is considering implementing a balanced scorecard.

Design a balanced scorecard, suitable for presentation to senior managers on a monthly basis. Your scorecard should clearly indicate the perspectives and related measures you consider important for Mississippi Inc. and you should defend your choice of perspectives and measures.

(25 marks)

Total 100 marks

Case 4

EasyONline

Tony Brabazon and Tony O'Dea, University College Dublin

Overview of the Company

Ghodrat Moghadampour founded EasyONline, a chain of cyber-cafés, three years ago. The cafés provide 24-hour online access to the Internet, as well as selling a range of drinks and snacks. From an initial, single café in London, the chain has grown to 21 cafés, spanning major cities in several European countries. With heavy tourist traffic in many major European cities and only a 31% home PC penetration rate in several key European countries, the potential for sales growth seems assured for the immediate future. Sales in the current year are expected to be €50 million.

Despite this success, Ghodrat is puzzled by the latest month's financial report. Despite adding five new cyber-cafés to her growing chain during the month, and a stable customer volume at existing cafés, the financial report showed a small reduction in the chain's profitability. Ghodrat is concerned by this development as the business plan calls for an initial public offering (stock market listing) in 18 months time, and she wants to be able to show a record of consistent, annual, profitable sales growth. She holds half of the equity in EasyONline. One-quarter of the equity is held by a major PC supplier.

EasyONline competes against existing cyber-cafés by providing a top-quality service at a low price. Each café is large, typically in excess of 100 square metres, and is stocked with the latest PC models with flat-screen displays. Each café has a dedicated, high-speed optic fibre connection to the Internet. Costs are minimised due to the economies of scale that EasyONline is able to generate. For example, the cost of each café's high-speed Internet connection is reduced on a per-user basis because the café is open 24 hours per day. To ensure high utilisation of its cafés, EasyONline usually targets high 'footfall' locations in the centre of cosmopolitan towns and cities that have both a large domestic and a large tourist population. Average weekly traffic for established cafés is approximately 30,000 customers per week. Each location has a standard design, which reduces outfitting costs.

Café revenue arises from several streams. The user pays a flat-rate fee for computer usage, currently €1 for 30 minutes computer use. The time is rounded up to the next half-hour, thus a user spending 40 minutes on-line pays €2. The cafés sell a range of drinks and snacks and also generate revenue from printing services and sales of diskettes and CDs. During the past three months, EasyONline has launched a pilot programme in three of its cafés which generates revenue from advertising. The customer base, primarily 16 to 35-year-olds, is attractive to advertisers. A limited amount of on-screen advertising has been sold, and advertising space on walls and mouse-mats has also been sold. The pilot scheme has been successful and will be extended to the entire chain of cafés in the next month.

Following an examination of customer records, it has been found that a typical customer stays online for 25 minutes between 9.00 am and 6.00 pm, and for 48 minutes outside these times. Peak log-in times are typically between 3.00 pm and 7.00 pm but these vary between countries. For example, the chain's Spanish cafés show high traffic from 7.00 pm to midnight.

To date, EasyONline has operated a variety of café sizes, but no attempt has been made to determine the 'optimal' size of café in each country. Ghodrat feels that some of the cafés are the 'wrong' size and are losing money. If a café is too small, it is hard to recover the fixed costs of both staff and the high-speed Internet connection. If the café is too large, it suffers from low utilisation, resulting in excessive lease (rent) and Internet connection costs. The following information has been collected from two cyber-cafés in the UK:

(i)

	Manchester	London
Number of computers	200	600
Average monthly number of customers	40,000	180,000
of which:		
customers between 9.00 am and 6.00 pm:	12,000	80,000
customers between 6.00 pm and 9.00 am:	28,000	100,000

(ii) *Staff costs*

Each outlet must have at least one employee present 24 hours per day. This costs €120,000 per year. Previous cost studies have found that variable staff costs are approximately 10% of total revenue earned in the café.

(iii) *PC costs*

A major PC supplier holds an equity stake in EasyONline and supplies PCs to EasyONline under a revenue-sharing agreement. Under this agreement, EasyONline does not buy the computers in its cafés but pays the PC supplier a 'rental' of 10% of the computer usage fees earned in each café.

(iv) Lease costs

Leases are generally for five years. The current annual lease costs for the cafés are €240,000 for the Manchester café and €3,600,000 for the London café.

(v) High-speed Internet connection costs

These costs are similar in all major UK cities, and depend on the amount of bandwidth (capacity) required. This is largely determined by the number of computers in the café. Bandwidth can only be supplied in discrete amounts. For cafés with up to 300 computers, the cost is €15,000 per month. For 300–700 computers, the cost increases to €35,000 per month.

(vi) Other costs

General administration and overhead costs per café are comprised of a fixed element of €5,000 per month and a variable element of 5% of total café revenue.

(vii) Non-computer usage revenue

The pilot advertising programme operates in both the London and Manchester cafés. In each café, the non-computer usage revenues (sales of drinks, snacks, printing services, diskettes, CDs and advertising) are 40% of total revenue earned in the café. The contribution margin on these sales is 70%.

Required

Question 1

Calculate the average total monthly revenues earned in both the London and Manchester cafés.

(15 marks)

Question 2

Calculate the number of half-hour blocks of computer time (the 'product') that must be sold each month in order to break-even in the Manchester café.

(20 marks)

Question 3

Calculate the monthly profitability of both the London and Manchester cafés if customer numbers:

(a) remain at current levels;
(b) increase by 10%.

Note: assume that the customer mix (9.00 am–6.00 pm vs. 6.00 pm–9.00 am) remains unchanged when calculating **3(b)** above.

(20 marks)

Question 4

Considering the café chain's cost structure (fixed versus mixed) and other relevant information in the scenario, list two plausible reasons why the chain's profitability may have dropped last month.

(20 marks)

Question 5

Ghodrat is unhappy with the current flat-rate pricing system of €1 for 30 minutes Internet-access. She feels that this flat-rate pricing strategy encourages excessive use of the café at peak times, such as mid-afternoon, and underutilisation of the café at off-peak times.

Suggest alternative pricing strategies for the cyber-café.

(25 marks)

Total 100 marks

Case 5
Varsity plc
Joan Ballantine, University of Ulster

Company Background

Varsity plc is a multinational company which operates in a number of countries, including the USA, Australia, Japan and the UK. The company operates in the telecommunications sector, manufacturing a wide range of electronic components for sale in both the corporate and private sectors. In line with the company's strategy of improving environmental sustainability, Varsity plc has recently been investigating the commercial viability of developing the SunnyCharge, an eco-friendly solar charger. The company hopes to design a product that can be utilised to charge a range of new generation devices, including, mobile phones, games consoles and MP3 players. Whilst a number of basic eco-friendly chargers are already on the market, the Directors of Varsity plc know that the charger they design and bring to the market must be capable of beating the competition in terms of the range of features that it offers. Additionally, the Directors of Varsity plc are aware that the SunnyCharge will have a limited life-cycle given the fast-moving pace of the telecommunications sector and the ability of other companies to imitate products relatively quickly.

Historically, the finance function within Varsity plc has been poor in terms of analysing the viability of new product introductions. For example, the finance function has in the past failed to adopt a consistent and methodical approach to identifying not only the costs of manufacturing new products but also the other costs incurred across the entire life-cycle of new product introduction. As a result the company has a very poor record in terms of the profitability of new product introductions. For example, in the past three years a total of 25 products have been designed, developed and introduced to the market place by Varsity plc. However, a recent analysis of these by the newly appointed Finance Director, Dick Chaney, has shown that only 20% of these products have actually been profitable. The Finance Director attributes this result to the poor accounting procedures adopted by Varsity plc.

Finance Director Dick Chaney, a recently qualified chartered accountant, is all too aware of the importance of lifecycle costing. In a recent board meeting he recommended to the company's executive board that all new product introductions should be accompanied by a thorough analysis of product life-cycle costs before decisions are made regarding which products to proceed with. Such an analysis would not only need to consider the total life-cycle costs related to new products but would also need to treat all potential new product introductions as capital investment decisions. This latter element has been substantially ignored in the past by the finance function. The SunnyCharge is the first product that will be subject to Dick Chaney's more consistent and rigorous analysis. The Finance Director is therefore keen that a thorough analysis of the SunnyCharge is carried out, so that he can make a good impression on Varsity's Board of Directors at their next monthly meeting. You have recently been employed by Varsity plc as the Financial Controller. Your line manager is the Finance Director, Dick Chaney. The Finance Director has asked you to carry out a thorough analysis of the SunnyCharge, the results of which will be presented to the Board of Directors.

After receiving the task, you immediately enter into discussions with a variety of functions within Varsity plc. From discussions with the design and development staff, you ascertain that the SunnyCharge is expected to have a product life-cycle of four years, which includes research and development, design, manufacturing and sales and after-sales service activities. During the first year of the product's life-cycle, Varsity is expected to invest heavily in research and development and design activities. Additionally, towards the end of the first year of the product's life-cycle, capital expenditure of €2,000,000 will have to be incurred to purchase specialist machinery for the manufacture of the SunnyCharge. As a result of such investment, it is anticipated that a small number of SunnyCharges will be manufactured and sold to the market towards the end of the first year of the life-cycle. However, the majority of the manufacturing and sales activities related to the SunnyCharge will occur in years two, three and four of the product's life-cycle.

Further discussions with representatives from manufacturing, purchasing, marketing, distribution and after-sales service enables you to ascertain the following cost, demand and revenue information for the SunnyCharge (see Table 1).

Table 1: SunnyCharge – Cost, Demand and Revenue Data

	Year 1	Year 2	Year 3	Year 4
Capital Costs				
Machinery Costs	€2,000,000			
Research and Development costs	€900,000			
Design costs	€500,000			
Demand and Selling Price Data				
Units manufactured and sold	5,000	50,000	200,000	150,000
Selling price per SunnyCharge	€60	€60	€55	€55

Table 1 (continued)

Manufacturing Costs				
Variable cost per SunnyCharge	€16	€15	€15	€15
Variable cost per batch	€1,000	€550	€550	€550
Chargers per batch	200	200	200	200
Fixed costs	€150,000	€500,000	€500,000	€500,000
Marketing Costs				
Variable cost per SunnyCharge	€5	€5	€6	€7
Fixed costs	€50,000	€500,000	€500,000	€500,000
Distribution Costs				
Variable cost per SunnyCharge	€2.00	€2.00	€2.00	€2.00
Variable cost per batch	€100	€100	€100	€100
Chargers per batch	500	500	1,000	1,000
Fixed costs	€100,000	€250,000	€250,000	€300,000
Customer Service Costs				
Variable costs per SunnyCharge	€3	€2	€1.50	€1.50

In addition to the above, you ascertain the following information.

1. Varsity's accounting policy for depreciating non-current assets is to charge depreciation on a straight-line basis over the life of the asset. The residual value of the machinery purchased to manufacture the SunnyCharge at the end of year 4 is zero.
2. Varsity's accounting policy for research and development expenditure is to capitalise it on the balance sheet and to subsequently charge amortisation on a straight-line basis over the period of time in which sales revenue is expected to be generated.
3. The design costs incurred in respect of the SunnyCharge are to be treated as fixed costs which are expensed to the income statement in the period they are incurred.
4. Varsity plc currently has a total capital employed of €200 million, of which €80 million is debt financed and the remaining €120 million is equity financed. The current cost of debt is 6% per annum and the cost of equity is currently at a level of 4%.

As suggested earlier, Varsity plc has traditionally been poor at adopting a consistent and methodical approach to identifying not only the costs of manufacturing new products but also the costs incurred across the entire life-cycle of new product introductions. In addition to this, however, the previous Finance Director used investment appraisal techniques randomly, such as net present value (NPV), to evaluate the viability of product introductions. This was partly as a result of his lack of understanding of the technique and his inability to explain the workings of the technique when quizzed by the company's other directors at board meetings. Consequently, new product introductions have in the last couple of years been sadly lacking in rigour. Dick Chaney, the new Finance Director, is adamant that the profitability of new product introductions is calculated on a year-by-year basis over the full life-cycle to assess their commercial viability. However, he is also of the opinion that capital investment appraisal techniques, such as NPV, are once again employed in a consistent and rigorous manner to assess the viability of all new product introductions.

The Finance Director has asked you to help him prepare a report which assesses the viability of the SunnyCharge. The report will be presented to the Board of Directors next month. From discussions with the Finance Director, you ascertain that the other executive directors of Varsity plc do not have a good knowledge of life-cycle costing and its application to new product introductions. The Finance Director is therefore keen that the report produced should highlight the importance of adopting a life-cycle costing approach before decisions are made to proceed with the introduction of new product lines. Knowing that you have a good knowledge of cost-management techniques, including life-cycle costing, the Finance Director has asked you to prepare a first draft of the report. The report should address the following requirements.

Required

Question 1

Prepare a statement which shows, on a yearly basis, the total variable cost, contribution, total fixed costs and the budgeted profit the SunnyCharge is expected to make over its four-year life-cycle. Comment on your analysis and the results reported.

(35 marks)

Question 2

What percentage of the total budgeted product life-cycle costs of the SunnyCharge will actually be incurred by the end of the research and development and design stages? What are the implications of this for possible cost-reduction activity across the remaining life-cycle of the SunnyCharge?

(5 marks)

Question 3

How might the concept of life-cycle costing improve the success rate of new product introductions within Varsity plc? Are there any other cost-management approaches which might be used alongside life-cycle costing that you feel would enable Varsity plc to further enhance its success rate in terms of the profitability of new product introductions?

(10 marks)

Question 4

Is the SunnyCharge a viable project? In ascertaining viability, you are asked to calculate the profitability of the product using return on investment (ROI). As part of your discussion, you will need to carefully consider the alternative ways in which the asset base may be defined. You should also investigate the viability of the project using whatever capital investment appraisal techniques you consider appropriate. State all of your assumptions clearly.

(40 marks)

Question 5

Are financial measures the most appropriate way of ascertaining the viability and success of the SunnyCharge? Discuss.

(10 marks)

Total 100 marks

Case 6
Castlegrove Enterprises
Tom Kennedy, University of Limerick

Overview of the Company

Two partners, Larry Maloney and Sean McKenna, set up Castlegrove Enterprises some 20 years ago, shortly after they were made redundant from Digimac. Digimac had supplied parts to the Irish and European car industry, but decided to consolidate all of its European manufacturing operations in Eastern Europe. Maloney and McKenna had been employees of Digimac for 15 years and were offered a significant redundancy payment. Their families were well settled in the Galway area and were reluctant to move. Maloney had a degree in manufacturing engineering, and after 10 years of service with Digimac in a variety of positions was promoted to manufacturing manager. McKenna, who had a diploma in purchasing and logistics, had initially worked as a buyer before transferring to materials. He had been promoted to material manager some four years before being made redundant by Digimac.

Both men were keen golfers and had often spoken about the need to get away from the continually increasing work pressures experienced in Digimac. They had discussed the possibility of setting up their own business on a number of occasions, but did not have the capital or the courage to make the transition. Now that the opportunity presented itself, and with the encouragement of their families and the local enterprise board, they took the initiative. In doing so, they decided that Maloney was to be the managing director, with specific responsibility for production, engineering and facilities. McKenna was to be deputy managing director, with responsibility for purchasing, materials and administration.

Business Performance / History

After a difficult first two years, Castlegrove became a thriving business, primarily through the manufacture and supply of a small range of customised products for the building industry. It developed a very solid customer base and was the preferred supplier of a number of large building contractors. Ireland, labelled the 'Celtic Tiger', had just entered a phase of sustained rapid economic development, which allowed Castlegrove to capitalise on the huge demand for building and related products. Given the company's high dependency on this market and the public debate as to its sustainability, Maloney and McKenna were determined to diversify when the right opportunity presented itself. They had built up a successful management team and re-organised their responsibilities in late 2XX1. Kevin Holmes was hired to take responsibility for production, having previously worked for a competitor in Dublin. Mary McGuire had become familiar with the business as audit manager for a number of years and was attracted by the offer to work nearer to home. She joined Castlegrove as accounting manager. Liam Jones was promoted to sales manager, based on his excellent record as the senior sales representative for the past five years with Castlegrove. A local retired bank manager and a solicitor, who was recommended by one of Maloney's golfing partners, joined the board. The senior management team met formally every second Monday morning and the board usually met every three months. Castlegrove continued to maintain its original policy of staying with and developing its core business.

However, the sudden death of the owner of a small local garden accessories business, Rosemount, led to a decision to take over that business in late 2XX2. Rosemount had traded successfully for about 20 years, under the astute direction of Michael Murphy, in premises adjacent to Castlegrove. Murphy's family had no involvement in the business and his management style did not facilitate a management buy-out. Murphy had acted as mentor to Maloney and McKenna and they had valued his advice on a number of occasions. They were shocked by his sudden death and felt obligated to help his family. They moved quickly to take over the running of the business, with the encouragement of his widow, and completed the purchase some months later. They successfully integrated Rosemount into their own operations and it traded successfully for over two years.

All was to change with the entry of a new, low cost, multinational company Zip, in late 2XX4. Zip set up its own manufacturing facility in a new industrial estate in the outskirts of Galway and it was to present very serious competitive problems for Rosemount. Zip had recognised the market potential nationally and was in the process of rolling out a targeted expansion programme. Rosemount could not match zip's range of products, aggressive marketing and special promotions. Rosemount lost over half its customers in the first half of 2XX5 and, despite extensive efforts to recover market share, faced the inevitable decision to close down. This decision was finally made by Castlegrove at a special board meeting in September 2XX5. However, it was decided to defer making the decision public until a proposal from the new product development team had been considered.

New Product Development

Maloney and McKenna were always conscious of the need to invest in research and development and had set up a small new product development team in 2XX3. This team was made up of two engineering graduates and a production management student. It was decided to strengthen that team with the addition of John Somers in 2XX5. John was an electronic engineering graduate and had worked with Maloney and McKenna in Digimac. He went to Australia to work in the printing business when he was made redundant. He returned to Ireland on the death of his mother in April 2XX5 and was impressed by the huge change in the economic landscape since his departure. He ran into Maloney at the local golf club and was taken by his offer to join them on a trial basis. His brief was to assess the feasibility of a number of product ideas that were at an advanced stage of development and to bring them to the board for consideration. When he assessed the situation, he decided that the laser multi-purpose ruler and sensor unit were the most advanced technically. Following feedback from a number of trade shows and in conjunction with McGuire, he held a number of meetings with Jones and Holmes. This project team produced a comprehensive proposal for consideration at a specially convened board meeting in late October 2XX5. The proposal included draft operating income statements, market research, technical specifications, production and capital expenditure requirements. It made a strong recommendation to proceed with the manufacture of the laser unit. The board was impressed by the proposal and gave its approval. The unit was to be marketed under the name 'Pulse' and would be supplied to distributors in Ireland and England initially.

In making this strategic investment decision, the board was conscious of the need to find alternative work for the highly trained and long-serving production employees in Rosemount. The decision to develop 'Pulse' resulted in Castlegrove being able to retain them, based on the projections presented in the proposal and their suitability for the new production line. Critically, this meant that it did not have to pay out a significant lump sum redundancy payment or undertake a major retraining programme. Arising from the board decision in late October 2XX5, a capital expenditure programme was expedited. The commissioning of the automated equipment and the refurbishment of the production facility was to be completed in December 2XX5. Production and sales of 'Pulse' would commence in January 2XX6 and Rosemount would cease trading after Christmas 2XX5 in an orderly fashion.

Projected Operating Income of the 'Pulse' Product Line

The relevant costs and revenue associated with the 'Pulse' project are shown in Appendix 1. This shows that operating income was anticipated to be €30,600 in the year ended 2XX6 and €52,600 in the year ended 2XX7. Breakeven had been calculated at about 4,109 units and with sales estimated at 5,500 in 2XX6 and 6,500 in 2XX7, a very acceptable margin of safety was projected. This gave the project team and the board great confidence in the viability of the project. Somers was complimented by the board on his initiative and was asked to submit a timescale for the other new projects in the pipeline. He was offered and accepted the newly created position of product development manager, with an attractive remuneration package. His plans to return to Australia were put on hold for the foreseeable future.

During the preparation of the projected operating results, Jones spoke very strongly about the importance of setting realistic sales targets for the first year of any new product launch. He was very positive in regard to 2XX7 and, based on the market research data, was happy to commit to an approximate 18% projected increase for that year. He was less bullish about projections thereafter, noting that the 2XX7 projected performance was unlikely to be repeated. He thought it more reasonable to work on the basis of something in the order of a 15% annual increase for the foreseeable future. A lot of discussion took place before agreeing on a price of €85 per unit. Despite its uniqueness, some benchmarking was possible and this suggested a price per unit in the range €90–€100. The issue was unresolved until McGuire came up with a preliminary variable cost figure in the range €60–€70 per unit. This information quickly led to an agreement to go with an aggressive pricing strategy, given that it met Castlegrove's policy of achieving a minimum profit:volume (or contribution to sales) ratio of 20% on all product lines.

During this process, Holmes became somewhat agitated when he learned of the level of sales anticipated by Jones in the earlier years of the project. His analysis of the new plant capability and the quality of the operatives being made available from Rosemount was that he could comfortably produce 10,000 units per annum. This estimate took into account planned downtime and an allowance for other eventualities. He argued that it was important to keep the highly skilled operatives at his disposal working effectively and efficiently. He was proud of his record, as production manager, in utilising the assets of the company to their full potential and did not wish to have his record tarnished. Jones was adamant that he could not commit to more sales and that most of them would be to order. He added that there would be some benefit in building up a small stock reserve in order to cater for any unexpected sales and to ensure continuity of supply. Holmes was somewhat pacified by this and having reviewed his notes with his production supervisor, agreed to a production schedule of 7,000 units in 2XX6 and 8,500 units in 2XX7. His judgment was that this schedule would not necessitate any layoffs, but would involve running the machines at about 80% capacity. This, he accepted, was reasonable in the early stages of the life-cycle of a new product.

The discussion became somewhat heated again when McGuire warned about the undesirable effect of building up too much inventory and the impact that could have on the reported profit. Even though she had raised this many times before, she had always failed to convince the largely production-focussed management team to engage with her on the issue. She went on to talk about things like absorption costing and the need to understand the impact of using different levels of capacity for different applications. She advised the project team that Castlegrove always used the practical capacity level for financial reporting and stock valuation purposes. She emphasised that this was particularly important in terms of competitive pricing and in a new business with potential seasonality and cyclical cycles. She added that it would give some indication of the cost of idle capacity and that it would reduce the risk of the 'downward spiral effect'. As nobody really understood what she was talking about, it was suggested that, as this was only of relevance to her and the auditors, they should move on to agree the projected product costs. McGuire knew this was not the right time to pursue the matter further and, somewhat despondent, presented the cost figures that she had agreed with the relevant parties.

Based on the bill of material agreed with the design team, and after extensive discussions with McKenna, direct material was estimated at €5 per unit. As Castlegrove was heavily unionised, labour rates were based on industry norms. This resulted in a direct labour estimate of €25 per unit. This took into account the standard employer levies payable, the cost of annual leave and other labour benefits agreed with the unions. As regards overheads, McGuire had prepared a detailed analysis of each potential expense heading and classified these as either variable or fixed. Her four years experience with Castlegrove meant that she had an intimate knowledge of its cost structure. Throughout this time she had been complimented on her forecasting ability. The outcome of her analysis was that variable manufacturing overhead was projected at €30 per unit and variable non-manufacturing overhead at €3 per unit.

McGuire was fearful of raising the fixed overhead issue again, but knew that it had to be addressed. She advised her colleagues that her best estimate of the appropriate fixed overhead that should be charged to the 'Pulse' product line was €90,400 for the year. Both Holmes and Jones were adamant that they saw no basis for this charge as it would be incurred in any event and could threaten the viability of a new product that had great potential. Jones was concerned that this could have an adverse impact on the price, previously agreed, and that it could seriously undermine his sales performance. Holmes was proud of his cost control ability and did not understand why he should be responsible for costs that he had little control over. He spoke of his previous experience in Dublin, where the only thing that mattered to his manager was something called 'contribution'. Jones added that it was important to have some flexibility in the application of pricing policy in the first year of a new product launch and that this charge would undermine that strategy. The debate continued without any sign of reaching a consensus. It was decided to seek advice from Maloney, and he was invited to the next meeting of the project team.

At that meeting, the discussion continued in the same vein, until Maloney intervened to advise that it was important for all products to carry their fair share of overheads and if they could not, then it didn't make sense to go ahead with the project. In answer to a query from Jones, McGuire advised that €30,400 of the fixed overhead related to non-manufacturing activities and included expenses associated with his new sales office in London. Being weary of the process, all parties were relieved when McGuire reminded them that the product would make a positive contribution and was projected to record a healthy profit in the first year. She also told them that due to the low inflationary environment generally and the excellent experience to date by Castlegrove in managing its costs, she had anticipated the same costings in 2XX7. She added that these figures could be updated during the year as part of the usual performance review process. With that, it was agreed that Somers and McGuire would finalise the proposal and submit it to the board for consideration.

Concluding Comments/Substantive Issues

As they left the meeting, Maloney emphasised to McGuire the importance of getting the overhead issue sorted out once and for all, particularly as there would be more new product proposals coming to fruition in the near future. He was worried that it could lead to undue friction within the company and remembered that at a recent conference he was told that some costing systems could give rise to "dysfunctional behaviour". He said that he did not understand the term and added that the conference presenter noted that there are 'different systems for different purposes'. He asked McGuire, "As there are so many different costing systems, how does one know which one to use?" She responded by saying that "this would take some time to explain." She went on to remind him of her previous attempts to address the overhead issue and noted that it was of particular relevance now given their intention to incentivise senior management with a bonus scheme.

McGuire assured Maloney that she would give the matter some thought and prepare a presentation for the management meeting early next month. She headed back to her office with renewed determination and began to ponder how she would tackle the issue. She was conscious of the fact that her audience would be highly critical and would expect her presentation to focus on the specific situation in Castlegrove. In particular, she knew that any potential conflict between how they made decisions and rewarded performance would be closely watched. As she had a very good working relationship with the company auditors and was currently very busy, she decided to enlist the help of their consultancy service.

Required

As management consultant to Castlegrove, prepare a draft set of guidelines and briefing notes on how McGuire might structure her presentation to the senior management team. Your response should deal with the overall concerns expressed by Maloney and the specific issues arising from the new product decision.

Total 100 marks

Appendix 1: Projected Operating Income Statement for 'Pulse'

Period: 12 months ended	Dec. 2XX6	Dec. 2XX7
	€	€
Revenue	467,500	552,500
Variable costs		
Variable manufacturing		
Direct material	27,500	32,500
Direct labour	137,500	162,500
Variable manufacturing overhead	165,000	195,000
Variable cost of goods sold	330,000	390,000
Variable non-manufacturing overhead	16,500	19,500
Total variable costs	346,500	409,500
	121,000	143,000
Contribution margin		
Fixed costs		
Fixed manufacturing overhead	60,000	60,000
Fixed non-manufacturing overhead	30,400	30,400
Total fixed costs	90,400	90,400
Operating income	30,600	52,600
Note		
Projected sales (units)	5,500	6,500
Breakeven level of sales (units)	4,109	4,109

Case 7
Spektrik plc
Falconer Mitchell, University of Edinburgh

Introduction

Spektrik plc produces and sells a range of electronic measuring devices for a variety of manufacturing applications. New products are regularly added to its range. They are devised in the Design Engineering Unit of the company by a small team of electronic engineers who all have production experience.

Competition in Spektrik's main product markets has been intensifying and over the last few years profitability has deteriorated. The chief executive has attributed this to "an inability to control product costs as well as our key Japanese competitors have done." He has located one cause of this problem as being "technologically driven product design with a neglect of economic factors followed by an absence of continual cost-reduction effort when the product is in production – this has led to falling product profitability over the product life-cycle as prices are squeezed."

You are a newly appointed management accountant in Spektrik plc and you have been given the task of addressing the issues raised by the chief executive. Following investigation of Japanese management accounting practice, you have decided to follow the management accounting practices of your main competitors. Consequently, you have proposed the piloting of a system of target costing for the next new product launch.

The Pilot Target Costing Situation

The product for which the new target costing approach is to be applied is one which will replace one of the main products in the company's product range. With the help of marketing staff, you have drawn up the following financial specifications for the new product.

Product 107

1. Estimated total market life: 6 years

2. Projected sales profile:

	Product Introduction	**Product Maturity**	**Product Decline**
Duration	First three annual quarters	Next 12 annual quarters	Final nine annual quarters
Targeted unit selling price	€20	€18	€14
Budgeted sales volume for this life-cycle stage	50,000 units	360,000 units	180,000 units

3. Required initial investment:
   - Plant & Machinery €1,000,000
   - Space €750,000
   - Working Capital €250,000

4. Required return on initial investment: an average of 30% per annum.

Implementation of Target Costing Pilot

In order to implement the target costing pilot you have established a small four-man steering group comprising the heads of design engineering, production, marketing, and yourself. The group's objectives are to, first, specify the target cost to be set for Product 107 and, secondly, to plan how the target cost information should be used to achieve effective cost control. Finally, it should make recommendations on whether and how target costing should be extended within the company.

Required

Question 1

Calculate the target cost for Product 107. This should be done on the following two bases:

(a) a single target cost applying over the whole life-cycle of the product; and
(b) a set of target costs applying at each of the three stages of the product life-cycle, i.e. introduction, maturity and decline.

(40 marks)

Question 2

Discuss which of the above approaches to target costing would be most appropriate for Spektrik plc.

(20 marks)

Question 3

Make recommendations on how the company can best organise to facilitate achievement of the target cost/s set.

(20 marks)

Question 4

Make suggestions on how the existing target costing implementation could be improved.

(20 marks)

Total 100 marks

Case 8

Chicken Pieces

Peter Clarke, University College Dublin

Background

Jim Hanlon and Ray Fullam renewed acquaintances at a Christmas party of their former employer. Both had become good friends while studying and playing rugby on the 3rd Bs at College. Both accepted a job offer, on graduation, from Bates and Co., Chartered Accountants – after an endless round of tedious presentations by, and interviews with, the various accountancy firms.

Jim took up the position as a trainee accountant and Ray entered the management consultancy division. After a few years, their careers took different paths. Jim qualified as a chartered accountant and now owned a small accountancy practice on the outskirts of Dublin. Ray continued with his management consultancy career. Now, they had met again after five years and Ray was the more worried of the two. After a while, he explained to Jim that he had 'business problems'. Eventually, Ray explained his current situation.

Overview of the Company

At the start of the year Ray had been appointed as managing director of Chicken Pieces Limited, a company that manufactured ready-made chicken foods for consumers in Ireland. Cooking and eating habits of Irish people have been transformed during the past decade. For example, it is estimated that Irish people only spend one-sixth of their time on cooking meals compared with a few decades ago. This is a reflection on busy lifestyles and also on the fact that, with ready-to-cook foods available, there is generally less waste that requires disposal. Noting this trend towards convenience foods, the company began to produce packaged, ready-to-cook chicken pieces some years ago.

As a food, chicken is now more popular then ever to eat and the poultry market has recovered from the effects of the bird flu that surfaced in 2XX6. According to

Bord Bia, the Irish Food Board, production and consumption levels are increasing by about 2% per annum and modest future price increases are also expected. Chicken is economical, relatively low in fat and a good source of protein, and is increasingly appreciated for its contribution to a healthy diet. Chicken is also incredibly versatile since it lends itself to many different recipes and styles of cuisine – as any recipe book will demonstrate. Thus, modern consumers are prepared to pay a premium for the convenience of ready-to-cook meals.

Ray explained: "I took over the business last January and I hired a part-time bookkeeper to keep all the records straight, but he resigned a few days ago. I don't think he was very comfortable in the job. There is no management accounting system in place and I'd really appreciate some professional help, if you could afford the time."

Some days later Jim Hanlon arrived at the premises of Chicken Pieces. Jim's first impression of the plant and its surroundings was not very favourable, but he managed to hide his feelings as he shook hands with Ray Fullam and exchanged New Year's greetings. After the usual pleasantries, Ray outlined his business operations.

Current Operations

"At the moment we focus only on the convenience and ready-to-cook consumer market in chicken pieces. We have three major products, namely breasts, wings and legs. Next year we would like to expand our product range."

"Can you give me an overview of your operations?" asked Jim.

"Well, that's easy," said Ray. "There are a few different processes involved." As he spoke, he drew a rough diagram on a piece of paper (Appendix 1).

He continued: "We have one major supplier who provides us with all our chickens. When the carcasses are delivered they are inspected for quality and immediately put into cold storage. Subsequently, the carcass is taken out of storage, washed and cleaned and sent for jointing. This jointing process involves cutting through the elastic tendons and cartilage that surround the joint, rather than cutting through solid bone. This operation is highly labour intensive but involves little expensive equipment other than a good, sharp boning knife and a dishwasher-safe acrylic cutting board. The jointing operation ends when the different products first emerge, namely breasts, wings and legs. From each chicken we get two breasts, two wings and two legs. The leftovers are considered as waste and disposed of."

"The breasts are then transferred to a filleting process. Initially, deboning of the breasts cuts away the breastbone and ribs. Removing the bones from chicken parts makes them cook faster. Once everything is done, the product is sealed and is ready for distribution. None of our finished product is held in stock. The wings and legs undergo a similar but separate process and, in order to prevent confusion, we call this the finishing process. Basically, excess parts, including fat, are trimmed away from the wings and legs. When completed, the products are wrapped in cellophane and cardboard, dated and stamped and are ready for distribution. Again, we hold no stock of finished goods."

"Who are your main customers?" asked Jim.

"Well, at the moment we have only three customers – Buns, Mossgo and Superdim."

"So, what's the problem?" quizzed Jim.

"Actually, the immediate problem is a shortage of good operating and financial data, so it's difficult to say where the problem lies."

Ray Fullam continued: "At the start of the year I signed contracts with our three customers to supply them with chicken pieces for one year. This required me to take out extensive advertising space in their outlets. Then, they require special delivery dates and that's why our distribution costs are so high. Basically, I think the business has great potential. The concept of ready-to-cook chicken pieces is firmly established with consumers of all ages. However, we need to take a close look at our day-to-day operations since all the contracts with our customers are up for renewal. I suspect that we may be under competitive pressures, so I need accurate cost information. Certainly, the financial troubles of Cappoquin Chickens last Autumn made us all apprehensive."

"However, one advantage for us is that food sold in supermarkets in Ireland must indicate the country of origin on the label. Therefore, being an Irish producer gives us a bit of an edge since our produce must conform to EU food regulations. However, a measure known as 'substantial transformation' allows poultry products with minimal processing in Ireland, such as the addition of breadcrumbs, to be passed off as Irish. This loophole is official and above-board, created by EU legislation and therefore affecting other EU Member States. Irish poultry producers and the Irish government would like to see more stringent labelling, but this is being resisted by the EU politicians. Did you know that such labelling is not required for restaurants? So that if you ask for, say, Thai chicken when you eat out in Dublin, the odds are that you are, literally, eating Thai chicken! In fact, Ireland imports about four million chicken fillets each week, making Ireland the largest consumer of chicken per head in the EU. Poultry consumption accounts for nearly one-third of total meat consumed in Ireland. Asian chickens can be purchased at about 40% less than EU-produced chicken since production is carried on at density levels that would be unacceptable in Europe. Furthermore, the Food Safety Authority of Ireland (FSAI) once discovered animal DNA in some imported chicken fillets. While some of these imports are sold in supermarkets, about 90% are used in the catering trade and this has an adverse impact on the Irish poultry sector. Furthermore, the EU ban on Chinese poultry meat has recently been lifted, while the Thai authorities are confident in negotiating higher import quotas for their products. To survive, Chicken Pieces Limited will have to provide additional value to its customers while managing its cost base."

The Assignment

He continued: "The periodic accounting reports that I receive are useless and I could never find out what my unit cost was, but I was told that its calculation was too complicated! I don't see what the problem is, as I consider that the only real variable cost we have is the purchase of chickens. All our other costs can be considered fixed because they don't fluctuate with volume. For example, our distribution expenses are a fixed cost in the sense that sometimes we hire the courier to deliver a dozen chickens and at other times he delivers ten dozen to the same location."

Some time later that day, Ray Fullam gave Jim some operating data for the recent year (see Appendix 2) and was rather apologetic because that was all he had. He closed the door of Jim's temporary office very quietly.

Jim was grateful for the privacy and wondered just what he had let himself in for. He remembered how dull the topic of joint and process costing was at college. He now realised the relevance and importance of such issues. Accurate product costs were urgently required to allow future contracts to be negotiated successfully and for the company to engage in modern cost-management techniques.

His thoughts were disturbed by the vibration of his mobile phone. It was his wife. Since he intended to work all day, Jim enquired what was for dinner that evening. "Chicken," was the innocent reply and Jim declined to pursue the conversation further.

Required

You are to present a memorandum to Ray Fullam, to include coverage of the following tasks.

Question 1

Based on the limited information provided in this case study, identify four critical success factors (CSFs) of a non-financial nature for this business, and indicate how they should be measured by way of a key performance indicator (KPI).

(12 marks)

Question 2

Apportion the 'joint costs' of the storage/jointing operation on the physical output basis. Clearly show your calculations and briefly describe the limitations of using the physical units method for apportioning joint costs.

(18 marks)

Question 3

Prepare, in T-account format, the separate process accounts for:

(a) the preparation of chicken breasts, i.e. filleting; and
(b) the preparation of wings/legs, i.e. finishing.

(25 marks)

Question 4

Prepare a summarised cost/income statement for Ray Fullam's manufacturing plant for the recent accounting period. Your statement should be in the format of:

    Sales revenue

    Cost of goods sold (breasts)

    Cost of goods sold (wings/legs)

    Non-production expenses

    = Net profit or loss for the period

(20 marks)

Question 5

Calculate the breakeven point (in sales revenue) for the year.

(10 marks)

Question 6

The annual cost to the company of disposing of waste material in the 'jointing' process amounts to €14,000. Recently a pet food manufacturer, who is willing to collect such waste on a monthly basis, approached the company (previously it was disposed of by the company on a weekly basis). The company is interested in, effectively, outsourcing the disposal problem to the pet food manufacturer, as he is willing to pay an annual sum of €3,000. However, Chicken Pieces will have to invest in additional storage facilities, costing €8,000 per annum. Clearly present your calculation as to whether this proposal is financially attractive to the company, and identify other factors that should be taken into consideration before a final decision is made.

(15 marks)

Total 100 marks

Appendix 1: Chicken Pieces Manufacturing Operations

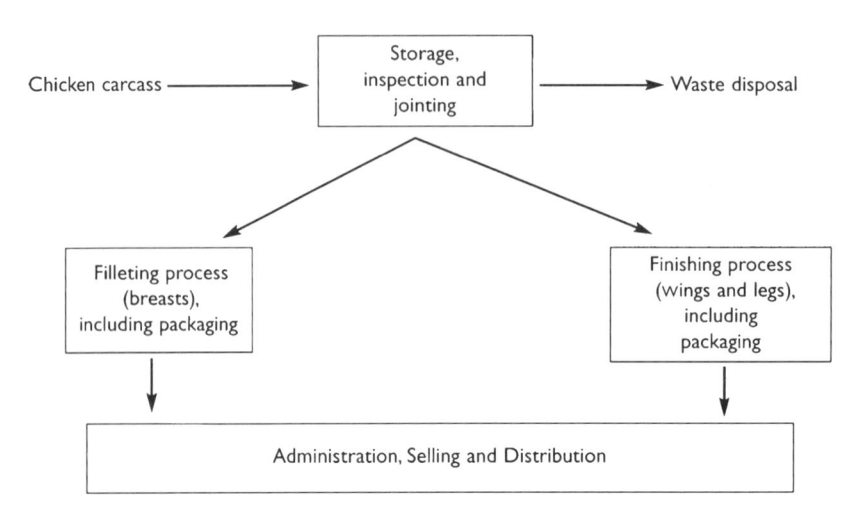

```
Chicken carcass ──→ Storage, inspection and jointing ──→ Waste disposal
                            │
                 ┌──────────┴──────────┐
                 ↓                     ↓
        Filleting process      Finishing process
        (breasts),             (wings and legs),
        including packaging    including packaging
                 │                     │
                 └──────────┬──────────┘
                            ↓
           Administration, Selling and Distribution
```

Appendix 2: Operating and Financial Data

1. Sales Data

	Buns	Mossgo	Superdim	Total
Sales – Breasts (units)	30,000	20,000	20,000	70,000
– Breasts (selling price)	€2.00	€1.90	€2.10	
– Wings and legs (units)	60,000	60,000	20,000	140,000
– Wings and legs (selling price)	0.80c	0.60c	0.90c	
– Cash received to date	€50,000	€20,000	€35,000	

2. Operating Data

Chickens purchased (carcass) and put into storage	40,000 chickens
Cost of chicken (carcass) purchased and paid for (total)	€24,000
Chickens in storage at year end (unprocessed and in storage)	5,000 chickens
Storage and other joining costs	€70,000
Waste disposal costs of jointing process	€14,000
Conversion costs of filleting process (re. breasts)	€32,500
Conversion costs of finishing process (re. wings/legs)	€31,000
Administrative costs	€25,000
Selling and distribution costs	€60,000

You may assume that, apart from the unused chicken carcasses at the end of the year, there was no other opening or closing stock of raw materials, WIP or finished goods.

Case 9
Horizons Group
Tony O'Dea and Tony Brabazon, University College Dublin

Horizons Group is a publicly quoted US company which operates in the educational sector. The group was founded in 1976 and currently has in excess of 240,000 students enrolled on various degree programmes spanning 219 locations in 39 states. Annual revenues of Horizons Group have increased from $610 million to $1,400 million in the last three years and there has also been significant profit growth.

Recent decades have seen a notable increase in the participation rate in higher education in the US. The US Department of Education estimates that the total size of this service industry exceeds $280 billion per annum. The increase in participation rates in higher education is due in part to the upskilling of many jobs with the expansion of the knowledge economy. Another driver of rising participation rates is the salary premium that college graduates attract. A recent US Census Bureau bulletin noted that college graduates earn, on average, about 75% more than non-graduates.

Horizons Group prides itself on its ability to anticipate student needs and on its ability to offer flexible degree programmes which cater for these needs. The majority of its students are working adults (its target market) and the degree programmes it offers have a strong vocational focus. The scale of the adult education market in the US is large. The US Department of Education estimates that approximately 39% of all students enrolled in higher education programmes are over the age of 24. The average age of incoming students in courses offered by Horizons Group is mid-thirties. Approximately 65% of its students are studying for a Bachelor's Degree and 30% are studying for a Master's Degree. Approximately 55% of its students are women and 45% are men.

Horizons Group considers that traditional universities do not effectively address the unique requirements of working adult students. Traditional universities and colleges were designed to fulfil the educational needs of conventional full-time students, mainly in the 18–24 age range. This focus results in a capital-intensive teaching/learning model, which is characterised by:

- a high percentage of full-time tenured faculty;
- fully-configured library and IT facilities with related full-time staff;
- student housing, sports facilities, catering infrastructure, health-care services and personal and employment counselling, designed to meet the needs of younger students;
- an emphasis on research activities, with a requirement to provide related staff and facilities;
- a traditional term structure with a summer break.

This teaching/learning model makes it difficult for traditional universities to effectively and cost-efficiently target the working adult student market. In contrast, Horizons Group was able to design its student recruitment and administrative systems specifically for this market. It has also reduced capital costs by hiring part-time faculty as required for courses (the group uses in excess of 19,000 part-time faculty), and by leasing space for courses as required. Colleges and universities run by Horizons concentrate on providing tuition services and do not undertake research activities. Consequently, Horizons Group is able to offer attractive tuition rates. The strategic objective of Horizons Group is to be the leading provider of accessible, high quality education for working adults and a preferred provider of workplace training to their employers.

Horizons Group offers its courses under a number of different university 'brand names'. The flagship brand is Thunderbolt University, which has its main campus in Nevada. Of the students at Thunderbolt University, approximately 60% are taking degrees in business, 20% are studying computer science, 10% are studying education and a further 10% are studying health sciences. A wide array of new degree programmes has been created in recent years and the university is constantly looking for new market niches to target with course offerings. Examples of new degree programmes initiated in the past year include a Master of International Management, a Master of Science in Nursing and a Bachelor of Science in Business (Retail Management).

Classes offered by Thunderbolt University are primarily held in the evenings or at weekends at its main campus in Las Vegas, its satellite campuses in other cities in neighbouring states, and in smaller learning centres in locations which do not justify a stand-alone campus. The dispersal of teaching venues means that many students are able to undertake their class work close to home or work locations. Alumni satisfaction with their educational experience has been high, with a recent survey indicating that 94% would recommend Thunderbolt University to others.

Master of Health Services Management Programme

Thunderbolt University is considering adding an additional programme to its existing offering. Although a Bachelor of Health Services Management degree programme already exists, no Master's level programme is offered in this area. Based on feedback from employers and past alumni of its undergraduate programme, there appears to be a substantial untapped demand for a Master's degree offering. Students would complete the degree by taking a series of 12 course modules. The modules would be offered several times a year and students could take them in any order they wished. The course would be offered solely by classroom instruction. Students would be required to complete a number of assignments and to complete a final exam for each course module.

All degree programmes in Thunderbolt University are required to 'pay their way'. Before any new degree programme is approved, it must be able to show that it can cover all the direct costs associated with the programme, cover a portion of general university overheads and also earn a required profit of at least 20% on tuition revenue.

Having undertaken initial market research on competing products in the market and having also taken account of the tuition costs of other Master's programmes offered by Thunderbolt University, it is considered that a tuition charge of $2,500 per course module will prove attractive to potential students.

The costs associated with each degree programme can be split into three main groupings:

- instructional costs;
- selling and promotional costs; and
- general and administrative costs.

Instructional costs include the cost of hiring faculty, the cost of instructional materials, the cost of renting/leasing the classroom location and the costs of organising end-of-module exams. Selling and promotional costs include the costs of student acquisition and the costs of promoting the programme to prospective employers of its graduates. General and administrative costs include the costs of registering students, maintaining student records and processing tuition payments. General and administrative costs also include a share of the general administration costs of Thunderbolt University, for example, general IT costs, costs of the personnel department and costs of central management of the university.

Instructional Costs

A key element in ensuring that Thunderbolt's courses are of a consistent standard across multiple teaching locations is the preparation of very high-quality standardised course materials. The average investment in the materials when setting up a new course module is $150,000. The copying and printing costs of the instructional materials for each student average $200 per module. Copying and printing costs are driven by student numbers. End-of-module exam costs are also predominantly variable and are $100 per student.

Faculty costs vary directly with the number of class groups formed. Class sizes are kept small (in the range 18–22 students) in order to offer a quality teaching experience. As more students enrol in a programme, new class groups are formed and extra faculty are hired to teach these classes. The cost of engaging a faculty member to teach a typical class of 20 students is $10,000 per module.

Additional classroom space is hired on an 'as required' basis as student numbers grow. As classes usually run outside normal office hours in the evenings and at weekends, it is usually fairly easy to rent additional space. The cost of hiring a classroom for a typical size class (in the range 18–22 students) is $1,000 per module.

Selling and Promotional Costs

All new courses are heavily marketed in the three months before tuition is due to start in order to ensure a good level of initial student enrolment. Initial pre-commencement marketing costs for the Master's programme would be $300,000 and this money would be spent on web-based marketing of the programme via Google and other search engines, a limited amount of traditional media advertising in a small number of key markets and targeted e-mail marketing to alumni of Thunderbolt. Once the programme actually commences tuition it is expected, based on past experience, that on-going marketing costs would be 15% of tuition revenue.

General and Administrative Costs

General administration costs consist of both student-related costs (registration, records and payments processing) and general university overheads. Under the current university accounting system (an absorption costing system) all of these costs are absorbed (charged) by students, based on a rate of 35% of course tuition fees.

Activity-based Costing Project

Concern has been raised regarding the accuracy of the current system of absorbing general administration and university overheads to students. Some of the programme managers feel that the current method of allocating central university overheads, especially IT costs, is unfairly penalising 'IT light' degree programmes and creating a subsidy to 'IT heavy' programmes, such as degrees in computer science and degrees in design.

After an analysis of overhead costs, the IT support costs have been analysed into two cost pools: those of general e-learning support, which are borne by all programmes, and those relating to specialist IT resources, which only apply to programmes in design and in computer science. The Master's Degree in Health Service Management will not require any specialist IT resources. The following information has been uncovered concerning overhead costs.

Cost Pool	Activity Driver	Rate Per Unit of Activity ($)
Registration costs	Number of students	$50 per student
Student records	Number of students	$40 per student
IT teaching support	Number of classes	$3,000 per class of 20 students
IT special resources	Number of design/computer science classes	$4,000 per class of 20 students
Central administration	Number of classes	$3,000 per class of 20 students

In calculating the rates per unit of activity, the total budgeted cost for the current year for each cost pool has been divided by the estimated volume of that activity that is expected to occur this year. Seventy-five percent of the rate per unit of activity for all of the above overheads relates to variable costs, and the rest to fixed costs. There is currently surplus capacity in each of the above processes. Adding the new course will not impact on the fixed overhead costs of any of the cost pools.

Outtel Inc. Proposal

Apart from offering degree programmes, Thunderbolt University offers a range of in-house training programmes for large firms. These training programmes are customised to the requirements of the firm and take place at their premises. The programmes may also count as credits towards a related degree programme. Hence they are attractive to employees.

The basic structure of in-house training programmes offered by Thunderbolt is similar to the model it uses for degree programmes. A set of customised course materials is written for the programme, classes are taught in groups of 20, and part-time faculty are hired to teach individual class groups. As for the degree programmes, most instruction takes place in the evenings or at weekends in order to minimise employee downtime.

Outtel is a major manufacturer of microprocessors. It is interested in running a management development programme for its mid-level managers in order to groom them to take more senior roles in Outtel in future years. The training director of Outtel has asked Thunderbolt to quote a price for running a 'single module' programme initially.

Thunderbolt has never dealt with Outtel before, but is particularly interested in getting business from the company. The training programme will encompass a total of 2,000 employees (100 class groups with 20 employees in each) and it is possible that a substantial number of these employees would follow up the training programme by undertaking an MBA with Thunderbolt. It has therefore been decided by senior management in Thunderbolt that the university is prepared to offer an attractive price to Outtel in order to win the contract to give the management training programme. The price for the quote will be set at the relevant cost of offering the training programme.

The following quote has been prepared by a new accountant in the executive programmes division.

	$
Instructional costs	
Faculty costs (100 classes × $10,000)	1,000,000
Instructional materials	150,000
Selling and promotional	
Marketing costs (15% of bid total)	575,000

General and administrative	
35% of bid total	1,341,667
Required profit (20% of bid total)	766,666
Bid amount	3,833,333

On seeing this quote, the director of company training programmes at Thunderbolt called the accountant for a meeting and expressed surprise that the quote was so high. The accountant noted that he had used similar costings to those used when evaluating a proposed new degree programme. The faculty costs were the same as for a class on a degree programme, as were the costs of creating the instructional materials. The marketing costs were the 'usual' 15% of tuition, although the accountant was willing to concede that these costs were not really applicable here as Thunderbolt would not need to spend any money marketing the programme. The calculations of general and administrative costs were also based on the 'usual' 35% of tuition, with the required profit being calculated as 20% of the bid total (tuition costs). The accountant argued that, regardless of the calculation of individual costs, the bid amount worked out at only $1,917 per employee trained, which he argued represented a 'good deal'.

The director of training was still unhappy with the bid calculation and restated that the bid should have been based only on the relevant costs of undertaking the training programme. The director then supplied the accountant with the following additional information.

(i) The faculty cost figure seems OK. We pay faculty the same amount to teach an in-house training programme module as a degree programme module, as both entail similar amounts of work.
(ii) We could design new instructional materials from scratch, but the course content on the training programme overlaps with an existing degree module. The existing materials could be reworked for the training programme at a cost of $35,000.
(iii) There will be no ongoing marketing costs for this programme. However, we have spent approximately $10,000 to date on cultivating Outtel as a potential customer.
(iv) The general and administrative costs of running in-house training programmes are similar to those of degree programmes because records have to be kept of all attendees, and of their performance on module assessments, as they are entitled to course credits for the module.

The director of training has heard of the ABC project and specifically wants the ABC costings to be used as she considers them more accurate than the basic 35% levy. This course will require specialist IT resources and support because it will make extensive use of video-conferencing and other IT services.

The director of training asked the accountant to prepare a revised quote for the training programme.

Required

Question 1

Master of Health Services Management Proposal

(a) Calculate the allowable target cost of a module for a single class of exactly 20 students in the Master of Health Services Management course.

Note: in answering this requirement, ignore all the initial one-off costs of developing the course materials and the initial marketing launch costs for a module.

(5 marks)

(b) Calculate the expected cost and the expected profit per module for a single class of exactly 20 students:

 (i) if absorption costing is used and the university's 35% levy for general and administration costs is applied to each student;
 (ii) if activity-based costing is used to allocate the university's general and adminstrative costs.

Note: in answering this requirement, ignore all the initial one-off costs of developing the course materials and the initial marketing launch costs for a module.

(24 marks)

(c) Comment on the significance of any differences between your results for (b)(i) and (b)(ii).

(5 marks)

(d) If the absorption costing system is used and the 35% levy for general and administrative costs is treated as a variable cost per student, calculate the number of students that must enrol in a single class in order for Thunderbolt to:

 (i) breakeven;
 (ii) make a profit of $5,000.

Note: in answering this requirement, ignore all the initial one-off costs of developing the course materials and the initial marketing launch costs.

(24 marks)

(e) Comment on your answer to requirement (d), bearing in mind the expected class size.

(5 marks)

(f) Calculate the breakeven number of students that are required in total for an individual module, if the costs of developing course materials and initial marketing costs are included in your analysis.

Note: in answering this requirement, assume that all classes will contain exactly 20 students. Also assume that the absorption costing system is used for general and administrative costs. You can ignore the 'time-value-of-money' in answering this part of the question.

(12 marks)

Question 2

Outtel Proposal

Calculate the relevant cost of offering the training programme for Outtel.

(25 marks)

Total 100 marks

Case 10
Newtown Manufacturing Limited
Tom Kennedy, University of Limerick

Overview of the Company

Power Corporation plc is a major supplier of boilers, power-generation equipment, components and related support services worldwide. It was organised around product groups, each with its own manufacturing facilities. In 2XX5 it made a strategic decision to purchase Newtown Manufacturing Limited from its founder, John Grimes, rather than develop a greenfield site. Grimes was a self-trained engineer with many years experience in a similar business in America and had accumulated sufficient capital to realise his life-long ambition of returning to Ireland and setting up his own business. He did this 10 years ago by setting up Newtown Manufacturing to supply boilers and components to the Irish and European markets. The timing was ideal in that it coincided with the beginning of the economic boom in both Ireland and the UK. Grimes recognised that he did not have the requisite managerial skills to run a business and hired Joe Scanlan as general manager. He formed an excellent working relationship with Scanlan and allowed him to strengthen the managerial team to support the continually developing and successful business. He recognised the excellent performance of the management team by allocating them 15% of the equity in 2XX2.

In 2XX5, after serious deliberation with his family and the other shareholders, Grimes decided to accept a very attractive offer for the business from Power Corporation plc. The terms agreed meant that Newtown would continue to trade independently and Grimes would work in a consultancy capacity for a minimum of five years. The senior management of Newtown would be retained and aggressive performance targets were agreed. At that time, Newtown Manufacturing employed 160 people in a plant on the outskirts of Dublin. It operated two shifts a day for five days a week. After the takeover by Power Corporation, Newtown was restructured into two distinct product groups: boilers and components. Each group had control over the manufacturing, engineering and sales/distribution of its products.

They were supported by a small general management team in Ireland and were to make a contribution to corporate services and support.

Business Performance/History

Newtown Manufacturing was profitable from the beginning. By the time it was sold to Power Corporation in 2XX5, its turnover was €15 million and its return on investment (ROI) was in the order of 8%. Power Corporation senior management had identified Newtown as a well-run organisation with untapped potential. It was particularly interested in its components business and had developed a strategic plan that would result in a significant investment in that area. Power Corporation had been impressed with the quality of the products presented by Newtown at a number of trade shows. It had come to the conclusion that it could double its components business in five years and earn a minimum of 15% ROI. It was confident that it could achieve major changes in its operating systems and capitalise on the modern computer-integrated components manufacturing facility commissioned by Newtown in 2XX4. It planned to phase out the manufacturing of boilers at Newtown and service this business from its Munich plant, where it could achieve much greater economies of scale.

The overall market for components had increased dramatically in the last few years and Newtown had capitalised on that situation, particularly in the UK. It had built a reputation as a quality and reliable supplier. It had phased-in new technology and updated its product range in response to customer demands. It had made a strategic decision to invest in the development of a range of highly specified products for the aerospace industry. It manufactured these products in its Gamma product line and was extremely proud of its position as market leader. However, it had come under very severe pressure recently from its largest UK customer to reduce the basic selling price of this range of products or risk losing the business to another supplier. The issue became even more acute when Scanlan and Grimes visited the 2XX6 Birmingham trade show and learned that a competitor was now offering similar products from its newly commissioned Malaysian plant at 10% below Newtown's best price. Scanlan and Grimes took immediate action on their return by asking Bill Durkan, the finance manager, to investigate the situation as a matter of urgency. They knew that they would have to be well prepared before briefing the senior management at Power Corporation and were concerned about the performance targets that they had agreed during the takeover process.

Current Accounting System

Durkan ran a very tight operation. He was a competent accountant and had developed an excellent working relationship with the auditors and company bankers. He concentrated primarily on the company's statutory financial reporting requirements and the cash management of the business. He freely admitted that he had not the time or the expertise to introduce a more sophisticated system of accounting for managerial reporting, costing or control purposes. Monthly accounts were available within five working days of the end of the month. They consisted of a standard form of profit and loss account with year-to-date comparison against budget. The cost of sales figure was calculated by making the necessary adjustments for inventory movements. The monthly accounts were supplemented by a product line performance report. This showed the accumulated direct costs and a statement of general overheads. It was produced by using a traditional job costing system. The actual results for the first three months of 2XX6 for the components product lines are shown in Appendix 1.

Product costs were used to help determine individual product prices, to assess product profitability and, occasionally, to make product mix decisions. Actual direct material and direct labour were charged to individual jobs and accumulated by product line. Overhead was grouped under four headings, as shown in Appendix 1. A single overhead rate per direct labour hour was calculated to allocate the general overheads to each product line. The resulting overhead was added to the actual direct costs to determine the total product cost. Newtown's overall aim is to achieve a mark-up of approximately 20%. It allows for some discretion in terms of discounts and special offers. This strategy has worked well for Newtown since its inception. It has consistently achieved growth rates of over 10% in sales volume and profitability in the last five years.

Durkan had been concerned for some time about the integrity of the cost information and the need to reflect the changing cost profile of the organisation. He was conscious of the significant shift in the labour mix from direct to indirect, and the impact that this would have on the overhead rate being used for pricing purposes. He knew that the trend of introducing more technically sophisticated plant and services would continue. As Newtown had no difficulty retaining its existing customer base to date, and continued to grow its market share, the issue was not deemed a high priority. However, recent feedback from its sales people and an urgent telephone call from Scanlan meant that the issue had to be addressed now. Durkan met with his recently recruited financial analyst, Mick Dowd. They discussed the potential benefit of using different overhead rates and the possible impact on individual product costs. They reviewed expenditure by department and the available operating activity by product line. In both cases, performance was in line with budget. They noted that the actual overhead recovery rate for the components group was €39.16 per direct labour hour for the first three months of the year versus a budget of €40. They were happy that the direct costs were competitive and would continue on the expected downward trend year on year. Finally, they decided that the best course of action was to analyse how the general overheads expenditure was incurred, as it was approximately 60% of its total costs.

Dowd has previously worked as part of an implementation team with a large banking company that adopted activity-based costing (ABC). He convinced Durkan that the situation at Newtown was particularly suitable for the application of the ABC principles and process. Durkan had heard about ABC at a conference some years ago and had only a vague understanding of it. He remembered the speaker saying that "overhead should not be viewed as a cost to be added to direct material and labour. Rather, one should focus on the activities performed by the support departments and try to link the cost of performing them to the products." Durkan told Dowd he would look at his conference notes, if he could find them, and do some background reading on the subject. He knew that he needed to get the full co-operation of Grimes and the senior management team in order to make the task feasible. He expected resistance from some of them, whose only interest was in the introduction of the latest manufacturing technology and a reduction in the money spent on administration.

Product Costing Review Strategy

Durkan was proud of the job he had done at Newtown and his careful financial management was recognised as a major factor in its success. As he was not familiar with the ABC process, he did not wish to undermine his position by promoting investment in such a system at this stage. He decided to present a case to the senior management that suggested changing circumstances had undermined the ability of the current system to allocate a 'fair share of overheads' to individual products. He would remind them of the basis for using the traditional direct labour hours allocation method and the benefit of looking more critically at what was happening now in order to allow them to make a better assessment of how much each product was contributing to the bottom line. He would emphasise the steps he had taken to ensure that the direct material and labour costs were recorded and assigned accurately. He would recommend the carrying out of a pilot study in the components product group using other allocation methods. He would tell them of the potential benefits of refining the existing costing system and applying the ABC principles. He would commit to reviewing the outcome of the study with them before deciding on the next step. He would promise to give them some background information on the ABC system and an overview of its key attributes and features. He would emphasise that the pilot study would be largely driven by his financial analyst, Mick Dowd, but would require some co-operation from them. He knew that he would have Scanlan's full support for this strategy, particularly given the feedback from the Birmingham trade show.

After a robust debate, the Newtown senior management team agreed to support Durkan's strategy. The decision was greatly helped by the news of the competitive threat to the Gamma product range. Durkan was mandated to critically review the components product group cost structure and see if Newtown could or should revise its pricing policy.

In carrying out the brief, Durkan and Dowd decided to concentrate initially on the first three months of 2XX6. Dowd was freed up from his day-to-day duties to concentrate fully on the project. His initial ambition to trace some of the general overhead directly to the individual product lines gave rise to too much confusion and was quickly abandoned. In conjunction with Durkan, he identified the key data that was required and the process that was likely to succeed. He interviewed each support department head so that he could reclassify the main categories of general overheads into more homogeneous expense headings. This iterative process facilitated the identification of the key tasks or activities that were being performed by each support department. Dowd had learned from previous experience that it was critical to set a realistic limit on the number of activities chosen. In consultation with Durkan, he decided not to exceed 20 for the pilot study.

During the process of activity identification, Dowd also decided on the operational measure or driver that best reflected the use of that activity. This decision reflected the best attempt at identifying a cause-and-effect relationship between the activities chosen and the costs incurred. The choice of driver was also influenced by the ability to capture the relevant information in an economically feasible manner. The process stimulated much debate and was underpinned by the assumption that being approximately right was acceptable. The outcome of this stage of the process is presented in Appendix 2. Durkan and Dowd were confident that they had the information necessary to estimate a revised and much more credible product-costing model.

Concluding Comments

Both Durkan and Dowd were delighted with the degree of co-operation and communication developed by the exercise. Michael Doyle, the manufacturing manager, noted that it was great that manufacturing and accounting people were having an intense discussion about resources. He expected the study to clearly demonstrate what a tight ship he was running. Richard Davies, the sales/marketing manager, speculated on the possibility that this exercise would confirm his assertion that manufacturing productivity had stalled in the last year and that it was no surprise that Newtown was under competitive threat. Larry Williams, the engineering manager, was enthused by the expectation that his efforts to reduce the number of engineering charge orders would be vindicated and that Grimes's personal agenda could no longer block progress in this area. For his part, Durkan was confident that he now had a solid basis for his argument with Davies to be more discerning in his choice of customers and the need to achieve better economies in the delivery of its products.

Required

Question 1

Prepare revised product-costing models for the components product group, based on the information available.

(20 marks)

Question 2

Comment on the outcome of the revised costing models, with particular reference to the competitive position of the Gamma product line.

(40 marks)

Question 3

Advise on whether Newtown should adopt ABC.

(20 marks)

Question 4

In order to assist Durkan in making his presentation, prepare a brief set of notes setting out the circumstances in which you would expect ABC to be most beneficial and summarise its key attributes and essential features.

(20 marks)

Total 100 marks

Appendix 1: Components Group – Product Line Performance Report

(Traditional Job Costing System using Direct Labour Hours):
January–March 2XX6

	Product Lines (Gross)			Total	Rate per Direct Labour Hour *1	Product Lines (Unit)		
	Alpha €	Beta €	Gamma €	€		Alpha €	Beta €	Gamma €
Sales value	1,600,000	1,650,000	1,150,000	4,400,000		80.00	110.00	115.00
Direct costs								
Direct material	400,000	255,000	250,000	905,000		20.00	17.00	25.00
Direct labour	220,000	225,000	135,000	580,000		11.00	15.00	13.50
Total direct costs	620,000	480,000	385,000	1,485,000		31.00	32.00	38.50
General overhead								
Manufacturing	265,392	298,565	199,043	763,000	13.27	13.27	19.90	19.90
Engineering	98,435	110,739	73,826	283,000	4.92	4.92	7.38	7.38
Sales & distribution	192,522	216,587	144,391	553,500	9.63	9.63	14.44	14.44
Administration	226,783	255,130	170,087	652,000 *2	11.34	11.34	17.01	17.01
Total general overhead	783,132	881,021	587,347	2,251,500	39.16	39.16	58.73	58.73
Total Product Cost per Traditional System (Direct labour hours)				3,736,500		70.16	90.73	97.23
Profit by product line/unit (Before inventory adjustments)	196,868	288,979	177,653	663,500		9.84	19.27	17.77
				Mark-up 18%		14%	21%	18%
*1 Total direct labour hours	20,000	22,500	15,000	57,500				
Volume (units)	20,000	15,000	10,000	45,000				

*2 Includes contribution of €130,000 to corporate head office

Appendix 2: Components Group – Major Activities and Cost Drivers for First Three months of 2XX6

Activity	Cost Drivers	Alpha	Beta	Gamma	Total	Total €	Dept.	Total €
1 Mould design/manufacture	no. of parts – square feet	20	35	35	90	325,000	Mnfg	
2 Manufacturing operations	no. of machine hours	20,000	26,250	22,500	68,750	233,000	Mnfg	
3 Supervision of direct labour	no. of direct labour hours	20,000	22,500	15,000	57,500	120,000	Mnfg	
4 Quality inspection	no. of units audited	40	50	55	145	85,000	Mnfg	763,000
5 Plant engineering/utilities	square feet	12,000	7,500	9,000	28,500	157,000	Eng	
6 Process and test engineering	no. of engineering change revisions	20	18	15	53	126,000	Eng	283,000
7 Distribution	% traced directly to customers	30	30	40	100	437,500	Sales/Dist	
8 Sales & marketing expenses	% of sales revenue	36	38	26	100	81,000	Sales/Dist	
9 Invoicing	no. of invoices	25	30	25	80	35,000	Sales/Dist	553,500
10 Materials management	no. of stock transactions	85	65	85	235	118,000	Adm	
11 Procurement	% of direct material	44	28	28	100	130,000	Adm	
12 Order processing	no. of orders	20	35	90	145	95,000	Adm	
13 Customer administration	no. of customers	8	10	15	33	65,000	Adm	
14 Information systems support	no. of desktop units	56	32	29	117	39,000	Adm	
15 General administration	no. of direct labour hours	20,000	22,500	15,000	57,500	205,000	Adm	652,000
Total general overhead						**2,251,500**		**2,251,500**

Case 11
Lennon Department Store Limited
Bernard Pierce and Barbara Flood, Dublin City University

Introduction

Deirdre Lennon had been in the business long enough to know that major decisions may be required in the near future. As she walked down the corridor, she reflected on the fact that the meeting with her senior management colleagues had been tense and difficult – an all too familiar experience these days. Although the company had managed to maintain a modest increase in turnover, she was very conscious that margins were being squeezed, competition was increasing and predictions of a looming crisis might be closer to reality than some of her colleagues liked to believe. She reflected on the decision just taken by senior management to engage a firm of consultants to examine various aspects of the business and to recommend a strategy for the future. As she left her office that evening, Deirdre tried to imagine how the original founders of Lennon Department Store might have reacted in the circumstances. "I just wonder how they would have coped with these conditions," she thought, as she pondered the origins of the company.

Background

John and Emer Lennon returned to Ireland over 50 years ago, having emigrated to England 10 years earlier. A small amount of personal savings, supplemented by funds generated from the sale of a family inheritance, presented an opportunity to acquire a small retail outlet in the suburbs of Dublin for the equivalent of €8,500.

The location was well known to John and Emer and seemed to offer several advantages as a location for a small newsagent and general store. The surrounding area seemed set for significant housing development and was well served by public transport, being close to a train station and major bus routes. The particular site offered many attractions, being located on a corner between a major road and a quiet cul de sac. The main building was in a dilapidated state and refurbishment and fitting-out required some bank borrowings, but it offered a generous amount of space for the business and also provided modest upstairs accommodation for the Lennons and their young family. A further attraction was a small yard and some outside sheds, which the Lennons quickly realised provided scope for future expansion.

Although the initial years presented many challenges and much hard work, it became clear that the business offered major potential for development and Lennons' shop became well established, not only as a well-stocked retail outlet, but also as a social venue and recognised meeting place. Within a few years, the family moved to a new home and the store expanded to fill the available space. A major decision was required when the Lennons were offered the then astronomical sum of the equivalent of €900,000 by an international hotel chain, which wished to purchase the premises and build their first hotel in Ireland.

Overcoming sentimental attachment, the Lennons finally accepted a slightly higher offer and invested the money in two larger and more modern outlets, one of which became the responsibility of their eldest daughter, Deirdre. A few years later, Lennons' opened two further stores, continuing the strategy of seeking out areas of high housing density, within easy reach of urban commuters. A combination of sound business knowledge and shrewd financial management ensured that Lennons' stores continued to trade successfully and, about 20 years ago, a majority shareholding was sold to an investment consortium and Lennon Department Store Limited was subsequently formed. Deirdre Lennon, who had almost 20 years' experience in the business and had built up an excellent reputation with suppliers, was appointed chief buyer in the company. Her younger brother, Seamus, continued in his existing role as manager of one of the stores and John and Emer retired from the business.

Over the years, the company persisted with the strategy of controlled expansion, while continuing the Lennon tradition of carrying a full range of stock and seeking to locate stores in densely populated neighbourhoods near major suburban commuter routes. The company now operates department stores and supermarkets at 25 locations throughout the country. It is centrally managed from a head office building, but also has a manager and support staff at each location.

Details of Current Business

The company sells a wide range of products and, to facilitate more effective management, has classified its products into the following merchandise groups.

Group 1	Hardware products
Group 2	Ladies' fashion wear
Group 3	Men's fashion wear
Group 4	Children's wear
Group 5	Concession sales
Group 6	Supermarkets

Concession sales arise where the company has entered into an agreement that the concession owner may sell their products in specified stores and pay Lennon

Department Store Limited on a monthly basis a specified commission based on sales value. Where a concession agreement exists, staff are employed by the concession owner and Lennon Department Store Limited has no responsibility for payroll costs.

Store Details

Although the company has followed a consistent strategy regarding store location, variations in traffic patterns, competition and housing development mean that demand for products varies greatly in different stores and has resulted in the establishment of three categories of stores within the company.

Category A	Offering all product groups listed above, including a supermarket on site.
Category B	Offering product Groups 1–5, but excluding a supermarket.
Category C	Offering only Group 1 products

In order to standardise the offering as much as possible, all stores within each category are exactly the same size, i.e. all Category A stores are the same size, all Category B stores are the same size and all stores within Category C are the same size. The company measures size in terms of square footage, as shown in Appendix 1.

In addition, within each category of store the same amount of space is allocated to each group of products and they are located in exactly the same position within each store. Decisions regarding these issues are taken at head office, as are decisions regarding suppliers, purchasing conditions and selling prices. Management take the view that the Lennon reputation and brand is critically dependent on the implementation of company policy. Local management is responsible for ensuring compliance with these policies and for maintaining the high level of customer service associated with the Lennon name.

Management Information System

The company has a well established management information system and monitors key performance indicators on a daily, weekly and monthly basis. Cost and revenue behaviour patterns for the year ending 31 December 2XX7, together with other relevant data, are outlined in Appendix 1 and the board has requested a projected profit statement for the year, based on this information and on further relevant details set out below.

Sales are monitored daily – in absolute terms, by comparison with budgets, and also on the basis of sales per square foot. The VAT rate on the company's products is predominantly 21%, with the following exceptions: children's wear for children below age 10 has 0% VAT rate, so a blended rate of 10% is used for children's wear; for supermarkets, because of the different products at different rates, the blended rate is about 8%.

Gross profit margin is defined as the VAT-exclusive selling price of an item less the cost of that item. For Group 5 (concession sales), commission is treated in the same way as gross profit. The gross profit margin is calculated daily per product by the IT system, by taking the selling price of the item from the cash registers and comparing it with the cost price of the item, which is held in the product database.

Payroll costs are monitored weekly and are accumulated for the week and expressed as a percentage of VAT-exclusive sales. Overheads are monitored monthly from management accounts and totals expressed as a percentage of VAT-exclusive sales.

Depreciation is not included in overheads, but shown under a separate heading. Properties are all owned by the company and are not depreciated. The company has a standard fit-out cost per store and this is depreciated on a straight-line basis over seven years.

All central costs are accumulated for head office and charged to the stores as a percentage of VAT-exclusive sales.

Proposals Under Consideration

The consultants that have been engaged by Lennon have been requested to advise on two specific areas where proposals are being considered for year ended 31 December 2XX7. From a detailed analysis of cost behaviour, the consultants have concluded that the cost information set out in Appendix 1 is accurate and reliable for this level of activity. They have also advised that because of company policy to maintain a high degree of autonomy between product groups, a significant amount of payroll and overhead costs are committed for a lengthy period and should therefore be considered fixed for the purpose of changing levels of activity. These amount to 30% of payroll and 35% of overhead projected for the coming year and it is recommended that this information be used in calculating the financial impact of any proposed changes in activity levels or space allocation.

Proposal 1

Management is considering the possibility of discontinuing the supermarket business and devoting the space currently occupied by supermarkets to increasing the space available for Group 1 business. It is expected that such a move may result in some reduction in the number of customers frequenting the store (referred to in the business as footfall), and that this is likely to have some adverse impact on the level of business. There is some uncertainty regarding what this impact will be, and estimates vary from a possible decrease of 1% in projected turnover (probability 15%) to a decrease of 3% (probability 60%) or, in a worst-case scenario, to a decrease of 8% (probability 25%). Management would like to see an appropriate analysis that incorporates these estimates. Because of the difficulties in estimating the impact on footfall, management would also find it helpful to know what will be the critical level of footfall if proposal 1 is implemented, i.e. what percentage reduction in footfall could occur before profits fall below existing levels. Any reduction in demand is expected to apply uniformly to all sales of all product groups in the stores involved.

Proposal 2

A separate proposal has been put forward to be considered independently of proposal 1. Commercial director Thomas Reilly is proposing that space in every store be allocated to product groups in a way that maximises the company's annual profits, subject to 25% of the space in every store being devoted to concessions and a maximum of 25,000 sq. ft. being allocated to any one product group. A further requirement is that a minimum of 10% of space in each store will be allocated to each product group, except that Category B stores will not have supermarkets and Category C stores will only have hardware and concessions. Concessions in Category C stores are expected to show the same levels of profitability as those in Category B stores.

Conclusion

Deirdre Lennon reflected on the meeting just ended and how she had voiced her opposition to both proposals. She had expressed the view that the company should continue with the growth strategy that has been the foundation of its success, arguing: "I have a hunch that our bigger stores are proportionately more profitable and we therefore need to grow our stores as rapidly as possible. If we introduce concessions into our smaller stores, then the Lennon brand will very quickly become diluted and future growth potential compromised. Furthermore, we should continue the policy of stocking the full range of products with uniform allocation of floor space. This has been the foundation for Lennons' success."

As she left her office that evening, Deirdre wondered why her senior management colleagues seemed slow to support her position.

Required

You are required to present the following in the form of a report to the board of Lennon Department Store Limited.

Question 1

(a) A projected profit statement for the company for the year ending 31 December 2XX7, based on the data shown in Appendix 1 and showing appropriate analysis by store category and by product group.
(b) A commentary on the company's projected performance.

(24 marks)

Question 2

(a) Calculation of the financial impact of implementing proposal 1, incorporating the issues raised by management in connection with implications for footfall arising from the proposal.

(b) Your advice regarding what further issues should be considered before making a decision regarding proposal 1.

(28 marks)

Question 3

(a) Calculation of the effect on profitability if the company decides to proceed with proposal 2, showing the recommended space allocation.
(b) Your advice regarding what further issues should be considered before making a decision regarding proposal 2.

(28 marks)

Question 4

(a) Your response to Deirdre Lennon's arguments regarding strategic priorities.
(b) Your recommendations regarding the most important factors for management to consider in developing long-term strategic plans for the company.

(20 marks)

Total 100 marks

Appendix 1: Relevant Data

	Store Category A	Store Category B	Store Category C
Number of stores	5	12	8
Size of each store in sq. ft.	90,000	50,000	25,000
Allocation of space			
Group 1	15,000	10,000	25,000
Group 2	10,000	7,500	
Group 3	7,500	5,000	
Group 4	7,500	5,000	
Group 5	20,000	22,500	
Group 6	30,000		
Total	90,000	50,000	25,000
Sales per sq. ft. (including VAT)	€	€	€
Group 1	500	500	500
Group 2	450	450	
Group 3	425	425	
Group 4	400	400	
Group 5	600	600	
Group 6	1000		
Gross profit margin	%	%	%
Group 1	40	40	40
Group 2	35	35	
Group 3	34	34	
Group 4	30	30	
Group 5	20	20	
Group 6	25		
Payroll as % of VAT-exclusive sales	%	%	%
Group 1	13	13	13
Group 2	15	15	
Group 3	14	14	
Group 4	15	15	
Group 5	0	0	
Group 6	15		
Overheads as % of VAT-exclusive sales	%	%	%
Group 1	16	18	20
Group 2	16	18	
Group 3	16	18	
Group 4	16	18	
Group 5	16	18	
Group 6	10		
Cost of fixtures and fittings per store	€3m	€2.2m	€1.4m
Annual head office costs			€10m

Case 12

Genting Theme Park

Iqbal Khadaroo, Queen's University Belfast

Genting Theme Park (GTP) is a privately owned company which operates an amusement park. It is located in the rural scenic highlands area of Wonderland, which has a sunny tropical climate all year round. It is accessible by cable car and a twisting, steep road.

The amusement park comprises a large open area (that is, a fairground) containing fairs, fun rides and numerous other attractions designed to appeal to people of all age groups. The park is open for 350 days in the year and is closed for 15 days for conducting repairs and maintenance. A typical day spent by a guest at the park is termed a 'Visitor Day'. During the year ended 31 December 2X10 a total of 2,100,000 visitor days were paid for and were made up as follows.

Visitor Category	% of Total Visitor Days
Senior citizens	5
Adults	40
12–16 years of age	15
Under-12 years of age	40

The company sells two types of admission pass to visitors: a 'One-day Visitor's pass' and a 'Two-day Visitor's pass'. These passes have a validity of one year and entitle the holder to admission to the amusement park on a particular day or on two consecutive days.

The management of GTP has adopted the following pricing structure.

(i) A One-day pass for an adult costs €40. Visitors aged 12–16 years and Senior Citizens receive a 20% discount against the cost of adult passes. Visitors aged below 12 years receive a 40% discount against the cost of adult passes.
(ii) A Two-day pass costs the purchaser 25% less than the cost of two One-day Visitor's passes.

(iii) 30% of the total visitor days were paid for by the purchase of One-day passes. The remainder were paid for by the purchase of Two-day passes.

Total operating costs of the park during the year ended 31 December 2X10 amounted to €42,500,000.

GTP also receives a percentage of the income of traders who provide catering and other facilities to visitors to the amusement park. There are 40 such traders from whom payments are received.

The amount of the payment received from each trader depends upon the size of the premises occupied in the amusement park, as follows.

Size of Premises	No. of Traders	Annual Payment per Trader €
Large	10	50,000
Medium	16	30,000
Small	14	15,000

The income from each trader is received under a three-year contract, which became effective on 1 January 2X10. The income is fixed for the duration of each contract.

All operating costs of the theme park incurred during the year ended 31 December 2X11 are expected to increase by 5%. This has led to a decision by management to increase the selling price of all categories of admission passes by 5%, with effect from 1 January 2X11. Management expect the number of visitor days, visitor mix and the mix of admission passes purchased to be the same as in the previous year.

GTP also owns a 500-bedroom hotel with leisure facilities, which is located in the capital city of Wonderland, about 10 miles away from the amusement park.

During the year ended 31 December 2X10, the charge per room on an all-inclusive basis was €100 per room, per night. The total operating costs of the hotel amounted to €10,000,000.

Average occupancy during the year was 300 rooms per night. The hotel is open for 365 days in the year.

It is anticipated that the operating costs of the hotel will increase by 5% in the year ended 31 December 2X11.

Management have decided to increase the charge per room, per night by 5%, with effect from 1 January 2X11, and expect average occupancy will remain at the same level during the year ended 31 December 2X11.

A statistical analysis carried out by the management accountant has determined that the revenue of the hotel and the number of visitors to the amusement park are independent.

Required

Question 1

Prepare a statement showing the budgeted net profit or loss for the year to 31 December 2X11.

(18 marks)

Question 2

The management accountant of GTP has conducted a sensitivity analysis for a range of amusement park activity levels and hotel occupancy and prepared a table showing the budgeted net profit for the year to 31 December 2X11 (see Appendix 1). Discuss the potential use of this table to the management of GTP.

(10 marks)

Question 3

(a) Another organisation has recently opened an amusement park and hotel about 20 miles away. The management of GTP are uncertain of the impact that this will have on the number of visitors to its park and hotel during the year to 31 December 2X11. Current estimates of the number of visitors to the amusement park and the average percentage occupancy of the hotel are as follows:

Amusement Park		Hotel	
Visitors %	**Probability**	**Occupancy %**	**Probability**
Increase by 5%	0.15	70%	0.10
No change	0.70	60%	0.65
Decrease by 10%	0.15	50%	0.25

Using Appendix 1, prepare a summary which shows the range of possible net profit or loss outcomes, and the combined probability of each outcome. The table should also show the expected value of net profit or loss for the year.

(15 marks)

(b) Comment on the table you have prepared in (a) and the use of expected values by management.

(7 marks)

Question 4

Outline FIVE dimensions of performance that management should focus on and suggest measures (or criteria) that could be used for each dimension of performance.

(15 marks)

Question 5

Comment on the alternative courses of action that management could take to improve the profitability of GTP, in the light of competition from another organisation.

(15 marks)

Question 6

Discuss the benefits to management of adopting 'strategic management accounting' techniques.

(20 marks)

Total 100 Marks

Appendix 1: Table Showing Net Profit in the Year to 31 December 2X11 for a Range of Amusement Park Activity Levels and Hotel Occupancy

% Increase/(decrease) in Visitor Days (using 2X10 as Base)

Hotel Occupancy %	-25% €000	-20% €000	-15% €000	-10% €000	-5% €000	No Change €000	+5% €000	+10% €000	+15% €000	+20% €000
75%	4,804	7,453	10,103	12,752	15,402	18,052	20,701	23,351	26,000	28,650
70%	4,045	6,694	9,344	11,993	14,643	17,292	19,942	22,592	25,241	27,891
65%	3,285	5,935	8,584	11,234	13,884	16,533	19,183	21,832	24,482	27,132
60%	2,526	5,176	7,825	10,475	13,124	15,775	18,424	21,073	23,723	26,372
55%	1,767	4,417	7,066	9,716	12,365	15,015	17,664	20,314	22,964	25,613
50%	1,008	3,657	6,307	8,956	11,606	14,256	16,905	19,555	22,204	24,854
45%	249	2,898	5,548	8,197	10,847	13,496	16,146	18,796	21,445	24,095
40%	-511	2,139	4,788	7,438	10,088	12,737	15,387	18,036	20,686	23,336

Case 13
Autoparts SA
Tony Brabazon and Tony O'Dea, University College Dublin

Overview of the Company

Autoparts SA is a large, diversified French firm operating in several countries. Total sales for the year ended 30 April 2XX7 were €535 million, with profits before tax of €58 million. Its primary activities concern automobile and truck sales and repairs. The stated strategy of the firm is to grow through acquisition. Early in 2XX7, following a review of the group's activities, it was decided to search for potential acquisition targets in the fast-growing Chinese market. Shortly afterwards, in February 2XX7, two subsidiaries were acquired. The first subsidiary, Varin pte, operates a large chain of truck maintenance depots in China. The second acquisition, another Chinese company, Yatese pte, produces a range of generic truck spares. These are typically installed on trucks during repairs once the truck's warranty period has expired.

A variety of management and staff incentive schemes are in operation throughout the group. At present, the incentive scheme operating in the two new subsidiaries has two components (these schemes were in existence before the subsidiaries were acquired by Autoparts SA). The first component of the scheme is a bonus pool, which is calculated as described in the two paragraphs below. The calculated bonus is paid to managers in two instalments, half at the end of the year in which the bonus is earned and half one year later. For example, if a bonus is earned in the financial year ended 30 April 2XX7, half of this would be paid shortly after the year end, while the remaining half would be paid in May 2XX8.

Varin

The truck repair market in China is highly competitive. Varin aims to provide a premier service and this has been successful in attracting a loyal, stable customer base. The entire management team shares in a bonus pool that is calculated annually, based on 10% of profit before taxes and bonus. Non-management staff do not receive a bonus, but in order to encourage staff loyalty and good morale, the salaries paid to non-management staff are approximately 10% higher than those offered by similar employers in China.

Yatese

The generic truck spares produced by this subsidiary are sold to repair depots across China. The company has established a reputation as a supplier of reliable, low-cost spares. Although sales are currently limited to the domestic market, the board of directors of Autoparts SA is currently considering a proposal to make a substantial investment in Yatese to allow it to expand its sales overseas. The management team of Yatese shares in a bonus pool calculated as 10% of gross profit, having deducted the cost of the bonus in the calculation of gross profit.

In addition to sharing in the management bonus pool, the general manager of each subsidiary is paid an extra bonus of €30,000 once the return on capital employed (ROCE) of its subsidiary exceeds 22%. ROCE is calculated as:

$$\frac{\text{Profit before interest, tax and all managers' bonuses}}{\text{End of year book value of net assets}}$$

The following financial information relating to each of the two subsidiaries has been provided.

	Varin	Yatese
Book value of assets at 30 April 2XX7:	€000	€000
Buildings	500	2,000
Machinery and equipment	200	2,000
Net current assets	2,100	2,600
Capital employed	2,800	6,600

	Varin	Yatese
Year to 30 April 2XX7:	€000	€000
Sales	4,000	5,500
Raw materials	1,200	1,000
Direct labour	1,500	2,300
Gross profit	1,300	2,200
Management compensation	300	350
Other costs	100	450
Profit before tax	900	1,400

Note: the abbreviated profit and loss accounts above do not include any expense for management bonuses. Fixed assets are currently being depreciated on a straight-line basis over their remaining life of 20 years (all fixed assets are currently being depreciated). The depreciation cost is included in 'other costs'.

You are also supplied with the following information.

(1) A post-acquisition valuation of the assets of the two subsidiaries revealed that buildings are undervalued by 100% on the above balance sheets, machinery and equipment is overstated by 10% and a deduction of 5% should be made from net current assets to reflect irrecoverable debts. Although these adjustments have been made for the purposes of preparing group consolidated financial statements, they have not been reflected in the books of either subsidiary as shown above. During the revaluation process, it was estimated that the residual life of the assets averages 10 years.
(2) Divisions with a similar business risk elsewhere in the group are expected to earn a ROCE of 30% in the case of Varin and 25% in the case of Yatese.

The chief executive officer (CEO) of Autoparts SA has asked the chief financial officer (CFO) to investigate the current bonus schemes of each of the two subsidiaries. In turn, the CFO has asked you to undertake a preliminary analysis. The CFO has suggested that the revised bonus scheme could consider including a share of general head office overheads in measuring the profitability of the two subsidiaries. He commented that "these costs are incurred for the benefit of all the subsidiaries in the group, and each of them should pay their fair share."

Required

Question 1

Calculate the total bonuses in respect of each of the divisions for the year just ended (30 April 2XX7):

(a) using the existing book asset valuations;
(b) if the assets are revalued, using the information in note 1 above, *with effect from 1 May 2XX6*.

(30 marks)

Question 2

Critically evaluate the current bonus scheme from the viewpoint of both the group and the subsidiary management teams.

(20 marks)

Question 3

Comment on the CFO's suggestion that the profitability of each of the subsidiaries should be measured after they have been allocated a share of general group administration costs.

(20 marks)

Question 4

Outline a suggested compensation plan for the management teams of both divisions. Your suggestion must:

(a) defend the scheme you have chosen, outlining both its strengths and weaknesses; and
(b) include a sample calculation of the bonuses payable to each division's management team under your chosen scheme.

Clearly state any assumptions you make in presenting your calculations.

(30 marks)

Total 100 marks

Case 14
IXL Limited
Joan Ballantine, University of Ulster

Overview of the Company

IXL Limited has been engaged in the automotive industry for some 20 years and is now specialising in the manufacture and sale of components for heavy goods vehicles. The company operates from a number of sites located throughout the UK and the Republic of Ireland. For accounting purposes, each site has been set up as an investment centre with responsibility for both profits and return on capital investment. The company's head office is based in the Republic of Ireland, which enables it to benefit from low levels of corporation tax. IXL Limited's customers represent some of the world's major manufacturers of heavy goods vehicles and are located throughout Europe.

During its history, IXL Limited has been a profitable company, holding a respectable share of the market for automotive components. More recently, however, IXL Limited's financial performance has been poor relative to that of its competitors. At a board meeting in late 2XX5, the finance director, John O'Leary, presented the financial results of the company, which showed the company's continual financial decline in terms of both sales volume and profitability.

You are employed as the financial controller within IXL Limited and your immediate boss is John O'Leary. As part of your ongoing education, you are undertaking a Master of Business Administration (MBA) at a prestigious UK university. To this end, your studies have provided you with useful insights into the problems of running a profitable business. Lately you have been giving the problems within your own company some thought and you are of the opinion that some of the problems which IXL Limited currently faces are as a result of poor management of working capital, in particular stock management. In the past you have shared some of your concerns with the finance director.

The finance director, John O'Leary, has responded to your concerns by recently attending a high-profile conference in Europe devoted to the issue of stock management. During a number of presentations, enterprise resource planning (ERP) systems were reported as being instrumental in enabling organisations to effectively manage their stock levels and bring about improvements in revenue generation. On his return, John O'Leary asks you to investigate the concept of ERP systems as a potential solution to the problems which IXL Limited is experiencing. Your search leads to the identification of a software package, SAP ERP Automotive Supplier Packaged Solution, which its vendors (SAP AG) suggest is a fully integrated solution for improving business processes and boosting competitive advantage. The promotional material for the SAP ERP Automotive Supplier Packaged Solution states the following:

"Far too often, companies lose valuable time and money because business units must customise IT solutions. This cripples your ability to support customers and facilitate expansion. To unlock business value and make information work for you, you must align and standardise your processes across critical business areas. This is what the SAP® ERP Automotive Supplier Packaged Solution can do for companies like yours. Offering the most complete solution of industry-specific best practices available, the SAP ERP Automotive Supplier Packaged Solution supports your business processes up and down the supply chain – from start-up orders to sales orders delivered via electronic data interchange (EDI) right down to production planning and control.

"The SAP ERP Automotive Supplier Packaged Solution delivers comprehensive documentation and configuration information for use in many industry-specific scenarios that help promote user buy-in, simplify project management, and quickly implement optimised business processes. Right out of the box, this packaged solution serves as the foundation for daily customer interaction and execution in many areas, including material requirements planning, inbound delivery, goods receipt, production, delivery note creation, shipping, billing documents, and invoice creation and settlement."

When you report your findings to the finance director, he further asks you to undertake an analysis of the potential benefits of implementing a SAP ERP Automotive Supplier package within one of IXL Limited's manufacturing sites based outside Dublin, which would subsequently act as a pilot site for the remaining manufacturing sites should implementation be successful.

The Dublin Site

The Dublin site is currently managed by Jack Duggan, an MBA graduate. Jack has recently taken over management of the site from John Forsythe, who was general manager for 18 years. Jack Duggan is keen to adopt new working practices in order to improve the site's efficiency. The site currently manufactures one main component, which it exports to a small number of major European manufacturers of heavy goods vehicles.

After a number of meetings with Jack Duggan, you ascertain that the ERP package would have the greatest potential for improvement when used as the basis for reorganising business processes and adopting a just-in-time (JIT) system. The adoption of the ERP and the JIT manufacturing system would enable the Dublin site to respond to customer demand more promptly, thereby providing it with a competitive advantage leading to increased sales volumes over the next five years. The adoption of the ERP system would also enable the production manager to manage stock more effectively. These changes would, however, necessitate modifications to the factory layout, which would involve significant capital investment in production machinery. On the negative side, the increased sales volumes arising as a result of the implementation of the ERP system would need to be managed carefully by the Dublin site. Indeed, you are already aware that the Dublin site has in the past found it very difficult to effectively manage its accounts receivable.

After a detailed review of the existing costs and benefits of the Dublin site, you ascertain the costs and benefits of implementing the SAP ERP system as per Appendix 1.

The estimates in Appendix 1 have not taken account of reduced stock-holding costs as a result of implementing the JIT system. Historically the Dublin site has had a poor reputation in terms of managing stock levels. However, the recently appointed Jack Duggan is convinced that initial cost savings are likely to be in the region of €250,000 and that these savings will rise by 5% per annum over the next five years. Finally, your estimates do not include the loss of rental income which is currently received by the Dublin site from leasing out its spare capacity to a third party. Jack estimates that the current rental income of €600,000 per annum will be reduced to zero by equal amounts in the next three years, starting in 2XX7.

You have been asked by the finance director to evaluate whether the board of directors should support the implementation of the ERP/JIT system within the Dublin site. Decisions of this nature have historically been made by IXL Limited on the basis of return on investment (ROI), which is currently set at a level of 22%. However, the finance director, aware that you are studying for an MBA, is giving you considerable freedom to use additional methods of appraisal that you feel might be more appropriate in arriving at a decision. In preparing your report you should be aware that the finance director will require you to clearly define any technical 'jargon' you use.

The company's cost of capital is currently 8%.

Required

Question 1

Prepare a report for the finance director advising whether or not IXL Limited should go ahead with the ERP/JIT project. You should use methods of appraisal which you consider to be appropriate given the time frame of the investment. However, since these are likely to be novel to the finance director, you should provide a brief overview of each additional method of appraisal used. You can ignore taxation and inflation in your analysis. Please state clearly all assumptions you have made in your calculations.

(40 marks)

Question 2

The finance director has in the past heard you state that ROI is an inappropriate method of appraisal when used as the only means of making investment decisions. You are required to outline the problems associated with using ROI and to suggest how the alternative methods of appraisal you have used in part (a) help alleviate these.

(20 marks)

Question 3

During your evaluation of the ERP/JIT project, you ascertain that risk might be an issue that needs to be addressed. Explain to the finance director the importance of risk and how it might be reflected in the appraisal you have carried out.

(10 marks)

Question 4

You are also aware of the dangers of ignoring taxation and inflation when appraising capital investment projects using discounted cash-flow techniques. Your report should consider how the calculations you have undertaken in Question 1 would need to be adjusted to account for tax and inflation. (Recalculations are not required.)

(10 marks)

Question 5

What actions need to be taken by the Dublin site to ensure that it manages accounts receivable arising from the extra sales volume in an effective manner?

(20 marks)

Total 100 marks

Appendix 1: Anticipated Financial Benefits and Costs of Implementing the SAP ERP Automotive Supplier Package Solution

Financial Benefits:

As a result of adopting a JIT system, it is anticipated that additional sales over the next five years will be as follows. The selling price of the component manufactured at the Dublin site will remain at its current level of €380:

Year	Additional Sales of Components
2XX7	40,000
2XX8	45,000
2XX9	50,000
2X10	52,000
2X11	48,000

Financial Costs:

Manufacturing Costs

The variable manufacturing cost of each component is as follows:

Direct labour	€107
Direct materials	€85
Variable overheads	€50

The fixed manufacturing overheads associated with the extra volume of production are estimated to be €900,000 per annum. However, when output increases beyond 49,000 additional components, this will necessitate additional supervisory costs and annual fixed manufacturing costs will rise by a further €250,000 per annum.

Non-manufacturing Costs

Variable selling and distribution costs are estimated to be €30 per component, while the fixed selling and distribution costs are expected to be €250,000. However, it is expected that the fixed selling and distribution costs will be step fixed in nature, with the result that these will increase by €125,000 when additional sales exceed 45,000 components, and a further €85,000 when sales exceed 50,000 components.

Additional fixed operating overheads of €100,000 per annum will be charged to the Dublin site as a result of implementing the ERP/JIT systems. The €100,000 represents overheads incurred by the corporate function. It is the company's policy to allocate such overheads to the manufacturing units on the basis of the unit's ability to bear.

In addition to the above costs, you ascertain the following:

Costs incurred to date on the ERP/JIT project to employee specialists to determine cost/revenue estimates	€50,000
Cost of purchasing and implementing SAP ERP Software	€1,500,000
Capital cost of production machinery	€6,000,000
Resale value of production machinery after five years	€150,000
Depreciation of production machinery (straight-line basis)	€1,200,000 per annum
Amortisation of software costs (straight-line basis)	€500,000 per annum

Case 15
Top Flite plc
Joan Ballantine, University of Ulster

Overview of the Company

Top Flite plc is a multinational company which operates in the USA, Canada and the UK. The company manufactures a wide range of electronic components, which it sells to a number of major electronics companies throughout the world. The company is structured along divisionalised lines, with major divisions located in Chicago, Boston, Toronto, Manchester and Belfast. All of the divisions of Top Flite plc operate as investment centres with minimal interference from the head office, which is based in Manchester. Historically, divisional performance has been assessed on the basis of return on investment (ROI) as this measure is widely used and accepted within the electronics industry. Divisional directors are required to report to the board of directors of Top Flite plc on a quarterly basis with respect to their performance.

Over the past five years the Belfast division has performed well in terms of ROI achieved. The financial data relating to the Belfast division is presented in Table 1, below.

Table 1: Belfast Division – Top Flite plc

	2XX1 € million	2XX2 € million	2XX3 € million	2XX4 € million	2XX5 € million
Invested capital	550	535	500	440	390
ROI	5.45%	5.98%	6.60%	6.82%	6.92%

ROI is calculated using divisional net profit divided by invested capital (after accounting for depreciation). Divisional net profit is arrived at after deducting central overheads, which are charged to the divisions of Top Flite plc on the basis of the divisions' ability to bear such costs. Since 2XX0, the Belfast division has been consistently charged central overheads equal to 4% of its invested capital.

The Belfast division is currently in the process of developing its three- to-five year plan. As part of the planning process, the finance director has asked managers within the division to submit capital investment proposals. To date a number of proposals have been submitted. Three of these proposals have been classified as 'significant' projects when compared to the division's current level of invested capital. Data relevant to the three proposals is presented in Appendix 1. Capital investment proposals within the divisions of Top Flite plc have historically been evaluated on the basis of ROI, and each division is set an overall target ROI against which its performance is evaluated. The Belfast Division's target ROI has been 6% for some years now.

The appropriateness of using ROI as the primary measure of performance has recently been the subject of debate at the head office of Top Flite plc. The debate has been fuelled by the chief executive officer (CEO) of Top Flite plc, who earlier in the year attended a high-profile seminar in the US, hosted by Robert Kaplan and David Norton, on the balanced scorecard. At the seminar, the limitations of using ROI were outlined and the advantages of adopting a multi-dimensional balanced scorecard approach as a strategic management system were discussed. In addition, the advantages of adopting alternative financial measures of performance, such as residual income (RI), were also outlined. On his return from the seminar, the CEO was keen for Top Flite plc to investigate the possibility of implementing alternative performance measures, such as RI and/or a balanced scorecard approach, within the entire organisation. In the interim, he has suggested that the basis for comparison of performance between divisions should be a controllable figure, where central overheads are to be excluded from the calculation of ROI. Additionally, he has suggested that the company investigate implementing a measure to either complement or replace the use of ROI. For the purposes of calculating RI, Top Flite's cost of capital of 6% should be used as the basis for the cost of capital charge.

The finance director of the Belfast division is aware that the implementation of a balanced scorecard approach within the division could have a significant impact on the way performance is assessed by Top Flite. However, within the Belfast division, there is currently very little knowledge concerning the balanced scorecard concept.

You are employed as the financial controller of the Belfast division. Your boss, the finance director, is aware that you are undertaking your accounting examinations and he asks you to prepare a report which investigates the implications of adopting alternative measures of performance, such as those outlined above. In particular, he has asked you to undertake the following.

Required

Question 1

Analyse the historical performance of the Belfast division using the data presented in Table 1, above. Comment on the ROI trend and any issues this raises.

(10 marks)

Question 2

Analyse the historical performance of the Belfast division using the data set out in Table 1 on both a controllable ROI and RI basis. Explain clearly the rationale for using a controllable figure for your calculations and comment on any issues raised by the results.

(20 marks)

Question 3

Appraise the viability of the three independent capital projects currently being considered by the finance director of the Belfast division using both the ROI measure and the proposed RI measure. You are required to consider the performance of each project on a year-by-year basis. Which of the projects would the finance director be likely to accept if he adopts a short-term or a long-term perspective? Would the decision reached by the finance director be congruent with the decision made by adopting a company perspective?

(**Note:** in evaluating capital projects the division normally charges depreciation on a straight-line basis over the life of the asset, which in the case of all three projects being currently considered is four years. You should use the beginning of year asset values for the purposes of calculating yearly ROI and residual income measures.)

(40 marks)

Question 4

Outline the concept of the balanced scorecard and how it might be used as a strategic management system within the Belfast division.

(15 marks)

Question 5

Discuss the key issues that the Belfast division would need to consider in advance of getting involved in the design and implementation of a multi-dimensional performance measurement system such as the balanced scorecard.

(15 marks)

Total 100 marks

Appendix 1: Belfast Division – Top Flite plc

Capital Investment Projects

	Project A € million	Project B € million	Project C € million
Initial cash outlay on fixed assets	−80	−80	−80
Net cash inflows in year 1	28	25	22
Net cash inflows in year 2	15	18	20
Net cash inflows in year 3	15	22	25
Net cash inflows in year 4	15	27	35

Case 16
Choco Group
Iqbal Khadaroo, Queen's University Belfast

Choco Group manufactures chocolate products, which it markets both under its own brand and in unbranded packs. Management have adopted a divisional structure for performance measurement and transfer pricing purposes.

Division M, which is based in a country called Mauriland, manufactures three chocolate products for sale in the domestic market. Budgeted information in respect of Division M for the year ending 31 December 2X11 is as follows.

Sales Information:

Product		Galactic	Venus	Saturn
Sales packs (000's)	Choco Brand	10,000	10,000	30,000
	Unbranded	30,000	40,000	–
Selling price per pack (€)	Choco Brand	2.50	5.00	10.00
	Unbranded	1.50	4.00	–

Cost of Sales Information:

Variable Manufacturing costs per Pack:	Material and Conversion Costs €	Packaging Costs €
Galactic		
Choco Brand	0.90	0.20
Unbranded	0.90	0.10
Venus		
Choco Brand	2.00	0.30
Unbranded	2.00	0.20
Saturn		
Choco Brand	4.00	0.50

Other relevant information is as follows.

1. Each of the three products is only sold in a single pack. During the year to 31 December 2X11 it is estimated that a maximum of 125 million packs could be manufactured. As all the three products are manufactured using the same process, management have the flexibility to alter the product mix. Management expect sales volume to increase by 10% in the year ending 31 December 2X12.
2. Advertising expenditure is committed under a fixed-term contract and is regarded as a fixed cost by management. Advertising expenditure in respect of the turnover of *branded* products in the year ending 31 December 2X11 is expected to be as follows:

Product	Advertising Expenditure as a % of Turnover
Galactic	10%
Venus	15%
Saturn	18%

3. The average capital employed in the year to 31 December 2X11 is estimated to be €300 million. The company's cost of capital is 12%.
4. Choco Group uses both residual income (RI) and return on investment (ROI) to assess divisional performance.
5. Division M is expected to spend €145,000,000 on budgeted fixed overheads (excluding advertising expenditure) during the year ended 31 December 2X11.
6. Manufacturing capacity between the years ended 31 December 2X11 and 31 December 2X12 are expected to be the same.
7. You should ignore taxation in all your calculations, except for part (c) of the question.

Required

Question 1

(a) Prepare a statement showing budgeted profit of Division M for the year ending 31 December 2X11 and calculate BOTH the residual income (RI) and return on investment (ROI) for Division M. The statement should show the annual budgeted contribution obtained from each branded and unbranded product.

(18 marks)

(b) Comment on THREE factors, other than profit maximisation, that the management of the Choco Group ought to consider when making product mix decisions for the year ending 31 December 2X12.

(8 marks)

(c) State THREE reasons why the management of the Choco Group may have chosen residual income (RI) in addition to return on investment (ROI) to assess divisional performance.

(8 marks)

Additional Information for Answering Subsequent Parts

Division Z of the Choco Group is based in Sunnyland. The management of Division Z purchases products from various sources, including other divisions of the group, for subsequent resale. The manager of Division Z has requested two alternative quotations from Division M for the year ended 31 December 2X11:

Quotation 1 – Purchasing 5 million packs of 'Saturn'.

Quotation 2 – Purchasing 12 million packs of 'Saturn'.

The management of Choco Group have decided that a minimum of 30 million packs of 'Saturn' must be reserved for Mauriland customers in order to ensure that customer demand can be satisfied and that the product's competitive position is further consolidated in the Mauriland market.

The management of Choco Group is willing, if necessary, to reduce the budgeted sales quantities of other products in order to satisfy the requirements of Division Z. However, they wish to maximise contribution to the group.

The management of Division Z is aware of the availability of another product that competes with 'Saturn', which can be purchased at a local currency price that is equivalent to €7.00 per pack.

Choco Group's policy is that all divisions are allowed autonomy to decide what transfer prices to charge and purchase from whatever sources they prefer. The management of Division M intend to use market price less 25% as the basis for each of the quotations.

Question 2

(a) From the viewpoint of Choco Group, comment on the appropriateness of the decision by the management of Division M to use an adjusted market price as a basis for the preparation of Quotations 1 and 2, and the implications of the likely decision by the management of Division Z.

(8 marks)

(b) Recommend the prices that should be quoted by Division M for 'Saturn', in respect of Quotations 1 and 2, which will ensure that the profitability of Choco Group as a whole is not adversely affected by the decision of the management of Division Z.

(8 Marks)

(c) Discuss the proposition that transfer prices should be based on opportunity costs.

(8 marks)

Question 3

(a) With regards to **Quotation 2**, Division M is not prepared to supply 12 million packs of 'Saturn' to Division Z at a price lower than market price less 25%. All profits earned in Sunnyland are subject to taxation at a rate of 20%. Division M pays tax in Mauriland at a rate of 40% on all profits.

Advise the management of Choco Group on whether the management of Division Z should be directed to purchase 'Saturn' from Division M, or purchase a similar product from a local supplier. You should support your advice with relevant calculations.

(15 marks)

(b) Comment on the major issues that can arise with regard to transfer pricing in a multinational company.

(12 marks)

Question 4

Explain how the management of Choco Group could use life-cycle costing in its product pricing strategy.

(15 marks)

Total 100 Marks

Case 17
Elveron Limited
Barbara Flood and Bernard Pierce, Dublin City University

Overview of the Company

Elveron Limited is an electronic component manufacturing company based in Greystones, County Wicklow. Since its establishment by Tom Bridge 30 years ago, Elveron has manufactured components for motorcar manufacturers. However, in the last decade, due to astute strategic planning by Tom, the company expanded its product range and also started to supply truck and bus manufacturers. Elveron is now one of the largest electronic component manufacturers in Europe.

Despite the phenomenal growth of Elveron, Tom Bridge maintained a hands-on management style within the company and was regularly to be found on the factory floor packing components to complete a big order. Tom always made an effort to get to know the staff who worked for Elveron and he values the role played by the company in the local community, not only by providing employment opportunities but also by supporting local sporting, cultural and other voluntary activities. As a result of his friendly participative management approach, Tom is well liked by the hundreds of staff who have worked for the company over the years and he is much respected and admired in the local area.

David Ledger graduated from university as an electrical engineer and immediately found employment with Elveron. He has enjoyed his career with the company and has had plenty of opportunities to take on responsibility and address new challenges, such that he became head of the company's product development team in 2XX3. Another reason David has enjoyed his time with Elveron is that Tom Bridge encouraged and supported his keen interest in sailing. Since a young age, David has engaged in competitive sailing at both national and international level, and his employer has always enabled him to work flexible hours to fit in with his training schedule. Indeed, Tom Bridge has also provided financial aid when David needed support to attend overseas training camps or faced expensive enhancement or repairs to some of his boats. In March 2XX5, David was approached to join a sailing team that was preparing to compete in the 'Around-the-world' yacht race in November 2XX5. David was obviously enthusiastic regarding this opportunity and was delighted and grateful when Elveron agreed to provide him with paid leave for the remainder of the year.

Following the race and on his return to Ireland in December 2XX5, David was looking forward to catching up with family and friends. He knew that in his absence there had been considerable changes in Elveron, but not having been on land for any length of time and having been consumed by his sailing activities, he was not aware of the details. When he met some work colleagues for a drink over the Christmas holidays, they were only too happy to inform him of the changes.

Changes in Elveron

In April 2XX5, Tom Bridge's wife, Lucy, fell ill. While Lucy received immediate medical treatment and was well on the way to a full recovery by June, the incident made Tom re-evaluate his work-life balance. Consequently, he decided that he had invested enough time in his business and wanted to spend more time with his wife, children and grandchildren. Thus, he decided to sell Elveron to Cooper Inc., a US-based multinational company which is the global market leader in the vehicular electronic component market.

Cooper Inc. took control of Elveron on 1 November 2XX5 and while the jobs of all Elveron employees were guaranteed for one year, a US management team, headed by Todd Lyman, has been sent to the Greystones plant to "whip the company into shape". Some of the changes which were introduced immediately by Todd and his team were as follows:

- the company has been restructured into three divisions to reflect the structure of Cooper Inc. companies around the world: Car Division, Truck Division, Bus Division;
- new work practices have been introduced and production workers not only have to work in their specialised areas but must also be willing to substitute into a variety of other roles;
- local suppliers have been replaced with Cooper Inc. 'preferred suppliers', who are typically based in Asia.

David Ledger, having listened carefully as his work colleagues recounted the story of change at Elveron, commented: "Well, that all sounds very dramatic, but I don't think it will affect me or the product development team too much." His colleagues laughed and said, "Oh, we forgot to mention, Todd disbanded the product development team and you have been reassigned."

Truck Division: Financial Performance January–March 2XX6

On returning to work on 2 January 2XX6, David is informed that he is now the general manager in the Truck Division and that the company has high expectations for enhanced performance in the division in the months ahead. Todd comments: "David, I'll be straight with you. Things have not been going well in the Truck Division since we took over. There seems to be inefficiencies and quality problems in the production process and the staff appear to be careless and unmotivated. We expect you to sort things out as soon as possible."

Although David has never worked previously in general management, he sets about his new role with enthusiasm. While he has to learn on his feet and encounters many speed bumps, he feels that he has developed a good understanding of the division's activities by the end of March 2XX6. He is also pleased that he has won the support of staff. However, his satisfaction is shattered when he receives, via e-mail, a 'Performance Report for the Truck Division for Quarter 1 2XX6' (see Appendix 1). David was not involved in the budget setting for his division and was not aware that quarterly performance reporting had been introduced and so is frustrated to receive the report unexpectedly. From a quick review of the report he is shocked to see that it portrays the performance of the division in a negative way and that there has been no attempt to analyse or explain the variances calculated. While he was aware that a budgetary control system was used by Elveron when Tom Bridge was in charge, he does not remember it being used in such an authoritarian, constraining way. He resolves to develop his understanding of best practice in budgetary control.

As David has little prior experience of financial performance review, he decides to request the assistance of one of his friends, who is a consultant specialising in management control systems. To assist his friend during the consulting process and to enable detailed variance analysis, he gathers together as much information as he can regarding the financial and operating activities of the division in the first quarter of 2XX6. This information is set out in Appendix 2.

Additionally, he feels that he will be able to seek advice from his consultant friend regarding a couple of other labour issues which have caused some difficulty in the division in the first quarter, details of which are provided below.

Labour Issues

Rate and Efficiency Standards

David is acutely aware that Todd Lyman has a negative perception regarding production workers, as he feels that the workers are not well motivated and their laziness is the root cause of negative efficiency variances.

David is not convinced that Todd's assessment of labour inefficiency is appropriate. In his new role as divisional manager, and to enhance his knowledge and understanding of the operation of the division, David has spent many days on the factory floor in the first quarter of the year. From this experience, he has a sense that workers are actually putting considerable effort into their activities and do not appear to be inefficient. Thus, he has concerns regarding the accuracy and appropriateness of the labour standards and so has gathered information about revisions to standards that, with hindsight, should have been implemented for the first quarter of 2XX6 (see Appendix 3).

Remuneration schemes

Todd Lyman is determined to alter the behaviour of production workers and has suggested that he will change their remuneration scheme from a time-based scheme to some form of incentive scheme. David is concerned about how the workers may react and wants to gather relevant information before approaching Todd to discuss the issue further. He has compiled remuneration data regarding a typical production worker (Appendix 3) and is seeking advice on the implications of the potential change.

Required

You are the consultant who has been recruited by David Ledger and are required to write a report that addresses the following issues in the Truck Division.

Question 1

(a) Discuss the problems which you consider exist in the budgetary control system operated by Elveron in the first quarter of 2XX6 and, in particular, outline the flaws which you consider are present in the form and content of the Performance Report which was issued to David Ledger concerning the Truck Division.

(18 marks)

(b) Describe, with explanation, the changes which you think should be made to the form and content of the divisional Performance Report in order to improve its effectiveness as a management control tool.

(10 marks)

Question 2

(a) For the Truck Division in the first quarter of 2XX6, prepare a statement which reconciles the static budget gross profit to the actual gross profit, showing the revenue and cost variances in as much detail as the available information permits. (Note: do not use the information in Appendix 3 in answering this requirement.)

(28 marks)

(b) Provide a commentary to accompany the statement prepared at (b)(i), which outlines the potential reasons for the occurrence of the variances calculated.

(14 marks)

Question 3

(a) Describe the potential impact of inaccurate labour standards in the Truck Division and outline a process to determine the accuracy of the revised standards proposed by David, as set out in Appendix 3.

(8 marks)

(b) Utilising the revised standards set out in Appendix 3, calculate planning and operating labour rate and efficiency variances and reconcile the static budget labour cost to the actual labour cost for the Truck Division for the first quarter of 2XX6. Briefly interpret your calculations.

(7 marks)

Question 4

(a) Prepare a schedule which compares the weekly wages that would be earned by John Murphy under the existing time-based scheme and the two possible incentive schemes at the following weekly activity levels:

- 1,000 components manufactured;
- 1,300 components manufactured;
- 1,600 components manufactured.

Indicate, with reasons, which scheme you think might be preferred by the workers.

(8 marks)

(b) From the company's perspective, outline the potential benefits and drawbacks of introducing an incentive-based remuneration scheme for the production workers in the Truck Division.

(7 marks)

Total 100 marks

Appendix 1: Truck Division – Performance Review

MEMO

To: David Ledger, General Manager, Truck Division
From: Todd Lyman, CEO, Elveron
Date: 5 April 2XX6
Re: Quarterly performance review

David,

You will find below the performance report for your division for the first quarter of 2XX6. In line with Cooper Inc.'s group management control system, you will receive such a report within five days of every quarter end. You have one week to respond in writing to the report.

As you will see from the report, the performance of your division has been poor in the quarter under review, with operating profit falling short of budget by over 36%. Costs appear to have escalated out of control and we are particularly concerned with the cost of labour. We thought the new work practices would improve things and reduce costs, but things appear to be getting worse not better and it may be that a round of redundancies in November will provide the best long-term solution to whip the work force into shape.

We look forward to receiving your report by 12 April.

Todd.

Truck Division
Performance Report – Quarter 1, 2XX6

	Budget	Actual	Variance
Sales and production units	70,000	85,000	15,000
	€	€	€
Sales revenue	420,000	501,500	+81,500
Materials	49,000	78,795	−29,795
Production labour	89,250	123,088	−33,838
Manufacturing overhead (variable & fixed)	138,250	165,367	−27,117
Gross profit	143,500	134,250	−9,250
Divisional non-manufacturing costs	25,000	21,000	+4,000
Allocation of central Elveron costs	15,000	22,000	−7,000
Allocation of Cooper Inc. HQ costs	21,000	39,000	−18,000
Divisional operating profit	82,500	52,250	−30,250

Appendix 2: Truck Division – Operating Data for Quarter 1 2XX6

The standard cost sheet for the component manufactured by the Truck Division shows the following:

	€	€
Selling price per unit		6.00
Materials:		
Material X: 100g @ €4 per kg	0.40	
Material Y: 50g @ €6 per kg	0.30	0.70
Labour:		
Grade I: 3 minutes @ €10 per hour	0.50	
Grade II: 2 minutes @ €12 per hour	0.40	
Grade III: 1.5 minutes @ €15 per hour	0.375	1.275
Manufacturing overhead:		
Variable: 6.5 minutes of labour-time @ €9 per hour	0.975	
Fixed: €1 per component	1.00	1.975
Total manufacturing cost		3.95
Standard gross profit per unit		2.05

The annual budget for the Truck Division for 2XX6 was based on achieving sales of 280,000 units in the year which, considering the estimate of the industry size in Europe, would provide a market share of 20%. At the end of the first quarter for 2XX6, the latest information indicates that the size of the European market is ahead of expectations by 10%.

At 1 January 2XX6 there were 1,000 kgs of Material X and 1,000 kgs of Material Y in stock in the division. During the first quarter, 13,000 kgs of Material X and 6,500 kgs of Material Y were purchased and at the end of the quarter 2,950 kgs and 1,550 kgs, respectively, remained in stock. Due to the inexperience of a new staff member who is responsible for the stock accounting records, the purchase prices for both materials have not been recorded separately. Since the purchase of the company by Cooper Inc., it is the Truck Division's policy to maintain a stock of finished goods at each quarter end amounting to 5,000 components.

The mix of labour set out in the standard cost sheet above is the optimum mix for the manufacture of the component. However, due to the new work practices introduced since Cooper Inc. took over the company, staff are required, when directed, to complete the work normally done by another grade. It should be noted, however, that regardless of the nature of the work completed by the worker, he/she is paid for the time at the rate at which they were originally recruited and for which they are trained. In the first quarter of 2XX6, the actual time worked by employees recruited at the three different grades and the actual rates of pay were:

Grade I:	3,980 hours @ €9.80 per hour
Grade II:	3,400 hours @ €11.76 per hour
Grade III:	3,000 hours @ €14.70 per hour

> **Appendix 3: Truck Division – Labour Issues**

1. Labour Standards

Having observed the activities of the workers in the Truck Division and spoken to the supervisors and the division's process engineers, David considers that the labour standards for the Truck Division should have been revised in the first quarter of 2XX6 as follows:

Grade I:	2.85 minutes @ €9.80 per hour	€0.4655
Grade II:	2.30 minutes @ €11.76 per hour	€0.4508
Grade III:	2.10 minutes @ €14.70 per hour	€0.5145 €1.4308

2. Remuneration Schemes

John Murphy is a typical employee working at the Grade II level within the production function of the Truck Division. He is currently paid at a rate of €11.76 per hour and works a standard 40-hour week. During the first quarter in 2XX6 he worked an average of six hours overtime per week (employees cannot work more than 10 hours overtime under the company's work-life balance policy), which was paid at time-and-a-half.

Possible new incentive schemes proposed by Todd Lyman:

1. Piece-rate with guaranteed minimum

Grade II workers would be paid at a rate of €0.36 per good component manufactured and there would be a guaranteed minimum of €380 per week.

2. Differential piece-rate

Grade II workers would be paid as follows:

Up to 1,300 components per week:	€0.34 per component
1,301–1,500 components per week:	€0.39 per component
1,501+ components per week:	€0.45 per component

Note: Todd assumes that under both of these schemes, employees will work faster, facilitating all production within the available work time.

Section B

Cases in Business Finance

Case 18

The Pottery Company Limited 1

Anne Marie Ward, University of Ulster

Overview of the Company and the Directors

This case centres on several issues relating to the management of working capital within the Pottery Company Limited (PCL). The PCL is about 60 years old, is located in Fermanagh and manufactures, distributes and retails two designs of fine china. The products it manufactures are considered to be luxury goods, and are more ornamental than practical. All manufacturing takes place at the Fermanagh site, though the company has a distribution depot in Dublin to service its sales in the south of the country. This depot stores inventories, and distributes them on demand to department stores and gift shops in the south of Ireland. PCL also sells some of its products to an Irish distribution company, which sells the china to large department stores in various foreign countries. The company has two retail outlets: one is situated at its distribution depot in Dublin and the other at its factory in Fermanagh.

The company has four directors, with differing backgrounds: T. Brewster is the managing director; M. McGrath is the sales and marketing director; B. Owen is the credit control director; and R. Gallagher is director of production.

The Principle Issues

The finance director (M. Lyttle) left the company two years ago as he and his family emigrated to Spain. The other directors have not yet replaced the finance director. The directors hold a meeting to discuss the current cash crises that the company is encountering and to determine whether a new finance director should be appointed. They decide at the end of the meeting that they should advertise for a new finance director, and recruit a candidate only if that person can deal with the issues faced by the company at present. You, a potential candidate for the post, are provided with the minutes from the directors' meeting, extracts from the financial statements for the years 2XX7 and 2XX9 (Appendix 1) and cost and revenue budget information for the growth strategy adopted by the directors on 1 January 2XX8 (Appendix 2). The relevant parts of the minutes of the directors' meeting are as follows.

Excerpt from the Minutes of the Directors' Meeting on 14 January 2XX8:

T. Brewster (when looking at PCL's statements of financial position and extracts of income and expense information for the years ended 31 December 2XX7 and 31 December 2XX9 – Appendix 1): "I cannot understand our current situation; PCL is a strong company. We seem to have done better since Lyttle left. He was always so negative about some of the ideas suggested and seemed to be stifling the development of the company. Yet, now that he is gone I cannot but help feel that we have maybe made some incorrect decisions."

M. McGrath: "I am also confused by the current situation. I do not mean to 'brag', but my team have performed brilliantly. In the past two years sales have more or less doubled. We have all worked so hard. The marketing campaign is a great success and only costs €1.5 million each year. The new sales staff have been very productive. Their salaries are only €400,000 per year."

R. Gallagher: "I do not think the praise should go to your team only. My team has really risen to the challenge. The shop-floor staff have worked tirelessly over the past two years. Indeed, all of them have worked every Saturday. They were paid an overtime rate, but it is only for one day each week. I made sure production was not disrupted by pursuing a good inventory management policy. The purchasing manager knows to keep three months raw material clay inventory in store; I check with him on a regular basis. In addition, I do not think that you (*McGrath*) can ever say that you had to wait for a product. We make it a priority to keep the stores as full as we can."

B. Owen: "I have been looking into the costings. R., your staff may have worked hard, however the Saturday overtime rates have increased the cost of wages to 63% of the average sales price of the product and this must have impacted on profitability. In addition, paying suppliers late has also affected the price of raw materials, which have increased to 12%. I was talking to the main supplier on Thursday and he stated that he would be willing to reduce the price to the 2XX7 level, if we returned to the original payment terms. With respect to my department, I also have additional costs to report to those originally expected. We did as well as we could, given the circumstances. The increased sales did place the company at more risk. We did not get sufficient time in some instances to appropriately check the credit risk associated with some of the new customers. The result–an increase in overall bad debts from 1% to 1.5%. Though, I suppose, a half a percent increase is probably worth it given the 96% increase in sales. We have managed to keep the credit days steady at about 50 days. However, other Pottery manufacturers give 30 days credit and incur bad debts of 1%, even with internet sales. My department may be able to achieve this if we could hire an additional member of staff. I expect this would cost about €36,000 per year."

T. Brewster: "I think when we decided to go ahead with the new marketing campaign and to increase our production we maybe did not consider the whole cost situation. I have been playing golf with a colleague who manages a successful retail factory and he says that his finance director keeps going on about the importance of working capital management and just how costly it can be to a business if an appropriate policy is not adhered to. He started to explain how different types of policies are suited to different economic conditions. However, it was a quick conversation. I think he said policies could be regarded as 'aggressive, neutral or conservative'. I did not enquire any further as I did not want him to think that PCL did not have a policy in place. Remember, Lyttle kept talking about working capital and its cost. I have been thinking that this maybe has been a factor in our deteriorating liquidity position. I have pulled together our initial proposals for this expansion and noticed that we do not have any cost for working capital (see Appendix 2). Do any of you know what this cost is?"

B. Owen: "It is something to do with the length of time customers take to pay. I am pretty sure that credit control is a part of working capital management, but must stress that the trade receivable days have not changed. Therefore there should not be any additional cost in that respect."

M. McGrath and R. Gallagher: "We both do not think that working capital has much to do with sales or production. I mean the money comes in and goes out. It's just larger amounts, isn't it?"

T. Brewster: "I am not so sure. I know that the purchasing manager is unhappy as he has to keep negotiating longer credit periods with suppliers because of our financial position. Anyway, I know that we all agreed that the four of us could manage the company without the assistance of a finance director; however, I am not so sure now. I think we need someone to take a look at the decisions we made again and to consider the cost of working capital. In addition, we need to get some advice on how to pull our company back into a stronger financial position. I mean, it is still profitable, though the bank is getting a little worried and is charging 15% on our overdraft. When Lyttle left he had a fixed rate agreed of 8%. The bank manager wishes to meet with us in March to discuss the future of the company. This gives us time to put corrective action in place."

B. Owen: "I agree. But let's not rush into this. A finance director costs a lot of money, circa €100,000 per year. Is it worth it? I mean it's not as if a finance director generates sales, produces the china, or gets the money in."

M. McGrath: "Maybe so, but the company did have a stronger financial position when we had one."

B. Owen and R. Gallagher: "That is true. We do need some guidance in our decision-making in respect of finance issues."

T. Brewster: "That is settled then; we all agree that we will recruit a finance director. Though I have been thinking they should justify their presence. So let's give the prospective candidates our initial proposal, copies of the financial statements from 2XX7 and 2XX9 and ask them to write a report evaluating the initial growth proposal."

R. Gallagher: "We should also get them to explain working capital to us."

B. Owen: "Yes, they could make suggestions on how to strengthen the company's cash position. Highlight the fact that we do not wish to lose any of our staff. Demand cannot be serviced without some overtime from our current team. R., are the machines working at full capacity?"

R. Gallagher: "No. There is excess capacity."

T. Brewster: "I'm getting hungry. I will prepare packs for each candidate and ask them to write a report and prepare a presentation of their key findings. I will even include the minutes of this meeting so they are fully aware of our views. Right then, let's have lunch."

Required

In preparation for your interview, write a report for the directors of PCL (to be forwarded to the directors with your CV by the deadline), and include the following:

Question 1

An explanation of working capital management and the different types of policy that can be pursued, suggesting which policy might be best for PCL under a boom economy in Ireland.

(25 marks)

Question 2

An evaluation of the company's performance, liquidity, working capital position and how it has changed over the period 31 December 2XX7 to 31 December 2XX9. Suggest improvements for PCL's working capital management.

(30 marks)

Question 3

An evaluation of the growth strategy schedule (Appendix 2) adopted by the directors in 2XX8. Adjust the original schedule to take into account any changes to costs as a result of the actual working capital policy followed and any errors or omissions.

(20 marks)

Question 4

A re-prepared growth strategy schedule wherein a similar working capital policy to that in existence in 2XX7 is maintained. Assume that the company can change its trade receivables credit period to match that of companies in the same industry.

(20 marks)

Question 5

In light of these workings, suggest immediate measures that can be implemented to ease PCL's current liquidity problems.

(5 marks)

(Assume no inflation)

Total 100 marks

Appendix 1: Statement of Financial Position for PCL for the Years Ended 31 December 2XX9 and 2XX7

	2XX9	2XX7
ASSETS	€'000	€'000
Non-current assets		
Tangible assets	21,500	24,000
	21,500	24,000
Current assets		
Inventories	42,500	9,000
Trade receivables	39,500	20,500
Cash	—	150
	82,000	29,650
Total assets	103,500	53,650
EQUITY AND LIABILITIES		
Equity and reserves		
Equity share capital	1,500	1,500
Retained earnings	42,000	45,900
	43,500	47,400
Current liabilities		
Bank	50,000	3,750
Trade payables	10,000	1,500
Total liabilities	60,000	5,250
Total equity and liabilities	103,500	52,650

Extract Information from the Income Statements for the Years Ended 31 December 2XX9 and 2XX7

	2XX9	2XX7
	€'000	€'000
Income	294,160	150,000
Gross profit	44,124	30,000
Net income	2,941.6	7,500

Appendix 2: Initial Proposal for the Growth and Development of PCL (Implemented on 1 January 2XX8)

Sales and Marketing Director's Contribution

Current Situation (see also the information in Appendix 1)

At present (2XX7) we sell six million units of china each year at a weighted average sales price of €25.00. Half of the units are priced at €27.00 and are sold in Ireland. The remainder are priced at €23.00 and are purchased by a distributor who distributes the items to overseas countries. Each unit costs approximately the same to manufacture. The distribution company does not take responsibility for any credit risk, claiming bad debts from future sales amounts owing from them to PCL.

New Campaign

Expenditure on marketing in foreign countries is expected to increase sales to the distributor by five million units per annum. It is expected to cost €1 million. Ten additional sales staff are required at a cost of €40,000 each.

An additional sales campaign is suggested for Ireland. This involves setting up an internet sales function based in the Dublin depot. A website will be established at a cost of €50,000 each year and advertising costs should amount to €0.5 million. Four more staff are required, at a total cost of €300,000. We expect to sell 1.2 million pieces in this manner. As internet transactions are 'virtually free' we can afford to sell the products cheaper (about 10% cheaper). Though we need to be realistic, most catalogue companies give credit, and we already give 50 days credit to the retailers and the distribution company. To be attractive we should use similar terms.

Production Director's Contribution

The finance director has an agreement with the suppliers wherein they deliver the raw materials required (clay) each day before the factory opens. We pay them very quickly to secure this arrangement, quicker than we get monies in for sales. I am sure that we could take a longer credit period. I think we should keep three or four months of the clay in inventories. It would be very costly if we ran out of clay, as all the staff would have to be paid anyway. It is only 10% of the average sales value of the china (as is indirect costs), whereas wages account for 60% of the average sales value of the items. There is nothing worse than not having sufficient inventory when trying to achieve growth. We will endeavour to keep the store houses full.

Credit Control Director's Contribution

I would be a little worried about the internet sales. We do not have a system in place to deal with checking the credit-worthiness of these customers. I would need another two staff to deal with the increased volume of business. I estimate that they will cost about €30,000 each. This should ensure that bad debt levels remain at 1%.

Growth Strategy: Expected Revenue and Expenditure

General Manager
The directors agreed the following expectations:

	Distributor €'000	Ireland €'000
Income (5,000,000 × €23.00)	115,000	
Income (1,200,000 × €27.00)		32,400
Cost of goods sold (115,000,000 × 80%)	(92,000)	
(32,400,000 × 80%)		(25,920)
Additional Contribution before fixed costs	23,000	6,480
Advertising cost	(1,000)	(500)
Additional sales staff	(400)	
Additional internet staff		(300)
Additional credit control staff (€30,000 × 2)		(60)
Internet software costs		(50)
	21,600	5,570
Total net contribution from additional sales		27,170
Bad debts (€115,000,000 + €32,400,000) × 1%		(1,474)
Expected additional profit		25,696

Case 19
The Pottery Company Limited 2
Anne Marie Ward, University of Ulster

Overview of the Company and the Directors

The Pottery Company Limited (PCL) is owned by a consortium of local individuals from Fermanagh. The company is about 60 years old, is located in Fermanagh and manufactures, distributes and retails two designs of fine china. The products it manufactures are considered to be luxury goods, and are more ornamental than practical. All manufacturing takes place at the Fermanagh site, though the company has a distribution depot in Dublin to service its sales in the south of the country. This depot stores inventories, and distributes them on demand to department stores and gift shops. PCL also sells some of its products to an Irish distribution company, which sells the china to large department stores in various foreign countries. The company has two retail outlets: one is situated at its distribution depot in Dublin and the other at its factory in Fermanagh.

The company has four directors, with differing backgrounds: T. Brewster is the managing director; M. McGrath is the sales and marketing director; B. Owen is the credit control director; and R. Gallagher is director of production.

Principle Issues

The finance director (M. Lyttle) left the company at the end of 2XX7 as he and his family emigrated to Spain. After M. Lyttle left, the company pursued a growth strategy which resulted in the company doubling its sales. However, the company is less profitable than it had been before the strategy was implemented and is having serious liquidity problems (see Appendix 1). The bank manager has stated that the bank is unwilling to extend the overdraft limit. Moreover, the bank manager has informed T. Brewster that the bank is considering withdrawing its support from the company. T. Brewster is meeting the bank manager in March (2X10) to discuss the company's future. At present the bank is charging 15% on the facility. This reflects the increased credit risk that the bank is facing. In 2XX7, the rate was 8%.

Changes to Income and Costs

Sales

In 2XX9 the company sold 12,200,000 units of china; 8,000,000 of these were to a distributor who re-sells the china in foreign countries. A special price of €23.00 is agreed with the distributor. In addition, 3,000,000 of the units are sold in Ireland for €27.00; the remainder are for internet sales, which attract a 10% discount on the normal sales price of €27.00. Sales demand occurs evenly over the year. Customers currently take on average 50 days to pay their accounts and bad debts are 1.5% of gross sales revenue. In 2XX7 the company sold 6,000,000 units of china at an average price of €25.00.

Cost of Sales

Before M. Lyttle left in 2XX7, the variable costs associated with producing each unit of china were about 80% of its average sales price at the time (€25.00). However, this has crept up to 85% of this original average sales price. The cost of direct labour increased from 60% to 63% of the average sales price, as all staff worked Saturdays to achieve the increased production targets. The cost of materials increased from 10% to 12% of the average sales price as PCL started to withhold payment to its suppliers. Suppliers are now being paid approximately 103 days after they supply the clay. Indirect variable overhead costs have remained the same.

At present three months clay is held in inventory. The balance of the inventory disclosed in the statement of financial position (Appendix 1) represents finished good inventories.

Your Recommendations as the Newly Appointed Finance Director

You have been recruited, provisionally for three months, as finance director. The current directors are unsure as to whether the benefits to be gained from having a finance director outweigh the salary cost (which is about €100,000). They have decided that if you can justify that a company of this size requires a finance director, then you will be hired on a permanent basis. As part of the assessment process, you were provided with the company's statements of financial position for 2XX7 and 2XX9 (reproduced in Appendix 1) and given details of the growth proposal that was adopted (the principle issues are detailed above). You informed them in this report that they have been overtrading and that the company is incorrectly financed. You also stated in this report that if the directors implement your recommendations, then the company's liquidity problems would be turned around in six months.

The Key Recommendations Emanating from the Report are as follows:

Sales

The directors have stipulated that they wish to maintain current sales levels. Your first recommendation is that PCL reduce the credit period allowed to 30 days, in line with other pottery manufacturers. This will not affect sales levels. Based on your discussions with B. Owen, the credit control director, it is expected that this reduction will be experienced gradually over one month. You also recommend that an additional member of staff be recruited, who specialises in the recovery of bad debts; the assumption being that bad debts can be reduced to 1%. This additional resource is estimated to cost €36,000 per year.

Cost of Sales

You recommend that the level of finished goods held in inventory be reduced to the levels held at the end of 2XX7. Theoretically, production could be stopped until the surplus is cleared. However, the company wishes to continue with the current sales levels, therefore it is important that no staff are made redundant or forced to go on a reduced week (i.e. less than five working days). Therefore, you have recommended that production on a Saturday be stopped until sales levels fall to the required amount. At this point additional permanent production staff should be hired. This will remove the need to pay overtime rates and should reduce the variable labour cost back to 60%. There are four working weeks each month.

You recommend that PCL pays the supplier an amount to align the current credit balance to that of the original credit agreement of 2XX7 (i.e. payment within 36.5 days). The suppliers of the raw material clay have indicated that they would be willing to return in full to the terms of the original agreement. This involves them delivering each day's requirements before the factory opens. Therefore, there will be no need to hold any clay in inventories (at present three months requirements are stored, amounting to €9,150,000 worth of raw material inventory). They have stipulated that they will reduce the purchase price of the clay to the 2XX7 level.

Financing

You recommend that PCL obtains a €20 million long-term loan, payable over 15 years in equal monthly instalments. You provide a conservative estimate of the cost of this loan at 8%.

You also recommend that PCL renegotiate the overdraft interest rate back to 8%. The directors have informed you that the rise in the interest rate to 15% reflects the banks adjustment for an increase in credit risk associated with providing an overdraft facility to PCL.

Proposed Action

The directors have discussed the recommendations you suggested in your initial report on their working capital problems. The severity of the liquidity problems faced by the company, combined with the deterioration in the company's profitability, has prompted the directors to act quickly. They all agree to implement your proposed changes to the working capital cycle and request that you source long-term funding as a matter of urgency. In addition, they require you to prepare projections for a six-month period from April 2X10 to September 2X10. These will be presented to the bank manager at the meeting in March (2X10). They have provided you with some additional information on PCL's costs and on non-regular cash outflows expected in the six-month period (Appendix 2).

Required

Write a report to the directors of PCL. In this report:

Question 1

Explain business finance and the role of and benefits to be gained from recruiting a finance director.

(20 marks)

Question 2

Substantiate your reasoning for choosing long-term debt over long-term equity as the source of long-term finance.

(15 marks)

Question 3

Calculate the funding that could be released from working capital were your recommendations adopted.

(5 marks)

Question 4

Provide a schedule detailing the expected monthly profits for the period April 2X10 to September 2X10. Assume that your recommendations are all capable of being implemented from 1 April 2X10. Outline any assumptions made.

(20 marks)

Question 5

Prepare cash projections for six months (from April 2X10 to September 2X10 inclusive). Detail any assumptions made.

(20 marks)

Question 6

Outline key information you consider the bank manager will wish to see in the business plan for the forthcoming meeting in which T. Brewster will request the long-term loan facility and will renegotiate the overdraft arrangements.

(15 marks)

Question 7

Prepare five slides detailing key issues emanating from Questions 1–5 for presentation to the directors at a briefing next week.

(5 marks)

Total 100 marks

Appendix 1: Statements of Financial Position for PCL for the Years Ended 31 December 2XX9 and 2XX7

	2XX9 €'000	2XX7 €'000
ASSETS		
Non-current assets		
Property, plant and equipment	21,500	24,000
Current assets		
Inventories	42,500	9,000
Trade receivables	39,500	20,500
Cash	–	150
	82,000	29,650
Total assets	103,500	53,650
EQUITY AND LIABILITIES		
Equity and reserves		
Equity share capital	1,500	1,500
Retained earnings	42,000	45,900
	43,500	47,400
Current liabilities		
Bank	50,000	3,750
Trade payables	10,000	1,500
Total liabilities	60,000	5,250
Total equity and liabilities	103,500	52,650

Extract Information from the Income Statements for the Years Ended 31 December 2XX9 and 2XX7

	2XX9 €'000	2XX7 €'000
Income	294,160	150,000
Gross profit	44,124	30,000
Net income	2,941.6	7,500

Appendix 2: Additional Assumptions Estimated for the Six Months from April to September 2XX0

1. The direct variable overhead costs are paid for in the month they are incurred.
2. Fixed costs remain at the same level as last year and are paid for in the month incurred.
3. At present, non-current assets are depreciated at an average rate of 10% per annum (reducing balance). No non-current assets were purchased or disposed of in 2XX9 and no non-current assets are scheduled to be purchased or disposed of in the coming year (2X10).
4. A tax bill of €1.2 million has to be paid in September 2X10.
5. The company usually pays a dividend of €500,000 each September.

6. The bank balance at the start of April is the same as it was on 31 December 2XX9. Interest is added to the statement at the end of each month and is calculated on the monthly closing balance at an amount equal to the yearly rate divided by 12. The bank has informed the directors of PCL that it will be willing to revert to the original interest rate if it is happy with the proposals for the company going forward.

Case 20
The Corner Café
Jill Lyttle, Queen's University Belfast

January 2X10

Bernie, the proprietor of a long-established and well-known café in the centre of a busy town in South-west Ireland, has decided to retire after many years of successfully running what was originally the family business. The café is frequented by local residents and businesspeople and is also popular with visitors to the area. Bernie has just given notice to the landlord that she wishes to leave when the lease terminates in March 2X10 and has confided this to her regular customers, including Sam and Sheena Sullivan. Sam and Sheena know the café well as they live in the town and visit it frequently. After Bernie told them of her intentions, they quiz her about what will happen when she goes as, like other regulars, they will miss the café and wonder if anyone else will take it over. The kitchen area is fairly well-equipped, although some of the equipment is getting old, and there is modest scope for expansion. There are 30 covers in the café and, in recent years, Bernie got tired of working long hours, so she only opens on Monday to Saturday from 10.00 am to 4.00 pm.

March 2X10 – Week 1

Sam has just been told that he is being made redundant and will only be paid to the end of the month, but he will also receive a lump sum of €30,000. After the initial shock, he is more than resigned – indeed, quite cheerful – about his situation as he had been getting restless and was thinking of applying for other jobs. Sheena has a secure, well-paid job and they have a manageable mortgage, which they should be able to service for the foreseeable future even without Sam's salary, especially as the lump sum will help to tide them over until he gets another job.

They were telling Bernie the news late on Saturday afternoon when she turned to Sam and said: "Didn't you say once that you had always wanted to run a café? Why not run this one? The landlord hasn't got anyone else yet, maybe he would let you take the lease over, I'll talk to him if you like."

Sam's eyes lit up at this suggestion and he and Sheena discussed it for the rest of the weekend. Initially, Sheena was much less enthusiastic about what Sam referred to as his "dream opportunity", but eventually admitted: "I suppose it wouldn't do any harm finding out a bit more. Maybe it would be worth trying for a while to see if you could make a go of it. After all, I'm sure the regulars will still come and the tourists won't know that it's changed hands anyway, it's not like you would be setting up a whole new business. But won't it cost a lot of money to do this? And I'm sure you won't be able to earn as much as you used to."

Sam points out that he has his redundancy money, which would help to finance the business, however Sheena is more wary and thinks it would be better to invest this to earn some interest or use some of it to help with general living expenses. "Aren't banks supposed to lend money to small businesses, why don't you talk to our bank manager and see what he will do to help?"

So the following week, Sam talks to Bernie again, then to her landlord and then to his bank manager.

March 2X10 – Week 2

Bernie

Bernie is willing to leave all her equipment and furniture if Sam gives her €4,000. He estimates that he would need to spend at least another €6,000 refurbishing the premises as privately he feels that the café could do with an upgrade and he thinks this could be done without closing for more than a few days at the start. It would also signal the change in ownership and herald a new era (as he put it more diplomatically to Bernie). He knows that Bernie worked full-time in the café as owner/manager and she has told Sam that she usually took home €150 per week for herself. She also said that her annual takings were about €85,000 and she earned a gross margin of 67% (see Appendix 1). Average spend per customer was €7, although she points out that this figure is derived from the till analysis of takings and the footfall is at least twice that. Sam hopes to increase the gross margin to 70% in the first year, 72% in the second year and then 75% after that, given that he will almost certainly expand the menu and raise prices accordingly, so the average spend is bound to increase in due course as well.

Bernie has sounded out her current staff and they are willing to work for Sam on a similar basis. The current staff, who are all part-time, comprise Naoimh, who has worked in the café for a long time and acts as relief manager when Bernie is not there, and three other ('junior') staff who work varying hours each day, depending on how busy the café gets. Bernie is quick to point out to Sam that these staff have never had the responsibility for cashing up at the end of the day, nor of opening and closing the café, only Naoimh or herself. Bernie advises Sam that she always has two people (including herself) on duty during opening hours and usually three people during the busiest time from 12 noon to 2.00 pm. Everyone is flexible and will work additional hours if required and will even cover full-time when others are on holiday. Sam has talked to all the staff (most of whom he already knows, of course) and has agreed to employ them all on probation at their current wage rates and hours, but tells them that he will review these after six months.

The Landlord

The landlord is willing to rent the premises to Sam for an initial three-year period, but at a much higher rent than he charged Bernie: he is proposing a starting rent of €15,000 per annum, payable quarterly in advance, and rising by 5% each year. Although Sam tries to negotiate with him, the landlord points out that Bernie's rent was agreed some years ago when someone else owned the building and that it is less than the current commercial rate. He also tells him that he has had one or two other enquiries, although these are for retail outlets rather than for a café.

The Bank Manager

Sam's bank manager has told him that he usually has to see a full business plan when considering loan requests. However, given that Sam is essentially taking over an existing business and the amount requested is relatively small, he has agreed to look at Sam's proposal if he is given budgeted profit and loss accounts for the next three years and a monthly cash-flow forecast for the next 12 months.

March 2X10 – Week 3

In arranging for the preparation of the projections for the bank manager, Sam has begun to think in more detail about some of the practicalities of running the café, in particular the menu, the prices and the opening hours. He is keen to change the menu, but accepts that it would be more sensible to carry on for now with what Bernie was doing and review it later on, as he realises that he does not have time to start from scratch if he is to open almost immediately after Bernie leaves. Most of the other cafés in the area are open longer – from 8.30 am to 5.30 pm – and Sam reckons that this is something he could change from the outset. He decides to open at 9.00 am and close at 5.00 pm as he estimates that this should bring him much more business, maybe a quarter as much again in the first year, with an annual increase thereafter of 5%. "After all", he says to Sheena, "I'm used to working from nine to five, and this will be a much pleasanter working environment. I'm sure I can manage on my own at the beginning and end of the day and I can get the staff to work extra hours, if necessary. I should still make more money than Bernie got."

Although Sam is hoping that the bank manager will agree to finance the business start-up by way of an overdraft or a loan (both of which would be charged at 5%), he wonders whether it would be better to put some of his redundancy money in the business instead, which is what he will have to do if the bank manager says no. If he does not put his money in the business, he knows he could invest it and get an interest rate of 3.5%. "Or perhaps I should borrow some money from the bank and use some of the redundancy money?"

March 2X10 – Week 4

The finance has been arranged; Bernie has agreed to leave a few days early so that various teams of workmen can get in to install some new equipment, replace the furniture and redecorate the café. The windows have all been covered over and a large sign proudly states: 'Closed for refurbishment. Re-opening under new management on 1st April.'

June 2X10

Three months after opening, Sam checks with his accountant to see how well he has done so far. He thought he would be careful at the start, so did not take any money for himself in April; he did, however, withdraw €1,000 in May and in June. Although he knows that the takings are not as much as he had hoped, he is disappointed all the same to see that the cash balance and the profits are not as good as he had expected they would be (see Appendix 2). Worse, he realises that the next rent payment is due in July and he will be unable to pay it without putting more money into the account. He decides to put €3,000 into the account at the start of July to cover this and tells Sheena that he will not withdraw money from the café over the summer.

The café has been fairly quiet early in the morning but quite busy in the afternoon, so Sam has changed the staff rota. His normal pattern of work from the outset has been that he opens up and spends his mornings in the café but usually leaves by 3.00 pm, although he stays all day on Saturday; Naoimh starts at 12 noon and locks up each weekday at 5.00 pm. He is able to cope on his own with one of the junior staff in the mornings. In order to have enough staff cover, the junior staff rota now totals 30 hours per week.

September 2X10

Six months – and one holiday – later, Sam is horrified to see that things are still not working out quite as he had planned (see Appendix 2).

Before the summer he had some casual customers early in the day, but increasingly, since he came back from holiday, business is quiet before 10.00 am and after 4.00 pm so he is not sure whether he should continue to operate his original opening hours. Junior staff hours have increased. Sheena reminded him that Bernie seemed to be able to make a good enough living with shorter hours: "Maybe it wasn't the long hours she disliked after all, she must have realised that there wasn't enough business for everyone at that time."

Unfortunately, in January Sam and Sheena had booked a two-week holiday during August and did not want to lose out on the deposit or a welcome break from work for both of them. Naoimh had originally said she would cover Sam's holidays, but as her son was getting married in Canada she was going to be away for the same two weeks. Sam therefore decided to shut the café for two weeks and now realises just what a dent this has made in his turnover for August. He is also concerned to see that his cost of sales has been much higher in August and September and wonders why. Worse still, the rent is due again shortly and there is not enough money to pay it.

Sam is an old school friend of yours and asks for your advice. "What went wrong? What should I do? I have quite enjoyed the last few months, but am not sure what to do next. I certainly need to look at the prices I'm charging but I don't know what else I should change."

Required

You may ignore the impact of all taxes.

Question 1

March

(a) Explain the financing options available to businesses in general and discuss which of these would be most applicable to Sam's situation.

(20 marks)

(b) Outline the relative merits of the financing options that Sam is considering and explain which you think would be optimal for him.

(10 marks)

Question 2

March

(a) Prepare budgeted P&L accounts for the next three years and a monthly cash-flow for the next 12 months, using Bernie's experience as a starting-point. Do these projections affect your financing recommendation in (b) and, if so, how?

(20 marks)

(b) What other issues should Sam consider when setting up this business?

(10 marks)

Question 3

September

(a) Outline two potential price-setting strategies, discuss their applicability to Sam's business and advise which would be more appropriate to adopt.

(10 marks)

(b) Compare Sam's projected P&L account and cash-flow with the actual figures for this six-month period and identify the main variances.

(15 marks)

(c) Suggest possible reasons for Sam's cash-flow difficulty and possible actions he could take to improve his income and his management of working capital.

(15 marks)

Total 100 marks

Appendix 1: Bernie's Estimated Accounts for Year Ended 31 March 2X10

	€	€
Sales	85,000	
Cost of Sales	28,050	
Gross Profit		56,950
Wages	22,230	
Rent	10,800	
Rates and Insurance	2,254	
Electricity and Gas	3,600	
Sundry	2,700	
Bank fees	800	
Accountancy fees	1,000	
		43,384
Net Profit		13,566

Notes

1. Rates and insurance are paid in advance in April each year.
2. Electricity and gas, bank and accountancy fees are paid quarterly in arrears.
3. Overheads are paid monthly throughout the year.
4. Suppliers (cost of sales) are paid monthly.
5. Naoimh works an average of 4.5 hours per day, Monday to Friday, between 11am and 4pm at €11 per hour; junior staff work a total of 20 hours per week, as required, at €9 per hour.

Other Assumptions for Sam's Projections

1. Annual increase in costs of 4% per annum.
2. Depreciation is to be charged at 25% RB.
3. Bank interest charged quarterly in arrears (based on €10,000).
4. Monthly drawings are to be €1,000 in the first year, €1,250 in the second year, and €1,500 in the third year.
5. Legal fees of €1,000 are to be paid in May.
6. Sales accrue evenly throughout the year.

Appendix 2: Sam's Cash-flow from April to September 2X10

	Apr Mth 1 €	May Mth 2 €	Jun Mth 3 €	Jul Mth 4 €	Aug Mth 5 €	Sep Mth 6 €
Cash Inflows						
Capital	15,000			3,000		
Sales	6,800	7,200	7,400	7,500	3,500	7,200
Total cash inflow	21,800	7,200	7,400	10,500	3,500	7,200
Cash outflows						
Bernie – F&F	4,000					
Refurbishment	6,000					
Purchases / CoS	2,380	2,520	2,590	2,625	2,000	2,800
Wages	2,362	2,362	2,362	2,557	2,557	2,557
Rent	3,750			3,750		
Rates and Insurance	2,344					
Electricity and Gas			700			700
Sundry	230	230	230	230	230	230
Bank fees			208			258
Bank interest			188			200
Legal fees		1,000				
Accountancy			260			260
Drawings		1,000	1,000			
Total cash outflow	21,066	7,112	7,538	9,662	4,787	7,005
Net cash inflow / (outflow)	734	88	(138)	1,338	(1,287)	195
Balance b/fwd	0	734	822	684	2,022	735
Balance c/fwd	734	822	684	2,022	735	930

Case 21
Calvin plc
Peter Green, University of Ulster

Calvin plc, an established Belfast-based company, manufactures building materials. Although the profitability of the company has been somewhat erratic, over the last three years Calvin has not needed to use its overdraft facility of €1.0 million. During the most recent financial year (31 December 2XX5) the company has reported a sharp increase in operating profits before interest and tax, from the €25 million level in 2XX3–2XX4, to €50 million. An analysis of performance indicates that whilst gross profit margins have remained more or less constant, the profitability of the company has doubled due to volume expansion as a result of an economic boom in housing developments.

Although the company has excess manufacturing capacity, due to the nature of the company's products and the associated transportation costs between Belfast and Dublin the company has decided not to export, even though market research has indicated that a substantial market exists in the Republic of Ireland (Appendix 1 provides data on the findings of the market research). The market research survey cost €0.25 million and this account has not yet been settled. As the company has substantial excess capacity, future investment requirements only relate to routine replacements, which are estimated to be less than €0.5 million per year over the next five years.

The company's chief executive is Mark Calvin. Mark, a chartered accountant, has historically followed a rather conservative financial policy, with relatively low gearing levels. The company currently has a large cash surplus and the board of directors has called for a meeting to discuss how this should be utilised.

The directors have made two main suggestions. One is to redeem the €20 million secured loan stock which had been issued several years ago to finance a capacity increase and which is due for redemption at par in 10 years time. The other is to increase the dividend payment to shareholders by the same amount. An analysis of the disposition of the current shareholders is provided in Appendix 2.

Calvin's capital structure as at 31 December 2XX4 is shown below:

	€ million
Issued share capital (25p par value)	140
Reserves	260
7% Secured loan stock 2X17	20

Corporation tax has been payable at approximately 33% and it would appear reasonable to assume that this rate will persist for the foreseeable future. The dividend paid by Calvin in 2XX3–2XX4 was 1.50 cents per share.

Industry averages with regard to dividend and borrowing levels for 2XX3–2XX4 have been collated as:

Dividend cover	2.4 times
Gearing (long-term debt/equity, calculated on book value)	45%
Interest cover	6.5 times

(Earnings before interest and tax divided by interest charges)

A more comprehensive set of comparative data for payout levels is provided in Appendix 3.

Required

In your capacity as a management consultant, write a report to the board of directors advising on the utilisation of the cash surplus.

For the purposes of this report, you may ignore differences in corporation tax between the Republic of Ireland and the UK, and answer only in relation to the information provided in the case study. State clearly any assumptions that you make.

(Approximately 40% of the marks will be awarded for calculations and 60% for the recommendations and report.)

Total 100 marks

Appendix 1: Data Supplied By Market Research Report

Projected Financial Data from Exporting (€million)

Year	1	2	3	4	5
Sales	1.0	2.0	4.0	8.0	20.0
Variable Costs					
Operating costs	0.70	1.40	2.80	5.60	14.0
Transportation costs	0.25	0.5	1.0	2.0	5.0

Transportation costs relate to the movement of finished goods from Belfast to Dublin. Initial set-up costs would largely relate to legal fees of €0.5 million, payable immediately and tax deductible against the profits for the current year just about to come to an end. Corporation tax will be payable at 33%, payable in the year in which income arises. After year five, it is estimated that performance would continue as per year five, indefinitely.

Additional Investigations

The market research team also identified an existing company manufacturing building materials and located in Dublin. Following an informal approach, the cost of acquiring this company has been estimated within the range of €16 – €20million. Additional investment of €4 million in new machines and €8 million in working capital would be required immediately, resulting in forecast post-tax net cash flows (after tax relief on capital allowances from year one onwards) from the acquired company in year one of €3.0 million rising to €5.0 million in year two and subsequent years, indefinitely. Due to the introduction of a just-in-time (JIT) stock control system, it is not expected that working capital will rise for the foreseeable future.

Due to the excess capacity in Belfast, machinery could be transferred to Dublin at a transportation cost of €0.5 million to the Dublin subsidiary, payable immediately. This machinery had originally cost Calvin €5 million. Capital allowances on new machinery can be claimed at 25% on a reducing balance basis. Corporation tax will be payable at 33%, payable in the year in which income arises.

The data supplied with regard to both exporting and acquiring the existing company has been prepared on the basis that the options are independent, that is the company could opt to both export and acquire the existing company, and the financial data would remain as above. If the machinery is transferred from Belfast to Dublin, however, then the manufacturing capacity in Belfast would no longer be sufficient to supply the export market. The improved manufacturing capacity in Dublin would be sufficient to service the entire Republic of Ireland market.

It may be assumed that all of the figures above have been adjusted for the likely impact of inflation and Calvin would require a return of 15% from any such investments.

Appendix 2: Equity Shareholdings (As at 31 December 2XX5)

Mark Calvin	managing director	5%
Shirley Morrison	sales director	5%
David Stevenson	technical director	5%
Gavin Rogers	business development director	5%
Institutional investors	(90% held by pension funds)	60%
Current employees	(approximately 150 employees)	10%
Retired employees	(approximately 100 employees)	10%

Appendix 3: Descriptive Statistics on UK Payout Ratios (2XX3/2XX4)

	Mean	Median	Mode	Standard Deviation
Full UK Sample	0.56	0.44	0.5	2.23
Industrial Classifications:				
Building	0.41	0.35	N/A	0.28
Chemicals	0.51	0.49	0.57	0.21
Engineering	0.51	0.45	N/A	0.33
Breweries & spirits	0.42	0.41	0.67	0.13
Food manufacturing	0.56	0.47	N/A	0.59
Distributors	0.63	0.45	0.64	1.43
Retailers	0.47	0.43	0.40	0.31
Electricals	0.54	0.47	0.59	0.41

Case 22
Darling & Company: Facing Future Challenges
Maeve McCutcheon, University College Cork

Facing the Future at Darling & Co.

Richard Darling arrived early at his new purpose-built premises on the outskirts of Athlone town. Richard believed that in spite of the turmoil of recent years, the future was bright. All manner of exciting opportunities now awaited Darling & Co. since its recent painful reorganisation; the problem was how best to position the company to meet those challenges. Richard knew that the Board was divided on the issue of future strategy and the non-executive directors would be looking to him to show strong leadership. The trouble was, he was still uncertain himself about the best path to take.

Background

Darling & Co. was founded in 1880 by Arthur H Darling, a native of Yorkshire who came to Dublin to marry the wealthy Bessie Kingston. Arthur, an engineer, brought with him a printing machine and set up in business in the coach house of his wife's family home off Parnell Square. Bessie was a leading light in the Dublin literary and musical scene and Arthur secured the business for concert programmes, literary pamphlets, poetry collections, etc. It was the couple's son, Gregory, who really set the business on the path to growth. In the early twentieth century he spotted a niche in the production and sale of educational books. As the education system grew so the company prospered, until 'Darling's' became the principal publisher of Irish-produced educational texts for all levels, from primary through to university texts. The company retained connections with the North of England and undertook significant contract work for Barrington's, a major publisher and printer in the North-east.

Edward Darling brought the company to the Irish Stock Market 49 years ago. The Darling family retained 20% of the shares in the company and retained a strong influence on the Board of Directors. Richard Darling acquired the family shares and took over as managing director in January 1998. Under his stewardship the company completely overhauled its printing processes and developed a state-of-the-art printing centre in Co. Westmeath. The restructuring, which commenced in 2XX4, had only just been concluded. Up to this the company had operated entirely from premises in Parnell Square in Dublin city centre.

The Restructuring

Darling's had an established reputation in Dublin as model employers, second only to the Guinness family. Moving out of Dublin had been a difficult decision for the company with its Liffeyside tradition. The finance director, Steve Porter, had persuaded Richard that the company could no longer compete given its current cost base. The workforce of 140 skilled workers needed to be drastically reduced. In addition, new digital printing systems meant that the company was finding it difficult to compete on quality unless it significantly re-tooled. The subsequent negotiations with the trade unions were difficult and protracted; generous redundancy packages were paid.

The restructuring, which was completed in 2XX7, cost the company €10 million, of which €6.5 million represented the capital costs of acquiring and re-furbishing the new premises and €3.5 million represented redundancy and other payments to employees. The company's reserves were rapidly depleted, especially as the Board decided to maintain the dividend at the 2XX4 level of 22 cent per share. The company had one million shares in issue. The restructuring was financed by a €10 million loan secured by a first charge on the Parnell Square premises. The loan, on an interest-only basis, was at 6% fixed rate for a 10-year term, with an early repayment option. In June 2XX8, when it was valued at €20 million, the company had signed a 10-year lease on Parnell Square premises at an annual rent of €800,000.

Market Sentiment

Richard was disappointed by the company's recent share price performance. While the restructuring had been generally welcomed when it was announced in 2XX4, the company's share price, which had advanced form €18 to €23 at that time, had generally hovered around €24 since then. In early 2XX8 the company had one million shares in issue, which gave a total value for the company of €34 million. However, following the turmoil in the financial markets in late 2XX8, the share price had fallen as low as €16 and was now hovering around €18. With the Dublin property currently valued at €16 million, this effectively values the core business at only €12 million. Richard was sure that, at this price, the market was ignoring Darling's growth potential.

Prior to the crash, returns on the stock market had been around 10%, representing an equity risk premium of 5%. The company's traditional business has an un-levered Beta of 1, but the multimedia aspect, which currently accounts for 10% of revenue, has an un-levered Beta of 1.5. The traditional business is expected to grow at 2%, but a rate of 10% is not unreasonable for the multimedia business for the foreseeable future. A reinvestment rate of about 15% would be needed in both areas.

The company had recorded losses in the years 2XX4–2XX6, but had returned to profitability in 2XX7. Its 2XX8 results have not yet been posted, but are broadly in line with market expectations (see Appendix 1). While no tax has been paid in recent years due to the losses sustained, the company can expect to pay tax at 12.5% in 2XX9.

A Growth Strategy

Jeff Masters, a native of San Jose, California, joined the company in 2XX3. Jeff, who is married to Richard's sister, Rose, had cashed out of his software business just before the dot.com collapse. He was impressed by the high level of technical expertise in Darling's staff and their network of contributing authors. He was interested in working with a small group of employees to develop new educational software packages. "This is a worldwide market," he enthused, "and you've got the network to really cash in. You won't grow the traditional business at more than 2–3%. We should re-orientate towards this growth area. Sure it's risky, but we have a lot of strengths in this area."

Jeff believes that the way forward for the company is through a Management Buy-out of the core business. They could purchase the entire company, having pre-sold the Dublin premises for €16 million. They would then pay down all of the existing debt of €10 million. He was ready to commit €5 million and, through his connections in the Venture Capital community, was confident he could readily raise the balance needed in high-yield debt finance at around 9%. "We could take the company private at €21 per share," reasoned Jeff. "We really don't need the listing and the buy-out will bring back control of the company to the family. When we have this puppy turned around, we can go back to the market and make a killing."

Conserving the Assets

Steve Porter, the finance director, has little time for Jeff's growth ambitions. He believes that the company now needs a period of consolidation. The tenant of the Parnell Street premises is looking to renegotiate the lease rental down to €650,000. However, he argues they could refinance at 5%, which would still represent a positive rental yield. He feels that disposal of the premises for €16 million would be a panic reaction to a volatile situation. "We should hold steady," he argued, "and wait for the rebound, after all, it is a unique premises in a unique location. At a conservative estimate this property will be worth €20 million again by the time the lease runs out."

Cashing Out

Ambrose Zachary Moriarty, the ebullient director of AZM Printing, has been circling Darling & Co. over the last few years. His business has mainly grown from 'Free Sheets' retail flyers and cut-price trade brochures. It is privately owned and he is understood to have outsourced some of his production to Eastern Europe. During a recent encounter he had bellowed: "Darling, I could take that old albatross of a business off your hands for €20 million, but don't be surprised if my offer is down to €15 million if you hang about. After all, Darling, fortune favours the brave." Richard wondered whether these overtures were worth pursuing. "€20 million for the equity in the company compares favourably with the current share price, but is the company worth more than that and would I be acting in the interests of everyone involved if I sell to someone like Moriarty?"

Evaluating the Choices

Richard could see problems with each course of action. He was excited by the prospects in educational software and multimedia products and agreed that that should be the target growth area. While a buy-out made sense with undervalued stock, what would happen if it didn't succeed? He was unsure about how much the core business was really worth without the Dublin premises. Richard was also concerned about the amount of debt involved. Traditionally, Darling's had been debt-free and he was not convinced that they should commit to future borrowing. He might consider increasing his own investment in the business, if necessary.

In relation to retaining the premises, he wondered whether his finance director was right to suggest they weather the storm in the property market. True, if they could lease the premises for €650,000, it would still be a solid investment, but there were significant risks with this course of action, even if in 10 year's time the market had stabilised and the premises was worth €20 million. What rate of return would this investment yield?

"Questions, questions, questions," thought Richard. "What I really need are some answers."

Required

You are an independent consultant employed by Richard to write a confidential report evaluating each of the options currently being explored by Darling Plc. In particular your report should include the following.

Question 1

With respect to the Management Buy-out strategy:

(a) A financial analysis of the buy-out option. This should include consideration of the value of the core business, the financing requirements for the buy-out and the ownership structure post-buy-out. You may assume that Richard maintains his current shareholding.

(30 marks)

(b) An assessment of how the buy-out option would affect Richard personally. You should include consideration of any adjustments he might wish to make to the buy-out proposal and of the circumstances in which the buy-out might fail.

(15 marks)

Question 2

With respect to the Property Lease Option:

(a) An evaluation of the internal rate of return on this proposal, assuming that the property is currently valued at €16 million, is leased for nine years at €650,000 and has a value on disposal in year 10 of €20 million.

(5 marks)

(b) A summary of the main risks in the leasing proposal.

(10 marks)

Question 3

With respect to the potential takeover bid:

(a) An evaluation of how each of the key stakeholders would be affected by the takeover.

(15 marks)

Question 4

A recommendation on the appropriate course of action for Richard.

(25 marks)

Total 100 marks

Appendix 1: Recent Financial Results for Darling Plc

€ 000	2XX3	2XX4	2XX5	2XX6	2XX7	2XX8*
Gross revenue	4450	4495	4674	4852	5012	5162
Operating Costs	3560	3371	3272	2911	2757	2839
Gross profit	890	1,124	1,402	1,941	2,255	2323
SG&A	356	360	374	388	401	413
Depreciation	167	282	246	243	209	226
EBIT	367.0	482.1	782.3	1309.6	1645.4	1684
Interest	26	632	618	645	609	610
Extraordinary						
Tax	0	200	400	2000	900	100
Net Profit	341.0	−349.9	−235.7	−1335.4	136.4	974
Dividends	209	209	220	220	220	**

* Not yet published
** Not yet finalised

Case 23

Sun Shine Limited

John Cotter, University College Dubin

Overview of Company

Sun Shine Limited is a computer software specialist based in Silicon Valley in California. It currently employs 72 staff. Its history is short, but very successful. It began business when its founder and current chief financial officer (CFO), James Brown, left Microsoft less than four years ago. James Brown, who was a new products specialist for Microsoft, believed there was a new niche in what he called "old but new" products, where non-computer technology products are reinvented with software innovations and support. The first product they developed was a palm pilot (or electronic diary) that had a number of extras, including telephone, radio, MP3 player and large memory storage. The Sun Shine Creation™ was very successful and quickly drove a large expansion in the size and fortunes of the company. Market share and revenues also grew, especially outside of the US. It currently has the following revenue sources:

- servicing the EU economies that have signed up to the Euro (45% of its trade);
- servicing the UK market in Sterling (25% of its trade);
- servicing the Asian markets in Japanese yen (10% of its trade);
- servicing the US (20% of its trade).

James Brown is very interested in developing and expanding by investing directly in Europe. His market research has suggested that continued growth in European markets is very promising, but expansion in the domestic market and Japan will be more difficult because of competing firms.

James Brown has commissioned a consultancy company, International Ideas, to analyse the relevant information for the further development of Sun Shine Limited. John Oglewski, a specialist on country risk analysis, has been given the task of developing the report for Sun Shine Limited. There are two main issues to be addressed in the report. First, the possible expansion of Sun Shine Limited: where to expand? In particular, International Ideas are asked to assess an expansion for Sun Shine in Scotland and the Republic of Ireland (the two were chosen for their membership of the EU but also because James Brown felt Irish/Scottish as his father was from Ireland and his mother was from Scotland).

John Oglewski sought clarification on the project as he felt that expanding in Silicon Valley should be assessed. The reply from Sun Shine, in a meeting with James Brown, was that whilst the company had plans to expand domestically in the future and would remain a US company by keeping its headquarters and research and development department there, nevertheless the expansion currently being assessed should concentrate on servicing Europe (EU without UK, and UK), which that would avoid the associated tariffs from US exports. (Non-EU tariffs ranged from 12% to 25% for the types of goods that Sun Shine produced and would represent a very large fixed cost to exporting to Europe.)

John Oglewski also received further clarification that he had not sought at all but felt it was relevant to the project. On meeting James Brown, it was clear to John Oglewski that James Brown had already made the decision on where to locate. James recounted John with tales of his latest trip to Ireland and the great time he had fishing on the Shannon. More importantly, James Brown also pointed out that the trip was part business, and that he had several meetings with representatives of Irish trade and development organisations, including the Industrial Development Authority (IDA), Enterprise Ireland and Forfás. The outcome of these meetings was very successful and James had made his decision to locate in Ireland. It was made very clear to John Oglewski that Ireland was the preferred location and that justifying choosing Scotland would be a very difficult and possibly fruitless task. John Oglewski felt his role was merely to give Sun Shine an independent 'rubber stamp' of its decision to locate in Ireland.

This exuberance of James Brown was clear as he enthusiastically discussed the possibility of developing even stronger ties with Ireland. James Brown noted that Ireland offered a very attractive corporation tax rate of 10% (compared to 16% in the US) and he felt that this could be exploited further by the possibility of fully relocating production (but not research and development) to Ireland, with the parent company remaining registered in the US. This would allow Sun Shine to benefit from access to its main markets and avoid customs, etc., while allowing for profits to be reported in Ireland that would be taxed at a low rate. The net profits could then be transferred back to the holding company in California. Also, profit manipulation could be further enhanced by transfer pricing between the parent company in the US and its subsidiary in Ireland. The main concern that James Brown voiced about relocation was the potential foreign exchange exposure it would face from exporting from Ireland to the US, Japan and the rest of Europe. James Brown was also enthusiastic about the quality of other inputs into computer software development that was present in Ireland, such as the expertise of potential employees and the overall structure of this industry in Ireland. Hence the second main issue to be addressed in the report is the potential foreign exchange exposure that would result from a full production transfer to Ireland and the continuing servicing of Sun Shine's markets.

Cash-flow Data

Details of the projected cash-flows of locating in Ireland and Scotland are given in Appendix 1. The discount factor that is recommended for any analysis is 5% and is based on the current cost of capital that Sun Shine is facing (based on US figures). The figures in Appendix 1 represent net values for any year (inflows minus outflows). Sun Shine wants the analysis to be based on five years of expansion and it is thought that after an initial net outflow, both operations will tend to be profitable thereafter. The financial support of respective governments and the potential large turnover are key drivers for the quick profitability of the expansions.

Country-specific Data

John Oglewski gathered comprehensive country-specific data for the purposes of analysing the new investment. Some summary data is given in Appendix 2. The data is to be used to help make a decision on whether the investment and expansion should take place and, if so, which economy should be chosen. The macroeconomic data provides average forecasts of some leading indicators over the next few years. These provide estimates of how the economies would do given the information that is available at the time of forecast and if the current situation was to hold going forward. Rankings of the skillbase, infrastructure, profit opportunity rankings (POR), fiscal responsibility and monetary instability represent values looking back over the last 10 years and are measured subjectively. The corporation tax and grants and support information give an indication of the respective government's financial support for foreign direct investment. In addition, it is noted that both Ireland and Scotland are open economies that are heavily dependent on international trade.

Foreign Exchange Data

Given that there were two main issues of concern (where to invest and potential foreign exchange exposure), John Oglewski felt he needed to get foreign exchange data in terms of dollars and Euro and also data over differing time-periods.

At the moment Sun Shine exports a large proportion of its product to the EU and Asian markets. In both cases it incurs exchange rate exposure (potential for exchange rate changes and for exchange rate risk). Due to this, Sun Shine Limited has developed a system where it receives payments on a six-monthly basis. This policy has worked quite well in managing exchange rate exposure, as the company is only concerned with exchange rate exposure on a semi-annual basis. John Oglewski obtains exchange rate changes for the relevant economies in dollars on a six-month basis over the last five years. The values are given in Appendix 3 for six-monthly intervals, detailing movements in the Euro, Sterling and the Yen in terms of one unit of a US dollar.

In addition, John Oglewski calculated monthly exchange rate changes in Euros for its main trading partners (the values are given in Appendix 4). Here, summary statistics (minimum value, maximum value, average value and standard deviation of values) are presented for a monthly analysis of exchange rate changes in Euros for the three leading world currencies and Sun Shine's main trading areas if they were to relocate to Ireland (US, UK, Japan and rest of Europe). The time period of the statistics was from 1992 to 2005 inclusive, representing 14 years, and sub sample values are given for an equally spaced period before and after the introduction of the Euro.

Required

You have been asked to act as an independent consultant to advise Sun Shine Limited on the best way to deal with its potential relocation and expansion. Also, you are required to advise on the foreign exchange exposure implications of moving to Ireland. A range of issues should be dealt with in your report.

Question 1

You have been asked to assess the relative merits of expanding in Scotland or in Ireland based on the projected cash-flows using present value (net present value analysis). Also support your answer using ratios (e.g. profitability index). Outline the breakeven internal rate of return for both locations based on the projected cash-flows.

(30 marks)

Question 2

Further illustrate your analysis by commenting on potential changing of the values relating to your answer in Q1 (e.g. discount factor). Confine your comments to the estimation of the net present value of the projected cash-flows (no calculations are necessary for this question).

(10 marks)

Question 3

Repeat the analysis of determining the relative merits of expanding in Scotland and Ireland using the country-specific details in Appendix 2. In particular, you should comment on the assumptions underlying these forecasts and whether you feel that any variability would affect your recommendations on where to base Sun Shine's expansion.

(20 marks)

Question 4

Repeat the analysis of determining the relative merits of expanding in Scotland and Ireland using the US dollar exchange rate changes in Appendix 3. In particular, you should comment on average exchange rate changes and deviations from the average. You should also comment on the extent to which Sun Shine's trade would be affected by this data.

(20 marks)

Question 5

Discuss the likely direction Sun Shine should take in terms of expanding revenues based on the foreign exchange rate changes (you should assume that each market is equally profitable on all considerations, with the exception of the exchange rate data), as shown in Appendix 4.

(20 marks)

Total 100 marks

Appendix 1: Projected Cash-flows for Potential Expansion of Sun Shine Limited

Net Cash-flows

	Ireland	Scotland
Year 0	−1000	−1000
Year 1	+300	+500
Year 2	+200	+200
Year 3	+400	+300
Year 4	+600	+400
Year 5	+700	+400

Notes: all figures are net (inflows minus outflows) and in $ millions over a five-year period. The initial investment in both economies is $1,000 million. Cash outflows deal with expenses such as wages, etc. Cash inflows include government grants and revenues.

Appendix 2: Country-specific Details for Sun Shine Limited

Macroeconomic Forecasts	Ireland	Scotland
Inflation Rates	3%	3.8%
Interest Rates	3.5%	5.0%
POR	86/100	84/100
Infrastructure	81/100	93/100
Employees	91/100	91/100
Grants and support	$22m	$6
Taxation	10%	21%
Fiscal Responsibility	96/100	97/100
Monetary stability	95/100	91/100

Notes: the Macroeconomic Forecasts are obtained from a variety of sources. For example, the economic information and forecasts are mainly obtained from OECD and IMF country reports. The grants and support information was obtained directly from individual country's industrial support bodies. Inflation, taxation and interest rates are averages of five-year forecasts in percentage form. The profit opportunity rankings (POR) represents a subjective estimate of the level of political risk entailed in doing business in a particular economy. The rankings (the higher, the more appealing) represent a proxy of the business climate to new enterprises. Infrastructure covers road network, telecommunications and other background facilities. 'Employees' measures suitability in terms of education. Grants and support are given by industrial development organisations to support new businesses. Tax is the prevailing corporation tax on offer and guaranteed for Sun Shine for the next five years in respective countries. Fiscal responsibility is a subjective measure of fiscal policies (e.g. taxation and budgets), with a higher ranking being more appealing. Monetary stability is a subjective measure of monetary policy, with a higher ranking being more appealing. The uncertainty relating to whether the UK would join the Eurozone is reflected in Scotland's score.

Appendix 3: US Dollar Exchange Rate Changes Data for Sun Shine Limited

Time-period	Euro	Sterling	Yen
1	2.3	1.8	2.8
2	3.1	1.6	3.2
3	2.1	3	4.1
4	2	2.3	2.9
5	1.9	2.1	3.4
6	2.9	1.7	4.5
7	3	2	3.5
8	3.1	3.2	3.2
9	2.7	1.2	2.9
10	4	1.8	4

Exchange rate changes (absolute values) are given for the previous five years representing six-monthly interval values. The exchange rate changes are given for each currency in terms of US dollars.

Appendix 4: Summary Statistics of Monthly Exchange Rate Changes for Euro

	Minimum	Maximum	Average	Deviation
Full sample				
Dollar	−9.37	6.97	−0.09	2.86
Sterling	−4.52	10.69	−0.04	2.01
Yen	−11.23	7.89	−0.12	3.26
Pre-Euro				
Dollar	−9.37	5.53	−0.20	2.82
Sterling	−4.52	10.69	−0.05	2.10
Yen	−11.23	7.89	−0.12	3.26
Post-Euro				
Dollar	−5.62	6.97	0.01	2.92
Sterling	−3.93	6.46	−0.03	1.91
Yen	−7.24	5.68	−0.16	3.25

Values are given as monthly percentage changes. All currencies are quoted in Euro. Deviation represents standard deviation of monthly values. The full sample is 1992–2005 inclusive, with the pre-Euro sample encompassing 1992–1998 and the post-Euro period encompassing 1999–2005.

Case 24
Blackwater Hotel Group plc
Peter Green, University of Ulster

The Blackwater Hotel Group plc, a company based in Dublin, is considering building a new luxury hotel located in the newly established dockland area in Belfast. The group currently owns six other hotels, located in Blackpool, Margate, Dublin, Galway, Limerick and Cork. The hotels located in the UK have been established by setting up wholly owned subsidiary companies and it is proposed that the new hotel in Belfast will be treated the same. The cost of the construction of the hotel, including a 100-year leasehold on the land, has been estimated at €90 million, 10% of which is payable immediately, 50% in one year's time and the balance on completion in approximately two years' time. Approximately €50 million of this expenditure is eligible for capital allowances on a straight-line basis at 4% per annum. Expenditure attracting capital allowances will occur at the same percentage rates as the estimated total cost of construction per year. Corporate taxes are levied at the rate of 32.75% per year, payable in the year that income arises. In addition, a working capital investment of €2 million will be required from the start of year three.

The hotel will have 320 bedrooms and 20 function rooms. For the purposes of analysis, the following data has been collated, based upon the financial performance of the hotel located in Blackpool, using an exchange rate of €1.65: stg£1.

On average, when a bedroom is occupied, expected occupancy is 1.5 people per night. The average charge per night is expected to be €140, which is valid whether one or more persons use the room. In addition, on average €60 per person, per day is expected to be spent on food and drink and €25 per person, per day on other hotel facilities. The gross profit margin on food and drink is expected to be 50%, and on other facilities, 20%.

Non-resident guests are expected to provide annual sales on food and drink of €3 million, and €1 million on other facilities. The rental of the function rooms will provide a pre-tax contribution of €1 million.

Expected annual outlays are: salaries, wages and pension costs–€5 million; gas, electricity, rates–€1.4 million; and all other costs, excluding major refurbishments–€1 million.

Every five years the hotel would require major redecoration and refurbishment. The most recent refurbishment of the hotel located in Blackpool cost €12 million. These costs were tax allowable in the year incurred.

The group normally evaluates its hotel investments over a 20-year operating time horizon. However, the financial director considers the proposed hotel in Belfast to be of a higher risk and has suggested that a 15-year operating time horizon should be employed. At the end of 15-years of operation the hotel is expected to have an after-tax value of €50 million, before any end-of-period refurbishment and excluding any working capital released.

All of the above estimated revenues, costs and values are stated at current prices; that is, no consideration of inflation has been made.

The market value of the group's debt is €37.8 million and the market value of equity is €165.6 million. The debt consists of 12% debentures redeemable at par value of €100, in 13 years time. The debt is currently priced at €114, ex-interest. The equity beta of the group's shares is 0.8 and the market return estimated to be 15% per annum. The current risk-free rate of return is 7% per annum.

Although the current rate of inflation in the Republic of Ireland is 4% and the rate of inflation in the UK is 2%, an appropriate rate of inflation for the purposes of the appraisal of the investment has been estimated at 4% per year and this is expected to continue for the foreseeable future.

The company has indicated that it will require a return of 12% nominal per annum from the proposed investment. You may assume that there are 365 days in a year.

Required

In your capacity as the group's management consultant, prepare a report to advise the board of directors of Blackwater Hotel Group plc of the financial viability of the investment, in particular the occupancy rate (the percentage of rooms occupied per night, excluding the function rooms) that would need to be achieved. Relevant calculations must form part of your report as an appendix. Your report should include a consideration of the following matters.

Question 1

A discussion of how accurate your evaluation is likely to be and which parts of your evaluation are likely to be subject to significant error.

Question 2

A discussion of how a formal consideration of all the risks of the proposed investment could be made.

Question 3

An analysis as to how the required rate of return has been derived, and whether this is likely to be appropriate for the appraisal of this proposal.

State clearly any assumptions that you make.

(*Approximately 40% of the marks will be awarded for calculations and 60% for the recommendations and report.*)

Total 100 marks

Case 25
Tannam plc
Louis Murray, University College Dublin

Following a sustained period of rapid expansion, Tannam has developed to become a listed company on the Dublin Stock Exchange. This rapid development and expansion means that it has, in fact, become a mini-conglomerate, with interests covering a wide range of activities, many of them relatively unrelated to each other. Initially established in the 1980s, Tannam began as a retail business, concentrating on television and audio equipment. Hugh Tannam had a well-developed and long-standing interest in specialised electronic equipment, and sourced a range of products that would appeal to both the retail and the rental markets. Rapid developments in the past few years mean that the business has expanded very considerably and now covers a range of relatively unrelated activities, including the provision of services to the television and film industries, manufacturing, property development, recording and musical equipment. Most of these activities are conducted through a number of subsidiaries, which were acquired following merger or the purchase of existing established businesses.

Due to the interests of its founder, Tannam began as a retailer of electrical and electronic equipment. It also developed a considerable presence in the rental market. Established as a limited company, it raised £4.25 million through an initial share issue. The first few years of trading were relatively uneven, however the business gradually stabilised as new outlets were opened in a number of towns and cities in Ireland. By the late 1980s, it had established a considerable presence, with annual turnover in excess of £4 million and a profit of approximately £250,000. To fund its continued development, Tannam applied for a stock market listing, and this was granted in 1991. However, trading patterns in the early 1990s remained relatively unstable, and Tannam was not able to record continued stable profits every year. The business remained highly exposed to relatively short upturns and downturns in the electrical and electronic equipment market. Also, performance of the Irish economy remained relatively poor throughout this period. At this time, it was commonly remarked that Tannam had all the features of a high beta business, as it was excessively exposed to short-term and long-term movements in the underlying economy. In response to this, the issue of diversification came into consideration. Both senior managers and major shareholders questioned the wisdom of continuing such a high exposure to short-term economic performance.

In order to achieve the objective of reducing the dependence on a relatively volatile market sector, the directors of Tannam decided to embark on a policy of expansion and diversification into other business sectors. They therefore decided to seek the advice of a management consultancy, which strongly recommended that they undertake this major change in overall strategy of the business. The consultancy identified its stock market quotation as one of the more attractive features of the overall business, and suggested that it examine the possibility of merging with other businesses that would be attracted by the possibility of a stock market quotation. This type of action could actually be viewed as a reverse takeover, if the unquoted firm or firms were larger than Tannam, as control of the merged group could pass to the owners or shareholders of the firms that are acquired. Although such a strategic move would have implications for the control of Tannam, the major shareholders decided that this was preferable to the high levels of uncertainty associated with their continued exposure to a single industry sector. A strategic decision was therefore made to seek unlisted firms as potential acquisition targets, the ideal partner being firms in an industry sector that is not related to electrical and electronic equipment.

Three separate unlisted companies were identified, and discussions were initiated with the directors of each of them. In all three cases there was a clear desire to reverse into a publicly quoted company. The main motivation for each was that it would make it considerably easier to raise further equity finance, which could be used to assist in financing further expansion and possible diversification. One firm, a Cork-based property developer, Spollen Properties, had been expanding very rapidly and had a very strong record of profitability. The directors of Spollen saw clear benefits in reversing into a publicly quoted company, such as Tannam. A second firm, CGU Distributors, was a distributor for one of the motor manufacturers, selling commercial vehicles in Ireland. The product range was relatively limited, so although this potentially was a major business, it remained medium-sized in Ireland. Again, clear opportunities for further growth and development could be identified, if sufficient funding sources were to become available. The final firm was Fastnet Media Services, which provided specialist services to the media and entertainment industries. Although established over 20 years, it had recently been enjoying a growing reputation as the Irish-based media, television and general entertainment businesses had been establishing themselves. As a result, by the mid-1990s its directors had also identified the potential for considerable expansion, should potential sources of funding be successfully tapped.

Discussions with the directors of all these companies proved to be highly successful, and agreement was quickly reached. Under the terms of this agreement, Tannam was reorganised as a holding company, with separate wholly owned freestanding units or divisions. Tannam PLC also changed its name to Tannam Holdings on 1 June 1997. New shares were issued in this holding company, and an agreement was reached regarding the pro-rata distribution of these shares to those who were shareholders of the four firms making up the new group. The terms of this distribution largely depended on the relative sizes of the four firms, however because of its particularly strong growth record and its considerable potential, shareholders in CGU received a slightly larger allocation. With the formation of this group, a new board of directors and a new chairman were put in place. A new managing director of the group also was appointed. Coming from CGU Distributors, the largest of the firms coming together to form this group, Tom Glover had a well-established reputation as a highly aggressive and successful manager, so he was offered this appointment. Since he had been a very sizable shareholder in CGU, Glover also became one of the largest individual shareholders of the group, as he controlled nearly six percent of all shares. As part of this arrangement, Hugh Tannam continued to have an active involvement with the group, however his interest was limited to an involvement with Tannam, now a wholly owned subsidiary of the group, concentrating on televisions and audio equipment.

Under its new leadership, Tannam pursued two major objectives. They decided to go for rapid growth, through a further series of acquisitions, and they also decided to reduce costs, in an attempt to generate increased profitability. In order to achieve the objective of cost reductions, two approaches were followed. Every one of the subsidiaries was closely examined, to identify possible sources of savings. Also, most major management functions for the group were brought together and centralised in one location. Although Tannam Holdings was responsible for a range of very diverse activities, senior management decided that there was a considerable potential for savings, following a major centralisation. Each subsidiary was also established as a strategic business unit, with its own profit centre, and reasonably tight budget constraints.

Over the next few years, Tannam also made a number of acquisitions. These acquisitions ranged from a number of relatively small businesses, each without a market quotation, to two very sizeable firms. These two firms were in the distribution, and the building supplies businesses. When considering the acquisition of quoted companies, management determined to acquire firms trading at a lower price/earnings (P/E) ratio than Tannam. This decision, to concentrate only on publicly quoted companies trading on a relatively low P/E ratio, was taken by Tom Glover, as he insisted that it was necessary to maintain company share price. The reason for this approach was a belief that it should ensure no dilution of earnings per share in Tannam, as a result of the acquisition. However, it has proved to be controversial with the senior management of Tannam, some of whom argue that these companies may be poor performers and may not contribute to the long-term success of the group. However, the managing director ensured that his policy was closely followed, so that both acquisitions of publicly quoted firms were of firms trading on lower P/E ratios than Tannam. A list of all the wholly owned subsidiaries currently in the Tannam Group is provided in Appendix 1.

A combination of retained earnings and new debt or equity capital was used to finance these acquisitions. As Tannam proved to be a profitable group, internally generated funds could be used to finance the purchase of a number of the smaller businesses. However, a number of the other acquisitions, including the two publicly quoted businesses, did require further outside funding. Accordingly, Tannam raised a combination of new equity and new debt finance to cover the cost of these acquisitions. As a result, in these cases, the acquisition consisted of a combination of share-for-share exchange, and a cash payment that was financed through the new debt issues. As the cash purchase of some of the smaller acquisitions also required external financing, through the issue of new debt, the capital structure of Tannam became more complex, and consisted of a combination of equity, convertible debentures, debentures and loan stock, and long-term bank debt. In every case, Glover and his senior management team took the decision regarding an appropriate source of finance. It largely depended on market conditions at the time, and the need to maintain a healthy debt ratio for the holding group.

Throughout this period of rapid expansion, the management team was able to maintain a healthy dividend policy. Annual dividends were either maintained at the previous year's level or were allowed to increase. Management were able to continue this policy, as annual earnings tended to remain reasonably stable. Clearly the decision to diversify the range of activities of Tannam had been successful, as the business established a strong record of annual profitability, with a relatively low exposure to downturns in the national economy. The original strategic decision to diversify business activities across a number of sectors was proving successful.

Throughout the period since Tannam Holdings was established, a budgetary control system was introduced, developed and gradually improved. Before establishment of the holding group, Tannam had employed a payback period approach to evaluate all investments above an established minimum value, which was low. Effectively, all investment appraisal decisions were evaluated by payback. A minimum cut-off period of three years was established. However, with the development of budgetary control systems, management agreed to establish an appraisal system that would allow for cost of capital, and the time value of money. Both net present value and internal rate of return were considered, and after considerable discussion, management expressed a preference for internal rate of return. Their reason was that a percentage rate of return on investment was a more meaningful measure. However, as there had been reasonably strong support for net present value, it was agreed that both would be prepared, and used as an input to the evaluation process. It was agreed, however, that the primary measure would be internal rate of return, so that all successful proposals must offer an after-tax internal rate of return that exceeds after-tax cost of capital for the group.

On a recent sunny day, the new finance director of Tannam Holdings, Gloria Knight, was considering a number of proposed new investments. As there had been a time lag between the departure of the previous office-holder and Gloria's appointment, a reasonably large list of new proposals was under consideration. Budgetary control procedures required that the finance director must evaluate all proposals above a pre-determined minimum value, so these proposals were awaiting her consideration before a final decision could be made. In each case, the subsidiary companies had prepared an evaluation of projects that had emanated from them, and an estimated after-tax internal rate of return (IRR) had been submitted. As finance director, Knight now had to decide which proposals she would support at an upcoming meeting of the board of directors. As well as submitting a recommendation, she decided that a report would be necessary, to justify the decision that she takes.

Total proposed expenditure came to €80 million. This investment would be financed in a similar manner to previous investments, through a combination of retained earnings, new debt capital and a new issue of equity capital. A recent income statement for Tannam Holdings is presented in Appendix 2. Although the precise details of the financing had yet to be finalised, it had been agreed with the board that whatever combination is employed, it will have minimal impact on the current structure of long-term finance in Tannam. To begin the assessment, Knight decided to calculate the current weighted average cost of capital for Tannam. As it had been agreed that assessment would be based on an after-tax IRR, she decided to prepare an estimate of the after-tax cost of capital, by allowing for the deductibility of interest payments, when assessing company taxes. Cost of debt was therefore calculated as the coupon rate, or interest rate, adjusted for this tax saving. Bank overdrafts were not included in this assessment, as they were considered to be short-term debt and therefore not part of the group capital structure. Also, as overdrafts tend to carry a low interest rate, Knight had a concern that their inclusion might overly reduce cost of capital. Cost of equity capital was estimated using the Capital Asset Pricing Model. Using an estimated return on the market equity index of 13%, a risk-free return of 6% and an estimated beta coefficient of 1.1 for Tannam Holdings, a cost of equity of 13.7% had been estimated. Details of the full calculations for weighted average cost of capital are presented in Appendix 3. Appendix 4 provides a list of the proposals that are under consideration. It largely consists of proposed investments by many of the individual subsidiaries, however one proposal for the purchase of a small unlisted business is also included.

Cost of capital calculations produce an estimated after-tax rate of 11.66%, so after allowing for error, an overall hurdle rate of 12% is implied. The implication is that all proposals offering an after-tax return in excess of 12% should be approved, regardless of which subsidiary of Tannam has submitted them. Using this measure, all but one of the proposals that had been submitted to her meet the minimum requirement for investment. After some consideration, Gloria Knight felt uneasy because she was fully aware that the various subsidiaries of Tannam were engaged in very different activities and therefore would be facing very different risk exposures. Her concern was whether it was appropriate to apply the single fixed hurdle rate across all these different activities. Perhaps the hurdle rate employed should allow for these differences in risk? For example, she was concerned that the huge proposed investment in a new head office building for Quirke Construction should be evaluated at such a low rate, considering the relatively volatile state of the construction industry. It is true that construction can experience years of steady growth, but there is always a concern that it may not be maintained. Also, an assessment of the proposed new warehouse facility for Tress indicated that it was not economical, but considering the particularly low risk exposure for the garden equipment sector and the potential value of this proposal to this business, Knight also wondered if the benchmark hurdle rate applied was possibly too high.

In order to develop her thinking, Knight decided to make an evaluation of the risk profile of each subsidiary company by identifying similar independent, publicly quoted firms on either the Dublin or the London Stock Exchanges. In order to minimise estimation error, she found firms that matched closely, after allowing for both size and industry sector. In each case, she then used publicly available sources to generate a beta estimate for each firm. Assuming that these values provide a close estimate of beta for each subsidiary in Tannam Holdings, she decided to adjust the hurdle rates to allow for a more precise measure of market risk. Estimated market risk or beta values for each subsidiary have been included in Appendix 1. In the case of Lennox Distributers, Knight estimated that the appropriate beta value is 0.9.

Gloria has also decided to conduct an extensive analysis of one of the proposed new investments. She feels that this detailed examination may be necessary, as there has been concern that discounting-based methods of appraisal may not have been fully understood and implemented correctly in all cases. In particular, there is concern that there may have been little assessment on the impact of error in the forecast cash-flows, on which appraisal decisions have been based. Within the timescale, it will not be possible to fully evaluate all of the proposals that are under consideration, so she identifies and selects a further proposed investment in new electrical equipment that has been planned by Fasnet Media Services. This proposal is at an earlier stage of investigation and therefore has not formed part of her initial assessment on the impact of hurdle rates on the acceptability of investments by the various subsidiaries of Tannam. However, when conducting this further investigation, she will again use an individual hurdle rate that is appropriate for Fasnet. This further proposal is of concern, as the media and entertainment industries do tend to experience volatile trading conditions. There is, therefore, a strong possibility that forecast cash-flows may be subject to considerable error. If this were to occur, it is possible that even the discounting-based methodology may produce an incorrect recommendation. The further investigation is therefore desirable.

In order to conduct a detailed investigation, Gloria gathers all available background information. Fasnet plans to purchase new film-making equipment for €5,850,000. They expect to use this equipment to assist with the provision of short programme- and video-making facilities for small- and medium-sized businesses that wish to find new methods of advertising their services. They also envisage that this service will be of interest to performers in the entertainment industry.

The equipment will be depreciated over a period of five years, to a scrap value of zero. Straight-line depreciation will be employed. However, based on past experience, it is likely that the equipment will be sold for approximately 10% of its purchase price, or €585,000. Should the investment be made, further working capital will be required. Again, based on industry experience, this will be equal to a level of 10% of the following year's forecast sales and rental revenue.

Revenue forecasts are presented in Appendix 5. Operation costs are expected to represent 45% of sales, however if average annual sales revenues fall by 5% or more, it is anticipated that operating costs probably will represent 50% of sales. Because of the timing of their accounting year, it can be assumed that all tax payments will occur in the same year as the associated reported profits. It can also be assumed that any anticipated losses associated with this proposal will be written off against other profits made by Fasnet, as there is a general expectation that this division will continue to be profitable. As with all other parts of the group, company tax rates of 15% will apply.

Although it is not the normal convention within the group, Gloria has a strong opinion that a sensitivity analysis on this proposed investment is essential. Initial calculations suggest that, although the proposal probably will meet initial requirements and will be profitable, volatile trading conditions may in fact mean that the forecasts may not be achieved. She is also concerned that the media and entertainment industries will be exposed to any downturns in the economy, and that revenue may be vulnerable. As a result, she considers it highly desirable that, as well as conducting an assessment based on forecast revenues, a further assessment should be conducted on the basis that forecast revenues only reach 95% of forecast values.

Required

Prepare a report on behalf of Gloria Knight, providing the background to the current appraisal decisions, and suggest an improved overall approach. Your report should be composed of two sections. The first section should concentrate on the related issues of hurdle rates, diverse subsidiaries and different risk exposures. The second section will relate to forecasting risk, sensitivity analysis and the detailed evaluation of an individual proposed investment.

SECTION 1

Question 1

Discuss the issue of diversification, as pursued by Tannam. Outline possible benefits and costs associated with this approach.

(10 marks)

Question 2

Review the policy adapted by Tannam, i.e. to only acquire companies trading on a lower P/E ratio than itself. Explain the reasoning behind this approach and consider whether it is always appropriate. Use numerical examples to demonstrate your points.

(12 marks)

Question 3

Critically outline how Tannam currently deals with appraisal decisions. In your discussion, consider the issue of whether a particular source of finance used to purchase a subsidiary or to cover the cost of a particular investment should be used to determine the hurdle rate in that case. Give reasons for your recommendation on a best overall approach.

(10 marks)

Question 4

Discuss whether a single hurdle rate is appropriate, considering the risk profile of the individual proposed investments. Using Knight's estimated beta values for the individual subsidiaries, use the Capital Asset Pricing Model and Weighted Average

Cost of Capital Formulae to determine an optimal hurdle rate for each subsidiary. You can assume that the balance of debt and equity capital in each subsidiary would be similar to that of the parent firm. Conclude this section with recommendations on each of the proposed investments.

(18 marks)

SECTION 2

Question 1

Discuss the issue of forecast error, and how it might impact on the accuracy of any recommendation on whether or not to invest. Suggest possible approaches to the issue of forecast error, and explain how they may ensure a more accurate final decision.

(20 marks)

Question 2

Prepare a detailed evaluation of the proposed extra investment by Fasnet. You should estimate both the after-tax Net Present Value, and the after-tax Internal Rate of Return. Based on your calculations, you should offer an initial recommendation on whether this investment will be profitable. You should use the appropriate optimal hurdle rate that was estimated in section 1 of your report.

(15 marks)

Question 3

Considering the fears regarding forecast error, prepare a sensitivity analysis on the assessments of Net Present Value and Internal Rate of Return. This analysis should be based on the assumption that forecast annual revenues fall by 5%. You should also allow for the likelihood that, in this event, operating costs will represent 50% of sales. Based on this analysis, discuss whether the recommendation should be changed.

(15 Marks)

Total 100 marks

Appendix 1: List of Subsidiaries Held in the Tannam Group, December XXXX

Tannam Ltd (β=1.9)	Electrical and Electronic Equipment – Retail and Rental
Spollen Properties Ltd (β=2.2)	Property Development
CGU Distributors Ltd (β=0.7)	Motor Vehicle Distributors
Fasnet Media Services Ltd (β=1.1)	Equipment for Media and Entertainment Industries
Quirke Construction Ltd (β=1.8)	Building Contractors and Providers
Kenge Haulage Ltd (β=1.3)	International Distribution
Tress Ltd (β=0.6)	Garden Equipment and Supplies
Cross Timber Ltd (β=0.8)	Furniture Manufacturer
Image Consultants Ltd (β=1.7)	Interior Design
Laheen Refrigerators (β=1.0)	Refrigeration Equipment for the Retail Trade

Appendix 2: Tannam Holdings

Consolidated Profit and Loss Account
Year Ending 31 December XXXX (€000s)

Turnover	410,812
Cost of Sales	−331,906
Gross Profit	78,906
Transportation Costs	−15,815
Administrative Expenses	−25,385
Overheads	−896
Interest Expenses	−14,398
Profit Before Tax	22,412
Tax	3,362
Profit After Tax	19,050
Dividends	6,477
Retained Earnings	12,573

Appendix 3: Estimation of Weighted Average Cost of Capital for Tannam Holdings

	Tax Adjusted Return	Weighting	Weighted Average Cost of Capital
10% Debentures	8.5%	0.175	1.48%
13% Loan Stock	11.05%	0.035	0.38%
9% Convertibles	7.65%	0.09	0.69%
12% Term Loan	10.2%	0.14	1.43%
Equity Capital	13.7%	0.56	7.67%
Weighted Average Cost of Capital			11.66%

Appendix 4: Investment Proposals under Consideration by Gloria Knight

	Initial Investment (€000s)	IRR (%)	NPV (€000s)
Improved Retail Premises – Tannam	2250	17	1450
New Electrical Equipment – Tannam	5875	15	3500
New Fleet – Kenge Haulage	10000	16	3800
Warehouse Facility – Tress	2500	11	−350
New Office Building – Image Consultants	5000	17	2250
Computer-controlled Equipment – Cross Timber	625	16	450
Land Purchase – Spollen Properties	22000	15	2500
Expanded Storage – Laheen	925	14	800
Head Office Building – Quirke Construction	25,000	13	1000
Purchase of Lennox Distributors	13175	12	2800
Total	91850		

Appendix 5: Forecast Annual Sales Revenues from Possible Further Investment by Fasnet

€000s per Year

Year 1	Year 2	Year 3	Year 4	Year 5
2	3.4	4	4	2.4

When conducting an investment appraisal, it can be assumed that all cash-flows arrive on the final working day of each year.

Case 26
Salmon Spray
Ray Donnelly, University College Cork

History of the Company

One rainy December morning in 1960, Arthur Pitt, the production director of QPS Foods, Staffordshire, received a phone call from an old friend, James Fallon, from Co. Mayo in the West of Ireland. James is the godfather of Arthur's daughter, Penelope. James was visiting England on business and wished to discuss a proposal with Arthur. The two men had lunch in Uttoxeter, during which they discussed Fallon's proposition. Fallon was sole owner and managing director of Salmon Spray Limited, a processed food manufacturer specialising in canned fish products. Its main brand is the Breaver brand of tinned salmon. James was approaching 55 years of age and wished to change his lifestyle. In short, he was looking for a partner who would look after the day-to-day operations while James himself took a less active role as Chairman. Fallon offered an attractive package. Pitt went home that night and discussed the move with his wife. Since she was Irish, she welcomed the move and his daughter was only two years of age so would adapt easily into the new environment. Pitt had no obstacles to taking up Fallon's offer. So, after 20 years as a senior manager in the convenience food business, Arthur Pitt decided to leave his native Staffordshire and move with his family to the West of Ireland.

Pitt never regretted the move. Salmon Spray proved a very successful company and grew substantially over the years. Fallon and Pitt were always conservative about borrowing and financed the expansion mainly from retained earnings. The 1980s was a decade of major change for Salmon Spray. Fallon died in 1980 and since he had no family of own, he bequeathed his shares to Penelope Pitt, who had joined the company having left school in 1976. Arthur retired in 1987 and Penny took over as managing director. Penny is far more aggressive than the company's previous managing directors. A major expansion was undertaken in 1989 when Salmon Spray took over two continental companies: DFC in France and DPC in Holland. Both specialised in processing seafood, with a particular emphasis on crab and shrimp. This expansion enabled Salmon Spray to access lucrative export markets in France, Germany, Spain, Holland, Belgium and Italy. The expansion was financed by borrowing and additional equity capital. The new investors comprise a publicly quoted company, a private venture capital company and some well-heeled individuals. The Pitts' combined stake remained at 55%. The company was now large enough to be quoted on the stock market, but since it did not require any additional funds and Penny wished to maintain control (her father is totally under her influence), it remains a private company. However, to appease the outside investors, Penny has recruited a number of non-executive directors. Some of these are associates of Penny, but most are appointees of the outside shareholders. The Chairman, Sir Rex Johnson, falls into the latter category. Sir Rex is a famous 'self-made' millionaire who is semi-retired. He currently spends most of his time enjoying his fortune; co-hosting a minor TV management game show; attending to two non-executive directorships in large UK-based plcs; and contributing to his role as Chairman of Salmon Spray. In Penny's opinion, Sir Rex is too narrowly focussed on the profitability of Salmon Spray. He is often heard saying, "so long as the company continues to earn profits, the shareholders will be happy." Penny does not care that much for Sir Rex or the shareholders. She sees them as moneychangers and sees her job at the company as continuing in the tradition of her father and godfather. She also considers that profits are not sufficient. Any project Salmon Spray takes on must earn a 'worthwhile' rate of return. She is therefore focussed on making the company as successful as she can make it on her own terms.

The Current Proposal

Salmon Spray is at a crossroads. It has continued to prosper and its profits since 1990 have enabled it to not only repay all of its borrowings but to accumulate a large cash surplus. Sir Rex has made it clear that he and the shareholders expect Penny to do something constructive with the cash surplus (i.e. increase profitability) or pay a large dividend. He has pointed out that a simple expansion of the existing business into Poland would be profitable, though not enormously so, and would solve the problem of the excess cash. He also thinks a share repurchase is worthy of consideration. Penny is not enamoured by the idea of giving what she perceives to be the company's cash to the shareholders. She personally has no immediate need of additional cash, so an additional dividend is ruled out. Given the situation with fish stocks in the EU, she does not believe that there is scope for further expansion in the canned seafood industry so has been looking further afield. She has spent all her working life involved with the seafood industry. The main processes involved here are flavouring, preserving and packing ingredients. She has noticed the trend toward healthier eating and while she herself has doubts about it, she reckons that many people are rather taken by the Mediterranean diet. She believes that the company could easily make the transition to fruit and vegetable processing, provided the project is managed carefully. She is currently considering the purchase of a small Spanish olive oil producer. The Spanish company has an extensive land bank on which a new factory could be constructed. Some of the existing land bank is surplus to requirements and could be sold to finance the building of the new factory to process fruit and vegetables. Since the project would require a major capital investment, the approval of the Salmon Spray board is necessary.

Penny asks Jack McBride, the company treasurer, to prepare a financial analysis that will help her make a decision and also convince the board of the viability of the project. He has also been requested to provide some figures regarding Sir Rex's plan for expansion in Poland. Jack has done a discounted cash-flow analysis for the project. He is recommending the purchase of the Spanish company on the basis that the project has a positive NPV. He does not consider the Polish project viable, but nonetheless has estimated the profitability of the project over the next five years, by which time the original investment would be fully depreciated (see Appendix 1).

Penny has perused Jack's analysis and is concerned that it will not assist her in persuading the board of the merits of the project. In particular, there are two parts of the analysis that bother her. First, she has major doubts about Jack's estimate of the cost of capital. He has estimated the cost of capital for the project to be 8%. His calculations are based on the notion that this is the rate at which Salmon Spray could borrow the money from the banks for the project. Penny reckons that since Salmon Spray will be using little if any debt to finance the project, this is not correct. Secondly, she has done a quick calculation of the accounting rate of return (ROR) from the project. She estimates the average annual ROR from the project to be just over 17%. She is disappointed by this because the company is currently generating an accounting rate of return of 27%.

Before the proposal goes to the board it must be approved by Penelope. Just before she meets with Jack she gets a telephone call from Sir Rex. He needs to devote the next three months to his TV series and a holiday in the Seychelles and wants to bring the board meeting forward by a week. Penny is not impressed: this proposal is the most important decision she has had to make since Salmon Spray took over the European canned food companies in 1989. She needs more time to think about it. She has had about as much of Sir Rex as she can tolerate. With Jack's analysis proving less than convincing, she is not best pleased.

Having listened to Jack drone on about cash-flow projections, shareholder wealth and costs of capital for half an hour, Penny finally loses patience. "I want to know the (accounting) rate of return on this project before I recommend this to the Board," she barks at Jack. "And what is this NPV stuff anyway? We never used such techniques before and have done well enough. The chairman, Sir Rex Johnson, and the other people on the board are only interested in profits. I cannot go to the board with this stuff. Is there any way we can reconcile your analysis with the profits this project will generate? I am also confused as to why you only used cash-flows for the first five years of the project. What about the cash-flows and profits from year six onwards?"

Jack admits to Penny that although he has not computed the ROR for the project, it is much less than the average earned by the company at present. However, he argues that this is a less risky project than Salmon Spray's current operation. Furthermore, he says, "we can borrow at 8% for it and the interest will be allowable for tax." Penny is confused about this and says, "my instincts tell me that this project could really be quite profitable, but how can I sell this project to the board if it will reduce the overall return on equity of the company? Also, since we have no intention of borrowing to finance this project I don't see the relevance of the cost of borrowing to the decision. As for the Polish project, it seems profitable, but I feel that it is not profitable enough to justify the investment."

After some discussion Jack and Penny decide that one possible way of convincing the board of the merits of the project would be to employ an outside firm of consultants to evaluate it.

Penny has approached you and asked you to consider both projects.

You establish the following facts.

The average beta for firms in the processed seafood industry is 1.3. The average beta for firms in the canned fruit and vegetables industry is 0.9. The market risk premium (Rm - Rf) is 5%. The risk-free rate is 6%. The average leverage in terms of the Debt over Equity ratio is 0.5 in both industries. Salmon Spray is an all-equity company and will remain so. Jack's projections for the Polish project are outlined in Appendix 1.

You also have a meeting with Jack and are informed that he has based his figures for the Spanish project on the following.

1. The cost of the Spanish company is €199.5 million.
2. Fees already paid to Salmon Spray's accountants for evaluating the net worth of the Spanish company: €0.2 million.
3. Legal fees incurred to date: €0.2 million; legal fees to be incurred if the Spanish company is purchased: €0.5 million.
4. Cost of building the new processing factory for fruit and vegetables: €20 million. It will take one year to complete. This can be financed entirely from the sale of part of the extensive land bank owned by the Spanish company.
5. Fruit and vegetable processing can begin immediately if additional production facilities can be rented for the first year. Rent will be €5 million.
6. Projected sales revenues from olive oil and fruit and vegetables and contribution margins and fixed costs of production and administration are outlined in the table below.
7. Depreciation will be €40 million per year in the first five years of the project.
8. Management of the factory will be delegated to managers already employed by Salmon Spray. The managers involved currently receive salaries totalling €1 million. Three hundred Spanish operatives will be needed, at cost of €60,000 per employee, for the first four years. In year five employee costs will rise by 22.22%.
9. Jack assures you that after year five the project should earn a rate of return equal to the cost of capital.
10. The projections for the first five years are outlined in the following table.

Year	1	2	3	4	5
Fruit and vegetables: Sales Revenue	460	500	580	620	640
Contribution Margin	25%	25%	25%	25%	25%
Olive Oil: Sales Revenue	415	365	265	165	165
Contribution Margin	20%	20%	20%	20%	20%
Fixed Costs: Fruit and vegetables Processing	50	60	60	80	91
Fixed Cost: Olive oil	55	40	40	40	40

Required

Answer the following questions. In each case fully explain and justify your approach.

Question 1

Sir Rex only seems to care about profits, Penny likes the accounting rate of return and Jack McBride uses DCF: what criteria should Salmon Spray use to evaluate the projects?

(10 marks)

Question 2

Outline and explain your own detailed analysis of the Spanish and Polish projects and make a recommendation as to whether the new projects are worthwhile or not.

(35 marks)

Question 3

Reconcile discounted cash-flow analysis with accounting profitability. Your answer should refer to Sir Rex's argument that the Polish project will return a profit and Penny's concerns regarding the ROR of the Spanish project.

(20 marks)

Question 4

Assess the strengths and weaknesses of Jack's approach. As well as considering his overall approach, pay particular attention to his computation of the cost of capital and his assumptions that the project will earn a rate of return equal to the cost of capital from year six onwards.

(10 marks)

Question 5

Comment on the interaction between the investment and financing decisions in the context of Salmon Spray.

(10 marks)

Question 6

How sensitive is the NPV of the Spanish project to your estimate of the cost of capital? Compute the internal rate of return to assist in this analysis.

(5 marks)

Question 7

Salmon Spray has a surplus of cash: is this a problem?

(5 marks)

Question 8

Comment on the conflicts of interest between the outside shareholders and Penny.

(5 marks)

Total 100 marks

Appendix 1: Jack's Projections Regarding the Profitability of the Polish Project

€ Million

Time	0	1	2	3	4	5
Net Cash-flows	−200.00	56.00	52.00	48.00	44.00	41.00
Depreciation (200/5)		40.00	40.00	40.00	40.00	40.00
Profit		16.00	12.00	8.00	4.00	1.00

Case 27
Waterlife plc
Evarist Stoja, University of Bristol

Overview of the Company

Waterlife plc is a company involved in producing wet suits and other equipment necessary for surfing and diving. It was founded by Joe and Nick, two childhood friends who are very passionate about the sea. They started surfing and diving when they were 15 years old and were often frustrated that their gear was not good enough to cater for their needs. They could not surf when the weather was cold, not to mention diving. Another problem with diving was that they really wanted to explore life in deep waters where the pressure was very high, but their gear could not cope. It was obvious that the companies producing the surfing/diving gear had not done much market research and hence were not fully aware of the specifications, design and flexibility required to cope with the situations encountered at sea.

Their frustration peaked when they went on a diving and surfing trip to South Africa, on which they spent all their savings. They had been planning this trip for a year and were really looking forward to it, but when they got there they were very disappointed. The water was not particularly warm and water pressure was so high that their wet suits and other accessories were totally useless, even though they were the best on the market. Their gear could barely cope with the temperature and pressure of the Mediterranean Sea, and Cape Town and Port Elizabeth were both next to the Atlantic and Indian Oceans, notorious for their cold waters and high pressure. Their trip would have been totally wasted had they not decided to go sightseeing.

When they got back home, they decided to do something to help all the disappointed surfers and divers, like themselves, who were out there. After persistence and help from their families, they finally managed to set up Waterlife 10 years ago as a private company. Cost control and niche marketing, as well as high performance design and investment in research and development, led to good performance and increasing market share. Although Waterlife started as a small firm covering only the regional market, it has now significantly increased its market share. A few years ago, Waterlife floated on a small regional exchange. It issued one million shares with a book value of €8 each (the current market value of shares is €10). Debt was issued recently with a book value of €2 million and an interest rate of 8% per annum. The firm also has €700,000 in retained earnings (see the current balance sheet in Appendix 1).

Current Situation

Although the market return of 12% and the risk-free rate of 4% mean that the cost of equity shouldn't be very high, this is not the case. A junior finance manager thinks that with a covariance between the market return and Waterlife share return of 150 plus a market return standard deviation of 10, equity beta should be pretty high. He thought that this was the main reason why equity was such an expensive source of finance: Waterlife was recapitalising at a very high rate. He suggested that by increasing the firm's leverage, the cash-flows would be discounted at a lower rate and hence the firm would be worth more (which in turn would drive up its share price). One of the directors was not convinced. He argued that increases in the leverage ratio would lead to an even higher cost of equity and hence the overall cost of capital would remain constant (he invoked the famous Modigliani and Miller's proposition II to support his argument). Although the junior manager was convinced that he was right, he could not make a case for his suggestion.

Nick, who recently completed an MBA at a prestigious European business school, could see the point of the junior manager's suggestion. However, at that time prospects for the economy were gloomy and he was worried about Waterlife being unable to meet the increased debt level commitments. Nick believes that these water sports products still remain expensive and hence are very sensitive to the performance of the economy. When the economy is doing well, people have more money to spend on Waterlife products and travel to exotic places. However, as soon as the first signs of recession become apparent, sales decrease significantly. For these reasons he believes it is a strongly cyclical business. Indeed, quite a few of Waterlife's competitors have now left the industry and some have even gone into liquidation.

More recently, however, although the economy had not picked up completely, the demographic and social trends appeared to be in favour of their business. Research showed that in the national market there are around one million young people, with this group predicted to increase by 4% per annum. It also showed that one in a 100 of them is likely to get involved in these sports and spend on average €500. However, Waterlife has not covered this market yet due to financial, production capacity and marketing constraints.

The company has adopted an innovative business model. Many companies in their industry own large amounts of fixed assets, which they place as a collateral to support their high leverage ratios of 45% debt to value. Waterlife rents some of its fixed assets, has a much lower leverage ratio and invests heavily on research and development. There has been some speculation in the financial press, however, that "... Waterlife management is taking it easy and they are not as efficient as they could and should be. The increase of the leverage ratio would make them more efficient…" Nick disagrees. He thinks that the low leverage ratio gives Waterlife the necessary flexibility to pursue its high growth investment strategies, which it wouldn't otherwise have due to restrictive covenants that are placed on bonds. Indeed, bonds issued by firms in their industry are very restrictive.

The Future

The research and development team has recently discovered a new material for making the wet suits that, as well as insulating, would also protect the divers from high pressure. It is expensive, however, and pursuing this idea would involve a large-scale capital investment of €6 million. Joe and Nick are exploring ways to finance the project. Accumulated retained earnings can only finance a minor part of this project. They need to decide whether to issue bonds, equity or a combination of both. Clearly, the cost for each source is different. In numerous discussions that Nick and Joe have had with the board of directors, some of them have stressed the importance of finding the appropriate capital structure mix to minimise the weighted average cost of capital (WACC). Joe opposes this view. He thinks that share value is what matters, and focusing on WACC would be a waste of energy and time. In his view, shareholders care only about the value of their shares, rather than owning a firm with a low cost of capital. However, after Nick took the time to explain to him that under certain conditions the two things are equivalent, he got the point. If this is the case, he thought, Waterlife can borrow more short-term debt and roll it over, effectively making it a long-term source of funds. He was keen to explore this idea because he knew that the interest rate on the short-term loan Waterlife is paying at the moment is 5%–substantially lower than the 8% it pays on the 10-year bonds it issued some time ago.

Nick, on the other hand, thinks that the answer is not so obvious. He is sure that while borrowing more short term and rolling it over would help, it is not the answer to financing the investment they are contemplating. Joe's idea was not very original. Nick had learned about companies tempted to pursue a similar strategy that had quickly got into trouble. He thinks Waterlife has to resort to long-term financing and the main options are debt and equity. But which one? He knows that both have their advantages and disadvantages. While debt is cheaper and also provides the company with a valuable income tax shield, the interest payments are mandatory and could lead to bankruptcy. Depending on the severity of problems faced, liquidation is also possible. Further, he thinks that although the proposed new debt level would not be different from that of other firms in their industry, Waterlife simply does not have the necessary asset type to increase borrowing to that degree. Equity, on the other hand, is the safer option, but would be significantly more expensive. To make matters worse, the market does not yet appear to be aware of the true value of the firm (and its future potential). With the growth opportunities they have, the share price should be at least €12. Issuing shares would simply make new investors richer at the expense of old investors. This was tough. He decided to ask one of his finance graduates to help him estimate the costs and benefits of each alternative.

They computed that issuing €5.3 million of debt at 8% would indeed be cheaper. It would also provide the company with a valuable tax shield of €1.59 million, which would increase the firm value. It would entail other costs, however. Simulations showed that if debt commitments could not be honoured, bankruptcy costs would be €5 million. They estimated how likely bankruptcy was given the current market coverage (the result is shown in Appendix 2). Another cost was that they would exhaust their entire debt capacity, which meant that they could not go to the debt markets again. Experience had taught him that flexibility was very important in their business. It looked like equity was the only choice. However, Nick was surprised to find out that issuing equity would decrease the already depressed share price of €10 by €1.4. He thought that this could be due to the holdings dilution of the current shareholders, but was not sure. The only thing he was certain about was that this was a tough choice that they could not make on their own.

Required

Nick outlined the previous issues to the board of directors and they agreed to hire you, as an independent consultant with extensive experience and technical knowledge on financing, to write a report in order to provide them with some objective views on the above and other related matters. This will help them in their decisions regarding the future. In particular, your report should include the following:

Question 1

A calculation of Waterlife's equity beta, cost of equity (re) and WACC. Why is the cost of equity so high? A discussion regarding the suggestion of the junior finance manager and the argument put forward from one of the directors. Who is right and under what conditions?

(15 marks)

Question 2

A discussion as to why negative prospects regarding the future of the economy have a more critical impact upon debt commitments rather than equity for Waterlife.

(10 marks)

Question 3

A discussion of the statement in the financial press regarding the low debt levels and efficiency of Waterlife. Is there any real reason for concern regarding efficiency? Is Nick right to think that the low debt levels give Waterlife the necessary flexibility that a fast growing firm must have? What other reasons might be behind the low levels of debt employed by Waterlife?

(15 marks)

Question 4

A discussion of the cost of capital minimisation and firm value maximisation objectives. Under what conditions are they equivalent for Waterlife? Support your answer with theoretical arguments.

(8 marks)

Question 5

A discussion as to why financing by retained earnings is the most preferred source of funds. Is Joe right to think that borrowing short term and rolling it over to invest in long-term fixed assets and a marketing campaign is the right strategy?

(12 marks)

Question 6

A calculation of the amount by which debt financing increases/decreases the value of Waterlife. A calculation of the value of Waterlife adopting the Trade-off Theory of capital structure. What is the implied tax rate? Are they right to assume that the tax shield equals €1.59 million and why? Does Waterlife have the necessary asset type to increase borrowing and why?

(13 marks)

Question 7

A discussion of the reasons why Nick thinks equity is safer than debt when interest payments are guaranteed but dividends are not. A discussion of the options Waterlife has to make the interest payments affordable if it decides to finance this project by debt.

(10 marks)

Question 8

A discussion on Nick's opinion that Waterlife's share price decreases as a result of dilution of the holdings of the current shareholders. What might be a better explanation for this outcome? On balance, what is your recommendation to Waterlife regarding the financing of the new project? Suggest some general points that a company should consider when thinking about changing its capital structure.

(17 marks)

Total 100 marks

Appendix 1: Balance Sheet of Waterlife plc 31 March 2XX5

Current assets:

Cash and marketable securities	1,200,000	
Accounts receivable	800,000	
Stock	2,000,000	
Total current assets		4,000,000
Fixed assets		7,000,000
Total assets		11,000,000
Liabilities:		
Short-term loan	300,000	
Bonds payable	2,000,000	
Total liabilities		2,300,000
Shareholders' equity:		
Common stock	8,000,000	
Retained earnings	700,000	
Total equity		8,700,000
Total liabilities and equity		11,000,000

Appendix 2: Forecast of Income Statement of Waterlife plc (€,000)

Probability	**35%**	**35%**	**30%**
Sales	2,000	3,800	5,500
Cost of sales	−1,000	−1,900	2,750
Gross profit	1,000	1,900	2,750
Expenses	−680	−1292	−1870
Earnings before interest and tax	320	608	880
Interest payable	−599	−599	−599
Tax at 30%	0	−2.7	−84.3
Earnings after tax	−279	6	197

Notes to Income Statement: interest payable is calculated as 8% of the total amount of long-term debt plus 5% of short-term loan. Waterlife cannot carry losses forward/backward for tax purposes.

Case 28
Mega Meals Limited
Donal McKillop, Queen's University Belfast

Overview of the Company

The Belfast-based business Mega Meals Limited began life 10 years ago in the form of a partnership between Peter Penney, an accomplished (if unqualified) chef, and his elder brother, James. In the early days, Peter travelled around surrounding fairs, markets and sporting events cooking and selling burgers, hotdogs and chips from his van. James, a solicitor, contributed the funds to purchase the van and initial stock, but acted as a silent partner, with a 50% share in the business.

The business was a reasonable success, generating a fair income for Peter and a good return on James' investment, but as time progressed Peter became increasingly disillusioned with the standard of food the company was providing, together with his peripatetic working lifestyle. Therefore, with James' consent, he employed a member of staff to run the mobile food van, while he began, using his culinary expertise, to offer high quality outside catering services. The primary events Peter provided food for were local social functions, such as funerals and weddings. Peter met Eddie Banks, the chief executive of FIFO, a Northern Ireland-wide chain of convenience stores, at the marriage of Mr Bank's daughter. Eddie was impressed by the calibre of Peter's food and asked him if he would be interested in providing a range of convenience meals and desserts, based on Peter's recipes, for sale on a trial basis in two of FIFO's stores. Despite Peter's misgivings about the general quality of such products and his ability to maintain his high standards as the number of meals produced increased, following discussions with James it was agreed that the FIFO proposal should be accepted.

The trial agreed upon turned out to be very successful, to the extent that Eddie Banks asked if Peter could supply a larger range of his products to be sold throughout the FIFO chain. To do this, investment in a new, expanded cooking and packaging facility would be required. At this point, the Penney brothers agreed to incorporate the business as Mega Meals Limited, with both owning half of the total equity. Peter would act as the managing director, while James would contribute the €400,000 required to build the new facility and meet the initial costs of hiring new staff from his savings. Although nominally a director of the new company, James' role would remain a silent one with respect to the entity's operations.

As in the case of the trial run, Mega Meals' food proved to be extremely popular throughout all the FIFO stores. As Mega Meals did not have an exclusivity clause in its agreement (to provide foods only to FIFO), this success led other retailers to become interested in the products. As the facility built at the time of incorporation had a large amount of spare capacity, the brothers were happy to agree to provide a range of their products to a number of other Northern Ireland-based retail chains.

Mega Meals' success has continued until today. Recently, Peter, in conjunction with James and Mega Meals' chief accountant, has negotiated two major new deals. The first is an agreement with Sparks and Dempster, a leading UK-based supermarket chain, to provide a wide range of convenience meals and desserts. The deal includes a guarantee that Sparks and Dempster will continue to source all their convenience meals from Mega Meals for an initial period of two years, with a five-year extension option if both parties are satisfied at the end of the period. In order to fulfil its obligations, Mega Meals is opening a major new facility on the outskirts of Birmingham. The initial investment required to do this is €3 million, which will be financed through debt. The returns generated through the Sparks and Dempster contract alone, should it be extended to the full seven-year period, will be enough to repay the debt within three years, while meeting the interest payments and providing a return to the company; that is, the project has a positive net present value (NPV). In addition, Peter is confident that Mega Meals will be able to negotiate further deals with UK-based companies.

The other deal negotiated by the company is for the supply of its products to Six-Twelve Inc., a regional chain of convenience stores based in Boston, Massachusetts. While primarily the same lines that are available in the UK will be sold, a greater emphasis will be placed upon identifiably Irish recipes. In this vein, the branding of the food will be changed to reflect the origin of the meals. Six-Twelve has agreed to supply all of its stores with Mega Meals' products for a guaranteed period of three years following the recent completion of a successful trial. As with the Sparks and Dempster contract, it will be necessary for Mega Meals to invest in a new facility in the Boston area at an initial cost of $1 million. As before, this project has been analysed by the company's finance department and found to have a positive NPV; the loan will be paid off at the end of three years. In addition, Peter is extremely excited about the prospect of breaking into the American market and feels that, with the excellence of his recipes, they can't help but be as successful as they have been to this point in attracting and retaining customers.

While agreeing that both deals appear to be superb opportunities for Mega Meals, James, who is naturally cautious but does believe in the quality of his brother's products and his enthusiasm in leading the company to date, can't help but be slightly concerned. Mega Meals' chief accountant had recommended that both deals be financed through floating rate borrowings. James is worried about the prospect of an interest rate rise, and would be happier if fixed rate finance were used. In addition, he is concerned that the returns from the US-based facility will be denominated in dollars, whereas the investment will be paid for in local currency. In response to James' concerns about the funding of the Birmingham facility, the chief accountant has suggested that the company could borrow at a fixed rate, which is higher than the current floating rate available, or undertake a swap with another company or financial institution (details of which are contained in Appendix 1). With respect to James' concerns about the risk of a weakening dollar, the accountant has identified an American company that would be willing to undertake a foreign currency swap with Mega Meals, thus allowing the company to borrow at a lower rate of interest than would be available directly from a US financial institution (details in Appendix 2). As a management consultant, James has asked you to advise him on the best way of funding Mega Meals' two new facilities.

Required

Your report to James should consist of two parts, (1) and (2), each of which should deal with one of the new investments.

In part (1), you should include the following.

(a) An evaluation of the benefits and drawbacks of using fixed or floating rate debt to fund the project.

(b) An evaluation of the benefits and drawbacks of undertaking a swap, either directly with another company or with a financial intermediary. This should include a calculation of the cost of the various options (including a description of how the swap should be structured), a calculation of the value of the swap, a qualitative evaluation of the risk involved and a discussion of the 'comparative advantage' argument for undertaking swaps (relevant information is provided in Appendix 1).

(c) Your recommendation as to the funding of the Birmingham-based facility.

In part (2), you should include the following.

(a) An evaluation of the relative merits of hedging, using a foreign currency swap, against other potential methods.

(b) A calculation of the benefit to Mega Meals of undertaking the swap, either directly or through the financial institution (details included in Appendix 2).

(c) An evaluation of the risk involved in undertaking the swap, particularly with regard to the credit risk related to Widgets Inc., the identified counterparty (you should deconstruct the swap into a series of forward contracts to help explain your answer).

(d) A recommendation as to how the US-based facility should be funded.

(Approximately 50 marks will be allocated to each question, with 40% of the total marks being awarded for calculations and 60% for the discussion and recommendations in both cases.)

Total 100 marks

Appendix 1: Data Supplied by Mega Meals' Accountant with Respect to its Borrowing Rates and Potential Interest Rate Swap Opportunities

	Fixed Rate (3 years)	Floating Rate (6 months)
Mega Meals	9.0%	LIBOR+2%
Cyco	7.0%	LIBOR+1%

Cyco Limited is a London-based firm which manufactures bicycles. It is willing to undertake a swap with Mega Meals, sharing any benefits (in terms of interest rates) equally between the two companies. Alternatively, an AAA-rated financial intermediary has been identified that will pay LIBOR in return for a fixed rate of 6.75%. Mega Meals requires a €3 million loan for three years. Any interest payments will be semi-annual, and the current rate of (local currency) LIBOR is 5% (six-month), with the LIBOR zero curve having a flat term structure.

Appendix 2: Data Supplied by Mega Meals' Accountant with Respect to the Potential Currency Swap

	€	$US
Mega Meals	9.0%	12.0%
Widgets	7.5%	9.0%

The rates quoted are fixed rates and have been adjusted for the effect of income taxes. The current exchange rate is 1.3$US/€, with US$ six-month LIBOR being 7.0%. The US LIBOR zero curve also has a flat term structure. Mega Meals requires $1 million for three years. Widgets Inc. is happy to undertake the currency swap for the amount and period suggested, either directly or through a financial institution. The principal amounts involved are $1 million and €769,231. If a direct swap is undertaken, the benefits will be shared equally between the two companies and Widgets Inc. will bear the foreign exchange risk. If a (AAA-rated) financial institution is used, its commission will be 20 basis points, and the financial institution will bear all the foreign exchange risk in the transaction.

Case 29

First Financial

**Ronan Gallagher and Donal McKillop,
Queen's University Belfast**

The Senior Management Team of First Financial, a leading Irish finance and mortgage company, has asked the Risk Management Division for a comprehensive assessment and update of the company's current market risk exposure. This is undertaken against the backdrop of continued deterioration in the Irish economy, which has severely impacted upon the economic fundamentals of First Financial.

The Senior Management Team has asked for summary reports from the Economics Division, Accounts Division and Business Strategy Division of issues likely to impact on the performance of First Financial over the coming year.

The summary report of the Economics Division has argued that the present recession will deepen during 2XX9 and 2X10. Indeed, it points to the most recent IMF survey, which forecasts that in 2X10 Irish gross domestic product will shrink by 4.8% in what the IMF describes as likely to be the *"deepest recession since the Second World War"*. The Economics Division also expects that this recession will be longer than the last two recessions because of pronounced imbalances in the housing and debt sectors and to support this contention it points out that the Governor of the European Central Bank (ECB) has described the current turmoil in financial markets as *"... the biggest financial crisis since World War I"*.

The Economics Division also points out that in May 2XX9 the ECB cut interest rates by a quarter of a percentage point to 1.00%, the lowest level since the single currency's creation in 1X99, with the door left open for a further 0.5% cut later in the year. The Economics Division also notes that the ECB has signalled that it will buy €60 million of covered bonds in a form of quantitative easing – buying corporate debt in order to pump cash and credit into the economy. This follows the lead, but stops short of the US Federal Reserve's and the Bank of England's moves to buy government bonds. A worry expressed by the Economics Division is that this policy of quantitative easing may trigger inflationary pressure, which will result in interest rate volatility with rates anticipated to rise from their current level of 1% by 3% in the medium term.

Table 1: First Financial – Summary Balance Sheet as of September 2XX9

Assets		Liabilities	
Cash and Deposits	€4m	Commercial Paper	€28m
Securities		Bonds	
Less than 1 Year	€5m	Variable rate	€8m
1 to 2 Years	€5m	Less than 1 year	€6m
Greater than 2 Years	€10m	1 to 2 years	€4m
Commercial Mortgages		Greater than 2 years	€4m
Variable Rate	€10m		
Fixed Rate (5 Year)	€10m	Bank Loans	
Commercial Loans		Less than 1 year	€15m
Less than 1 Year	€10m	1 to 2 years	€16m
1 to 2 years	€25m	Greater than 2 years	€10m
Greater than 2 Years	€15m		
Physical Capital	€6m	Capital	€9m
TOTAL	**€100m**	**TOTAL**	**€100m**

The Accounts Division has prepared an interim and summary balance sheet as of September 2XX9.

The Accounts Division is worried that First Financial may have more rate-sensitive assets than liabilities and with the recent downward trend in interest rates, the bank's net interest margin and income may well be declining at the moment. A further concern for the Accounts Division is that certain asset and liability classes are partially, but not fully, rate sensitive. For example, from past experience, 20% of fixed rate mortgages are repaid within a year. More generally, given the unstable market conditions for all financial institutions, the Accounts Division has some concerns about the effect of changes in interest rates on the market value of the net worth of First Financial. First Financial is required to adhere to a minimum capital ratio of 7%.

The Business Strategy Division also has concerns about the financial position of First Financial. It has identified an opportunity to sell off €5 million of the company's mortgages (€2.5 million of variable rate mortgages and €2.5 million of fixed rate mortgages). The feeling is that in the turbulent housing market, such an opportunity is well worth investigating. In addition, the Business Strategy Division suggests that First Financial might invest the proceeds of the mortgage sales in treasury bonds with a maturity of less than one year, a comparatively lower risk asset. The Business Strategy Division has identified a growth opportunity in the consumer loans market and suggests that this business could generate approximately €20 million of loans with a maturity structure of less than one year. It argues that one way of funding this loan tranche is through the issue of commercial paper, but is worried that this may have an adverse impact upon First Financial's interest rate risk.

Required

Question 1

The Risk Management Division is asked to assess which assets and liabilities have interest rates that are required to be reset (repriced) within the year and which mature between one and two years. Having identified rate-sensitive assets and liabilities, an assessment should be made of the sensitivity of First Financial's income to predicted short-term changes in interest rates. The Risk Management Division is asked to assess whether the predicted change in interest rates will cause deterioration in income and net interest margin.

(25 marks)

Question 2

The following durations have been calculated for the respective asset and liability categories of First Financial.

Table 2: Duration Values for Asset and Liability Categories

First Financial – Estimated Duration (Years)			
Assets		**Liabilities**	
Cash and Deposits	0.0	Commercial Paper	0.2
Securities			
Less than 1 Year	0.5	Bonds	
1 to 2 Years	1.7	Variable rate	0.5
Greater than 2 Years	9.0	Less than 1 year	0.2
Commercial Mortgages		1 to 2 years	1.2
Variable Rate	0.5	Greater than 2 years	2.7
Fixed Rate (10 Year)	4.0		
Commercial Loans		Bank Loans	
Less than 1 Year	0.6	Less than 1 year	0.3
1 to 2 years	1.3	1 to 2 years	1.6
Greater than 2 Years	4.1	Greater than 2 years	3.5

The Risk Management Division is asked to assess the effect of changes in interest rate on the market value of the net worth of First Financial. If, as expected, interest rates were to fall by 0.5%, what would be the implications for the market value of First Financial's net worth? What are the implications for the bank's capital position as a consequence of this interest rate decline?

(25 marks)

Question 3

Given the estimates of duration in Table 2, what will happen to First Financial's net worth if quantitative easing is successful in inflating the economy and interest rates jump by 3%? What implications does this have for the capital requirement of First Financial?

(25 marks)

Question 4

Assess the Business Strategy Division's advice regarding the offloading of mortgages and reinvesting in treasury bills. Assess the Business Strategy Division's advice regarding the expansion into consumer loans financed by the issue of commercial paper. How does this impact upon rate-sensitive assets, income gap, duration gap and the market value of net worth.

(25 marks)

Total 100 marks

Case 30

First National

Ronan Gallagher and Donal McKillop,
Queen's University Belfast

First National is an Irish Stock Exchange (ISEQ) listed manufacturing company. This company sponsors a defined benefit pension scheme for its employees. The defined benefit scheme is currently in deficit and the Board of Trustees, which looks after the governance of the scheme, has suggested that it is an imperative that this fund be rebalanced in terms of its asset allocation. To support this advice, the Board of Trustees has provided a commentary on why defined benefit pension schemes are currently in difficulty, profiled defined benefit pension trends across other ISEQ listed companies between 2XX3 and 2XX7 and provided a summary of trends for First National's pension scheme over the same period.

Required

Question 1

Analyse the following information in Table 1 and Table 2 to identify issues of importance for Irish defined benefit schemes.

(10 marks)

Table 1: Summary Statistics of ISEQ Defined Benefit Schemes (2XX3–2XX7)

	2XX7	2XX6	2XX5	2XX4	2XX3
Number of Disclosures	34	33	33	31	28
Number In Surplus	8	4	2	3	2
Number In Deficit	26	29	31	28	26
Average Pension Assets (€m)	506.3811	501.6784	442.6944	376.2043	337.2993
Average Pension Liabilities (€m)	567.3534	600.9299	578.8072	473.5377	424.0779
Average Deficit (€m)	60.97226	99.2515	136.1129	97.33342	86.77858

Table 1 (continued)

Asset Allocation – Equity	63.43%	64.64%	64.29%	65.60%	67.61%
Asset Allocation – Bonds	24.29%	22.20%	24.36%	22.05%	19.76%
Asset Allocation – Property	8.59%	8.61%	7.91%	8.95%	9.04%
Asset Allocation – Other	3.68%	4.56%	3.44%	3.39%	3.59%

Table 2: Percentage Asset Allocation – Top Ten Schemes By Equity and By Bonds for 2007

Rank	Top Ten By Equity Allocation 2XX7	Equity (%)	Top Ten By Bond Allocation 2XX7	Bonds (%)
1	First National Plc	81.32	Abbey Plc	84.40
2	UTV Media Plc	80.75	Waterford Wedgwood Plc	41.40
3	Ryanair Holdings Plc	80.20	Smurfit Kappa Group Plc	39.30
4	Aryzta AG	80.03	Anglo Irish Bank Corporation Plc	38.00
5	Origin Enterprises Plc	80.03	CRH Plc	33.10
6	C&C Group	80.00	Qualceram Shires Plc	29.40
7	Prime Active Cap.	79.20	Fyffes Plc	28.85
8	Grafton Group Plc	78.00	Irish Continental Group Plc	26.69
9	Elan Corporation Plc	77.00	Kerry Group Plc	25.90
10	Greencore Group Plc	76.89	Kingspan Group Plc	25.42

Question 2

The Board of Trustees has also provided a summary profile of First National's defined benefit scheme (see Appendix 1) and suggested that the scheme should be rebalanced in favour of greater holdings of corporate bonds. It has identified the following three corporate bonds which it is considering investing in to rebalance the pension fund.

1. Five-year corporate 6% coupon paid semi-annually (i.e. 3% every six months), 4% yield continuously compounded, Moodys rate this bond as Aa, €100 par, senior secured.)
2. Five-year corporate 8% coupon paid semi-annually (i.e. 4% every six months), 5.3% yield continuously compounded, Moodys rate this bond as A, €100 par, senior unsecured.)
3. Five-year corporate 10% coupon paid semi-annually (i.e. 5% every six months), 6.7% yield continuously compounded, Moodys rate this bond as Baa, €100 par, senior subordinated.)

Using the default intensity and recovery rate Tables in Appendix 2, map the bond credit ratings onto default rates and recovery rates provided by Moody's and provide a commentary on the relative riskiness of the respective bonds.

(20 marks)

Question 3

As well as using credit ratings to quantify the probability of default, it is also possible to estimate default probabilities from bond characteristics. The usual assumption is that the only reason that a bond sells for less than a similar risk-free bond is the possibility of default. Assume the risk-free yield curve is flat at 3% with continuous compounding. Assume that defaults can take place at the end of each year (immediately before a coupon or principal payment and that the recovery rate is as set out in Table 5 in Appendix 2 for each rating class). Assume that the default probability is equal across years. Assume that the bond par values are €100. Calculate default probabilities from bond prices using the simple approximation:

$$\bar{\lambda} = \frac{s}{1-R}$$

Where $\bar{\lambda}$ is the average default intensity per year, s is the spread of the corporate bond yield over the risk-free rate and R is the expected recovery rate. For the purpose of this part, assume a risk-free rate of interest of 3%.

(15 marks)

Question 4

The scale of the bond investments being considered is in each case €25 million. As a consequence of the scale of this investment, a more accurate estimate of default probability is required. Using the procedure outlined in Hull (2009) – Options, Futures and Other Derivatives, pp. 500–503 – calculate a more precise default probability. Use the same assumptions as set out in Question 3.

(40 marks)

Question 5

Compare the findings from historical default intensities and comment on the differences.

(10 marks)

Question 6

Given your calculations on the respective credit risk of the three bonds, which one do you recommend for the pension scheme to purchase?

(5 marks)

Total 100 marks

Appendix 1

Table 3: First National Defined Benefit Pension Scheme Summary Data (2XX3–2XX7)

	2XX7	2XX6	2XX5	2XX4	2XX3
Average Pension Assets (€m)	540.2589	535.6582	532.6878	492.6589	471.2312
Average Pension Liabilities (€m)	613.2214	615.2212	651.2221	599.5287	564.5897
Average Deficit (€m)	72.9625	79.563	118.5343	106.8698	93.3585
Asset Allocation – Equity	81.32%	82.00%	80.56%	81.57%	82.24%
Asset Allocation – Bonds	6.37%	6.58%	6.41%	6.22%	6.54%
Asset Allocation – Property	3.47%	3.87%	3.69%	3.88%	3.27%
Asset Allocation – Other	8.84%	7.55%	9.34%	8.33%	7.95%

Appendix 2

Table 4: Average Cumulative Default Rates

Average Cumulative Default Rates (%) 1970–2003 (Source: Moody's)

Term (Years)	1	2	3	4	5	7	10	15	20
Aaa	0.00	0.00	0.00	0.04	0.12	0.29	0.62	1.21	1.55
Aa	0.02	0.03	0.06	0.15	0.24	0.43	0.68	1.51	2.70
A	0.02	0.09	0.23	0.38	0.54	0.91	1.59	2.94	5.24
Baa	0.20	0.57	1.03	1.62	2.16	3.24	5.10	9.12	12.59
Ba	1.26	3.48	3.00	8.59	11.17	15.44	21.01	30.88	38.56
B	6.21	13.76	20.65	26.66	31.99	40.79	50.02	59.21	60.73
Caa	23.65	37.20	48.02	55.56	60.83	69.36	77.91	80.23	80.23

Table 5: Recovery Rates

Recovery Rates 1982–2003 (Source: Moody's)

Class	Mean (%)
Senior Secured	51.6
Senior Unsecured	36.1
Senior Subordinated	32.5
Subordinated	31.1
Junior Subordinated	24.5

Case 31
Good Eating Company plc
John Cotter, University College Dublin

Overview of the Company

Good Eating Company is a specialist food-producing company located in West Down. The number of employees in the company has been reasonably constant, with 102 on the books over the previous year. It has a great reputation for producing quality food products and, in particular, its handmade pies have won numerous national and international food awards. Traditionally, the company exported its products, with very profitable markets in many wealthy economies, including the US and Japan. Domestically, it was seen as a leader in producing high-quality food specialist products, although this market was fairly small. However, this domestic market was very profitable and has been developing quite rapidly in recent years. The finance director of the company, Mr. James Five-Bellies, believes that the company has reached its 'steady state' in terms of profitability and can continue to employ this number of staff for the foreseeable future.

Discussion of Pension

Good Eating Company has always been seen as an attractive employer in the local economy. A number of reasons have been cited, including the personal benefits bestowed on all staff. For instance, it was always progressive in providing pension contributions to its employees and it has a long-running defined contribution scheme operating for all members. This defined contribution scheme calculates the benefits accruing to employees based on the value of the fund when an employee retires. Details of the current assets and liabilities of the scheme are provided in Appendix 1.
   The finance director has prime responsibility for the operation and management of the pension scheme. In his role, he has required outside advice on a number of issues, but only followed those policies of which he was supportive. He has always

felt that the investment strategy of the pension funds should be mixed across a set of asset types, such as equities and property. He also recognised that these assets can incur high levels of risk that may not benefit the pension investment fund, so has also included relatively 'safe' fixed income-type assets.

The total fund is in many different assets, including: technology stocks, airline stock and financial stocks for equities; government gilts – five-year and 20-year; commercial paper; time-based deposits for fixed income assets and both commercial and retail property. The only investment rules governing the fund is the make-up of the portfolio of 50% equities, 30% fixed income and 20% property, and no investment is allowed in agricultural or related assets. He knew from experience that equities have the potential to be very risky, with a lot of downside price performance, and wanted to ensure that the pension investment fund diversified away from the core industry of Good Eating Company. Similar performances were recorded for Good Eating Company pension assets in 2XX1 and 2XX2 (falling by 10% each year). However, the fund performed very well in 2XX0, with a return of 26%, and since 2XX2 has achieved positive, if erratic, returns with an average of 8% per annum.

The liabilities of the fund are based on potential pension contributions for Good Eating Company, with advice been given by a consultancy firm that specialises in the investments and also in the pensions areas. The calculation is based on having an average pensionable number of employees of 100, with an average retirement lifetime of 10 years per person. Also, the average pension payments are €25,000 per annum. Thus the total calculated liabilities are calculated as:

No. Employees × No. years of scheme × pension payments
100 × 10 × 25k = €25 million.

Although the finance director has expressed confidence in the future performance of the company and the numbers employed, he has also suggested that an average pension payment of €25,000 is reasonable given the salary packages offered by the firm and others in the industry. However, he has not done any sensitivity analysis on the average number of years a pension member would receive payments from their retirement.

Part B of Appendix 1 details the expected return and risk performance of the assets of the pension scheme on a yearly basis. These are predicted estimates obtained from their consultancy findings. The report suggests that while fixed income investments offer low returns, they are also very safe with low expected deviation. The report uses the capital asset pricing model (CAPM) to discuss the relative merits of the assets chosen and the predicted returns and risk estimates are obtained from Ibbotson and Co., which estimates expected returns and risk based on past performance of assets using data from over 100 years.

Defined Benefit Pensions

As stated, Good Eating Company (plc) has a defined contribution scheme in place that pays according to the value of the fund when an employee retires. However, there are other pension funds open to the company, in defined benefit schemes, and the finance director is interested in examining the merits of these. Defined benefit schemes calculate the benefit according to factors such as final salary, length of pensionable service and the age of the member. The payments are made regardless of the value of a company's pension investment fund at the time of an employee retirement. If there is a deficit between the company's pension assets and its liabilities in the form of pension contributions, there is a government-backed scheme to support these pension schemes.

Note on Pension Protection Funds and Good Eating Company

The finance director, James Five-Bellies, has done some research on the current pension provision in the UK, detailing current legislation, current schemes and their operations. He provides the following information.

A new scheme, the Pension Protection Fund (PPF), was introduced in the UK as a result of the Pensions Act 2004. The idea behind the legislation was to help many pensions that faced financial difficulties as a result of poor investment performance and, specifically, to ensure that these pensions were returned to full funding, that is, the assets of the pension met the required liability contributions. Prior to the legislation many defined pension schemes were severely underfunded (and some insolvent) leading to a crises in financially supporting the retirement of many participating employees. The new system for defined benefit pension schemes, the PPF, has the following key functions. First, the PPF is required to pay compensation to members of eligible defined benefit pension schemes, when there is a qualifying insolvency event (defined as liabilities exceeding assets) in relation to the sponsor (company with defined benefit pension scheme). Secondly, the PPF receives its funds for compensation purposes by way of imposing compulsory levies on all eligible member schemes and it is this function that we are going to concentrate on in our discussions (for comprehensive information on the levies and the scheme in general see Blake *et al*, 2006).

The rationale for the development of the PPF from the UK government's perspective was to ensure that a guarantee system was in place so that employees and employers knew with certainty that full pension rights were guaranteed. Also the system should ensure that taxpayers are not required to bail out the system by providing financial support to ensure employees got their full future benefits. Essentially, the smooth operation of the PPF would require that the contributions (levies) imposed on defined benefit pension schemes be sufficient to meet future pension underfunding. For instance, speaking at the Labour Party annual conference on 1 October 2003, the Chancellor of the Exchequer Gordon Brown said the government will "legislate for a new statutory pension protection fund. In future every worker contributing to a pension will have their pension protected and be guaranteed their pension rights." This means that a promise made by a scheme sponsor to pay a certain pension is being guaranteed by the PPF.

Further details of the PPF are also provided. The PPF has a set of rules that are to be followed for defined benefit pension schemes. First, for each defined benefit pension scheme they have to pay a yearly levy. The fee from joining the PPF involved yearly levies charged with a cap of 0.5% of the sponsoring company's pension fund liabilities. The actual levy is set on a specific date, e.g. 31 March, and will not be required to be added to over the year following this date. Good Eating Company (and other sponsoring companies) may be able to manipulate the size of the levy required at this time by ensuring that its asset values are maximised and liabilities minimised at the time the levy is introduced, thereby reducing the cost of being protected by the scheme.

Secondly, for the pension scheme to receive financial support from the PPF it has to meet the criteria for entry into the scheme, namely, that the sponsoring employer has a pension scheme that has become insolvent with no chance of recovery. Thirdly, once insolvency is established, the PPF takes responsibility for the member scheme and, once in, the scheme will remain the responsibility of the PPF. There is a suggestion that this type of scheme may induce some undesirable behaviour amongst sponsors of defined benefit pension schemes. For instance, the scheme might allow participants to exhibit 'moral hazard', that is they change their behaviour after joining the pension fund relative to before joining the scheme. Also the fact that the PPF will guarantee pension rights for member schemes might encourage sponsoring firms to become members by underfunding their pension schemes in advance of bankruptcy (and thereby use the funds for some other, non-pension-related activities of the business). Also, the PPF has no authority to dictate the types of asset members are allowed to invest in for developing their pension funds, although they would like members to show prudence in their investment strategy.

After paying the levy, the member scheme (upon meeting the insolvency criteria) is eligible to receive financial support from the PPF. The PPF offers two types of compensation for defined benefit schemes that are of relevance to Good Eating Company. The PPF protects 100% of the pension for members above scheme pension age or already in receipt of a pension due to ill health or it being a survivor's pension (its previous employees), and 90% of the promised pension for the remaining members below scheme pension age (its current employees) up to a maximum of €25,000.

Required

You have been asked to act as an independent consultant to advise Good Eating Company on the best way to deal with its pension requirements. A number of issues should be dealt with in your report.

Question 1

You are asked to assess the current value of the assets and liabilities of Good Eating Company pension funds. Treating the pension assets and liabilities separately from the remaining assets and liabilities of the firm, calculate the working capital of the pension fund of the company. Also show, using ratios, (e.g. current ratio, etc.) the viability of the company's pension fund. Explain all assumptions that you make.

(20 marks)

Question 2

Repeat the analysis of Question 1 for the future value of the assets and liabilities of the Good Eating Company pension fund. In particular, you should comment on the assumptions relating to age of pension scheme, the discount factor used and the expected returns and risk of the assets.

(20 marks)

Question 3

Further illustrate your analysis by commenting on potential changing of the values relating to your answer in Question 1 (e.g. discount factor). Confine your comments to the estimation of the present value of the fund (no calculations are necessary for this question). Comment on the likely impact of the new results of Question 1 and how it would affect Good Eating Company in the actions it could follow in restructuring its pension plans.

(10 marks)

Question 4

Discuss the composition of the Good Eating Company pension's assets in terms of the capital asset pricing model and the views of the finance director, for example on diversification away from agricultural investments or related assets.

(20 marks)

Question 5

Assess the relative merits of joining the Pension Protection Fund. You should discuss the current defined contribution scheme and detail how a defined benefit scheme differs from this. Also you should suggest the best solution that the company could achieve before joining the Pension Protection Fund. You should also suggest the best solution that the company could achieve after joining the Pension Protection Fund.

(30 marks)

Total 100 marks

References

Blake, David; Cotter, John and Kevin Dowd, (2006), *The Pension Protection Fund*, Centre for Financial Markets, University College Dublin.

Ibbotson and Co. (2005), *Asset performance yearbook*, Ibbotson and Co.

> **Appendix 1: Details of Good Eating Company (plc) Defined Contribution Pension for year XXXX**

Part A: Pension budget	€(m)
Assets	
Equities	5
Fixed Income	3
Property	2
Total Assets	10
Liabilities	
No. employees	100
No. years of scheme	10
Pension Payments (€000)	25
Total liabilities	25

Part B: Expected performance of assets

	Returns (%)	Risk (%)
Equities	20	30
Fixed income	3	0.5
Property	20	12

Notes: there are two parts to Appendix 1. Part A details the assets and liabilities of the pension plan. The assets are based on their current market values, whereas the liabilities are based on their expected future requirements. The liabilities of the pension scheme is calculated as the No. Employees × No. years of scheme × pension payments. Further details of the estimates are given in the text. Part B details the expected return and risk annualised performance of the assets of the pension scheme.

Case 32
Personal Financial Planning: Tom Smith
Anne Marie Ward, University of Ulster

Personal Information (Tom)

Tom Smith has approached you for financial advice. During the course of your meeting Tom provides you with the following details about himself and his family.

Tom is 54 years of age. He is an only child and his mother lives only three miles away from his house in their family home. His father died four years ago and left him a large lump sum of money. Tom has €10,000 left. He keeps this money in a building society account (earning 4% interest). He is in full-time employment as a civil engineer. His take-home wages are about €2,900 each month.

Personal Information (Tom's wife – Angela)

Tom is married to Angela (aged 45). She is a public sector nurse who takes home about €1,400 per month. Angela works three 12-hour shifts in a row each week (usually Monday, Tuesday and Wednesday). A neighbour collects their youngest child from school whilst Angela is at work (cost €15 per day). Whilst chatting, Tom tells you that he loves sport. He runs, swims and plays soccer with his friends. You ask him about Angela. Tom states that Angela is not sporty. She smokes about 20 cigarettes per day, enjoys nights out with the girls and drinks about 30 units of alcohol per week. Angela also loves clothes shopping and has three store cards.

1. A 'Debenporks' card, which is being repaid at the minimum monthly amount of €100 (the balance outstanding is now €3,200). The card charges interest at the rate of 1.5% per month. The balance has been steadily increasing by about €100 per month. The card has a €4,000 credit limit.
2. A 'Dot Hawkins' card, which is being repaid at a minimum monthly amount of €80 (the balance outstanding is now €1,800). The card charges interest at the rate of 1.7% per month. The balance has been steadily increasing by about €80 per month. The card has a €3,000 credit limit.

3. A 'Succeeding' store card, which is being repaid at the minimum monthly amount of €120 (the balance outstanding is now €4,200). The card charges interest at the rate of 1.9% per month. The balance has been increasing by €80 per month in recent months. The card has a €4,500 credit limit.

Tom informs you that the repayments on each card are 'small amounts' and Angela's wages cover them anyway.

Personal Information (Tom's children – Dan, Sheila and Ted)

Tom tells you that they have three children: Dan (aged 22), Sheila (aged 16) and Ted (aged 10).

Dan has just graduated from university with a first class honours degree in Accountancy. He has received an offer for a training contract from KPMG. The starting salary is €12,000. However, Tom is unsure as to whether Dan should take up the offer, as Dan has also been offered a job from a local contractor who will pay Dan €16,000 per year. The contractor has suggested that he would pay Dan €4,000 through the books and would give him €1,000 per month in cash. The contractor has highlighted the tax saving that Dan would make. Dan is seriously considering the offer.

Tom had been financing Dan whilst he was studying. Tom paid Dan's yearly fees (€3,200 per year) and purchased a car for him (costing €6,000), because he lived at home whilst at university. Tom reckoned that this option was cheaper than paying for university accommodation. The insurance on the car is approximately €1,200 per year. The yearly tax is €165 and about €350 per year has been spent on repairing and servicing the car over the past three years. In addition, Tom had contributed €20 towards Dan's weekly petrol bill. Tom had also purchased Dan's textbooks, which cost about €200 per term, and had provided him with a weekly allowance of €40.

Sheila has just completed her Intercert/GCSEs. Though she did well in her exams (8 As and 2 Bs), she is considering leaving school and joining the bank. They will put her on their training programme and will give her a starting salary of €800 per month. Sheila considers this to be an excellent opportunity. Tom agrees. He comments on the fact that he spent a considerable amount of money supporting Dan over the past three years and the payoff does not seem to be worth it; Sheila can start her career in the bank at 16 years of age, earning only €200 per month less than Dan. Tom considers that perhaps it was not worth while supporting Dan through university. Tom informs you that he has a deposit account in his own name, with a balance of €6,000, which he has been building up over the past 30 months to finance Sheila's education (it earns interest at the rate of 3% – Tom has the interest paid directly into Angela and his current account). If Sheila were to take up the Bank's offer, then he would not require this fund so he is thinking of just giving the balance to Sheila instead. She would like to buy a car. To date Tom has been giving Sheila €15 per week for pocket money and Angela has been taking her shopping every second week to purchase clothes.

Tom has been transferring money from the current account into a deposit account in his own name for Ted's education (earning interest at the rate of 2% per annum). The current balance is €1,000. Dan is now unsure about whether to continue contributing to this account (€100 per month).

Tom's Savings/Investments

Tom tells you that he is reasonably risk adverse. However, he would not mind taking a chance with a proportion of his earnings, but is unsure how much he could afford to put into more risky investments. He would like to have a little nest egg of about €25,000 to materialise from his investments when he retires at 65. He also comments that he would dearly love to have his mortgage cleared by the time he retires and to have some wealth to pass to his children.

In addition to the accounts mentioned previously, Tom and Angela currently have the following bank/deposit/accounts:

Term deposit account (6 months)	€15,000
– (Interest receivable at 5% per year)	
Joint current account (Overdraft interest rate –18% per year)	(€3,950)
Deposit account (Interest receivable at 3% per year)	€10,000

Tom's Debt

Tom and his family currently have the following debt:

Car finance:
– Tom's car repayable at €360 per month (36 months left)
– Angela's car repayable at €400 per month (48 months left)

Credit card (joint)	(€12,000) at its limit
– Repayable at €800 per month	
(Interest is charged at 2.1% per month)	
Mortgage	(€75,000)
– Repayable at €1,100 per month	
(Interest is charged as 6% per year)	

The vehicles were both purchased new four years ago. Tom purchased his Volkswagen Passat for €18,500 and Angela purchased her Volkswagen Eos for €19,500. Both vehicles were purchased using 100% car finance: Tom's finance deal was fixed monthly repayments for seven years; Angela's finance deal was fixed monthly repayments for eight years. The arrangement fee in both instances was €500. Repayment of the arrangement fee was also covered by the finance deal. The vehicles are now starting to require some repair work and Tom estimates that they will have to start paying out between €250 and €300 per year on repairs. As a result he is contemplating changing the vehicles.

Insurance and Pension Information

The couple do not have any insurance as they consider insurance to be a waste of money. They also do not have any pension funds. They perceive the stock market to be too volatile and think that paying into a pension is a waste of money. The civil engineering company that Tom works for has an occupational scheme. It is company policy to contribute 5% to the scheme so long as the employee contributes 4%. Employees can opt out of the scheme if they so wish.

Other Assets

The couple's house has a current market value of €350,000 and they own 15 acres of land about four miles away from where they live. This was left to Angela by an old aunt when she passed away five years ago. Before she died the old aunt had received planning permission to build herself a nice new four bedroom house. Tom reckons that, in the current climate, they would probably only get about €50,000 for the land, if they were to sell it. He is not sure though. He commented on the fact that, though he would be happy to sell it, Angela has stated that it is an heirloom and she will never sell it. The land is not being used at present (well, a neighbour – who is of dubious character – has started to let a few of his animals wander into it). Tom does not know what to do with the land; he does not mind the neighbour's animals grazing it as it would cost him €1,500 to fence it properly and he does not think it is worth it.

Consumable Expenditure

Tom informs you that they spend about €600 per month on groceries, €50 each per week on diesel, €60 each per month for car insurance, €110 each per year for car tax, Tom spends €30 each week on consumables and Angela spends about €70. They spend on average €150 per week on household bills, including Sky (€30 per month), broadband (€18 per month), land line (€30 per month), mobile phones (Angela €50 per month, Tom €20 per month, Dan €30 per month, Sheila €40 per month and Ted €20 per month).

Other Income

Tom does a little consultancy on the side and usually earns about €300 per month from ad hoc jobs. He considers that this will continue into the future.

Required

Prepare a draft financial plan for Tom that considers all the issues referred to above. This plan should include the following as a minimum.

Question 1

schedules to portray the current situation as highlighted in the question:

(a) summary relevant background information;
(b) a current statement of net worth;
(c) a debt schedule;
(d) a statement of net income.

(Design proforma information-gathering sheets and include these (completed for Tom and Angela) as part of the appendices to the financial plan.)

(25 marks)

Question 2

A report to Tom that outlines the key recommendations that you consider will strengthen Tom's financial position and that should help Tom to achieve his financial objectives.

(35 marks)

Question 3

Schedules to portray Tom's financial situation if your recommendations were adopted by Tom and his family.

(a) A revised statement of net worth.
(b) A revised statement of net income.

Detail any assumptions made, where necessary.

(20 marks)

Question 4

As part of the financial plan, give Tom advice with respect to the decisions that his children are facing.

(10 marks)

Question 5

Tom also requests advice on investment decision-making, return and risk. Include a paragraph in the report which explains the principles underlying portfolio theory and how this might apply to Tom.

(10 marks)

Total 100 marks

Section C

Integrated Cases in Management Accounting/ Business Finance

Case 33
Bolo's Food Company
Maeve McCutcheon, University College Cork

Overview of the Company

Tom and Gus sat down to prepare the final elements of their business plan. They were due to have a second meeting with Richard White in one week's time. Richard, a business mentor with the South Western Angel Network (SWAN), had a reputation for picking winners and his opinion was respected among the venture capital community. A project endorsed by Richard would always get serious consideration. Richard had established a very successful range of coffee bars in the early 1990s at a time when no-one would have envisaged that the Irish would be queuing at 7:30 am to drink coffee outdoors out of paper cups. Having sold out his chain to an American multinational eager to get a foothold in the Irish market, he was now working full-time assisting companies to the first step on the ladder. He had been encouraging when he met them first, but sent them away to come up with a detailed business plan.

Tom Boland (aged 31) and Gus Grant (aged 29) had spent the past six months developing their plans for Bolo's, a company aiming to provide healthy food options designed for the school lunch trade. Tom is a marketing major who worked all his life in his family's restaurant business, Boland's, while Gus is a process engineer with a passion for food. The two have been friends since college and always dreamed of starting their own business. They recognised a gap in the market for healthy food dispensers suitable for installation in schools and clubs. The growing concern about teenage obesity was leading many schools to abandon traditional soft drinks and snack dispensers, yet a lot did not have the space or manpower to sell food directly to the students.

Tom and Gus saw themselves as men with a mission. Having been bullied in school because of his size, Tom was well aware of the difficulties in adopting healthy eating practices. "Look Richard," he had said when they met previously, "the products have to taste really good. Most health snacks taste like…well they taste pretty bad. Being healthy isn't enough when you can sneak out to the chipper on the corner. We've put a lot of time into designing a menu of pitta breads, wraps and bagels that taste as good as they are, and delicious fruit smoothies and juices that have to be nicer than a fizzy drink."

"The real challenge," added Gus, "is to get the food to the customer tasting the way it tastes when it's assembled. We are not interested in selling the kind of soggy product on sale in corner shops which tastes strongly of the wrapper and little else. We have put a lot of thought into our packaging and we will stock the dispensers daily and clearly label each product by date."

In the Beginning

Tom and Gus had each given up their full-time jobs to focus on getting the business off the ground. Tom had borrowed €50,000 from his father, while Gus had a personal loan secured on his home for €50,000. The two worked full-time out of Gus's garage and used the kitchens of Tom's family restaurant for food development. They were lucky to have secured help in the development stage from Tom's cousin, Mick, a full-time chef. Tom and Gus estimated that Mick had already contributed €25,000 in 'sweat equity'. Gus had worked for Henchard's Engineering, which produced refrigeration and dispensing equipment. He had persuaded David Henchard, the managing director, to develop a prototype of his design which would store and dispense 100 food products or drinks. They were dismayed at how quickly they had burnt through their initial funding and now had only €50,000 left, €40,000 of which would be required to fit out a new premises. In addition they would need to pay six months rental up front on their new premises. Securing funding was an immediate priority.

Getting the Show on the Road

The first food dispenser had been installed in the Ballymount Girls' School, a large State secondary school with 1,000 pupils located just one mile from Tom's family restaurant. Tom, who had the reputation of being persuasive, found that Miss Waters, the Principal, drove a hard bargain: "Five percent of revenue to cope with the cleaning costs. You supply two large bins which you empty daily. No access to the school between nine and three and I must personally approve any product changes. Have you insurance?"

The experience with the prototype was encouraging. After three weeks in operation the dispenser was sold out at 'first break' and Miss Waters had agreed in principle to a second dispenser. The two friends were very encouraged by this result. Teething problems with the dispenser had been quickly resolved. With a potential target population of 500,000 in the 12–18 year age group they reasoned that there is a market for at least 500 dispensers (200 in Leinster and 100 each in Connacht, Munster and Ulster). They also found that the product mix impacted on the level of consumption. A table of observed consumption patterns, showing sales patterns by product mix, is attached at Appendix 1.

Gus was working on an initial estimate of profitability based on a selling price per item of of €2. Their market research indicated that €2 was a significant cut-off point. They also factored in the short school year, which is only 30 weeks long (having allowed for mid-terms and break days). Their initial work showed that the costs are likely to vary by region as the transport cost and distribution element depend on the level of dispersal of the population. See Appendix 2 for estimates of costs.

Plans for Growth

Henchards had quoted an annual lease charge of €3,000 per dispenser, per annum, payable at the start of each year and to include a 10-year maintenance contract. The dispenser would have an expected life of 10 years. Gus reasoned that Henchards could produce up to 200 dispensers per year. If fewer than 100 dispensers were ordered at a time, the lease cost would be €4,000 per annum. New dispensers would be leased and installed during the summer months and in this way a full year's revenue would be available in the year of installation. Tom favoured rapid growth. He argued that they should order 200 dispensers for installation in Leinster for the coming school year and saturate the market. They would then expand to the provinces and ultimately have all the dispensers installed within four years. This would quickly achieve breakeven and minimise lease costs. Gus was more cautious. He argued that while they might breakeven more quickly with a programme of rapid expansion, they would also incur extensive funding costs. He suggested organic growth restricted to gradually expanding outwards at a rate of 40 machines per year for the first five years and only expanding out of Leinster at a later stage. The friends also disagreed on the prospects for the business for the longer term. Tom felt that there was a lot of potential in the fitness sector through gyms and sports clubs, while Gus felt that they should consider the primary school market.

Looking for Money

Tom and Gus hope to maintain control of the business and to allow Mike to participate as well. They had decided that they should restrict their salaries to €20,000 each, paying out profit as dividend only when surplus to investment needs.

They had made tentative approaches to the small business unit of their local bank, but were unhappy at the response. The bank offered them 8% variable rate on a €300,000 loan secured by personal guarantees with principal repayments of €50,000 per year, commencing in year three. The annual interest would be charged on the opening balance and there would be no early repayment option. They expected that would still be a significant shortfall from the capital required to start the business on the rapid growth trajectory envisaged by Tom.

Richard had advised that a venture capitalist (VC) could accept a year six valuation at three times year five earnings before interest, taxes, depreciation and amortisation (EBITDA). The VC would require conversion rights in year six to give a 35%

internal rate of return on the money advanced. For the VCs to advance the money they would need to be persuaded that the founders had a viable business plan.

Tom and Gus realised that they would require some help in putting their plans together as they still had some major areas of uncertainty and disagreement. Tom remembered Sally Lunn, a friend from their college days who had worked for some years with a Venture Capital organisation and was now a consultant to start-up companies. They made the call. "Look Sally we are really in trouble here, can you help us to sort things out?" Sally immediately recognised that there were problems with both the approaches suggested and that there was a considerable amount of work to be done before a credible business plan could be put together.

Required

You are Sally Lunn; based on the information supplied by Tom and Gus, prepare a report to advise them on the appropriate sales and growth strategy.

Question 1

Based on the costings supplied by Gus and the observed consumption pattern with the prototype, you should:

(a) determine the contribution margin for each product and the appropriate product mix for the dispensers;

(10 marks)

(b) compare and contrast the contribution margin per dispenser in year one based on Tom and Gus's growth plans. Discuss the the limitations of CVP in this context.

(30 marks)

Question 2

Produce financial projections for Bolo's, which should include:

(a) a five-year projection of earnings before interest taxes depreciation and amortisation (EBITDA) for each of the suggested strategies;

(15 marks)

(b) the funding requirement arising from each suggested strategy;

(15 marks)

(c) an alternative strategy which reduces the funding requirement without delaying the move to profitability.

(10 marks)

Question 3

Compare the terms of the bank financing and the venture capital financing and comment on:

(a) a comparison of cost and risk for the founders of each form of financing;

(10 marks)

(b) a consideration of the broader impact of venture capital involvement on a growth business.

(10 marks)

Total 100 marks

Appendix 1: Observed Consumption Pattern

Product Mix		Sales Pattern	
Food Stock	Drink Stock	Food Sales	Drink Sales
100	0	55	0
90	10	58	10
80	20	60	20
70	30	62	28
60	40	52	35
50	50	45	40
40	60	38	55
30	70	30	68
20	80	20	65
10	90	10	65
0	100	0	60

Appendix 2: Estimate of Costs

Item	Cost	Notes
Salaries	€60,000 per annum	At each 50 dispenser expansion point an additional staff member would be hired at a cost of €20,000 per year.
Distribution	€10 per machine, per day	These figures might increase where the population is more widely dispersed.
Advertising	€50,000 per annum	If rapid expansion were envisaged, this would increase to €100,00 per annum for the first three years.
Raw materials	€0.40 per food item €1 per drink item	
Packaging	€0.50 per food item €0.20 per drink item	
Wages	€0.30 per food item €0.20 per drink item	
Transport	€10,000 p.a.	Transport to distribution point from central premises (this does not apply in the Leinster area.)
Rent	€40,000 per year	Initial fit-out €40,000 50% of rent payable in advance.
Insurance	€6,000 per year	Payable in advance
Cleaning	5% of sales revenue	

Case 34
Toffer Group plc
**Ciaran Connolly and Martin Kelly,
Queen's University Belfast**

James Grant FCA is the chief executive of Toffer Group plc ('Toffer'), a large Irish company that manufactures satellite dishes, and he has recently appointed Ian Legg as personnel director of the company. Prior to joining Toffer, Ian had spent the previous six years as the personnel manager for a reputable medium-sized company, KTE Limited (KTE), and was under no illusions about the pressures and expectations that came with the new post.

Wherever he had worked, Ian had always tried to avoid the company accountants, as those he met tended to be reserved and uncommunicative. His involvement with the accountants at KTE was limited to polite enquiries on payroll and employment records, and the occasional commandeering of his office to 'house' the auditors. At Toffer, the accountants have a central role in the decision-making process. Before James Grant authorised any proposal, budgets were prepared, products were priced and ratios calculated, with considerable emphasis placed upon 'contribution'. It was contribution, not profit, which marked the difference between the acceptance and rejection of a proposal. Ian would have continued to leave the decision-making to the accountants and bowed to their financial wisdom if it had not been for one particular event that occurred approximately 14 months before he left KTE.

KTE was an established family business whose chairman, Sir Ryan O'Leary, was the last in the family line going back over a number of generations. As retirement age approached, Sir Ryan merged his firm with Toffer approximately three years ago, building in as many safeguards for his family and employees as possible. Consequently, the extension of Toffer's influence over KTE had been slow and gradual. James Grant was aware of the potential of KTE Limited, particularly if its production methods were modernised, but was reluctant to make radical changes too quickly, preferring to allow retirements to take their natural course. Indeed, James Grant had shown remarkable and uncharacteristic restraint in waiting to make the changes, but it could not last forever.

The end came in a deceptively mild way. The original budget, which is shown in Appendix 1, for KTE had already been approved for the forthcoming period. Unexpectedly, the routine board meeting for November was presented with market research findings conducted by a firm appointed by James Grant, who expanded on the research figures:

"The conclusions from the market research are that next year the maximum number of units that could be sold by KTE is:

Alpha: 5,000 units
Beta: 4,000 units
Gamma: 4,000 units

However, as you can see, these figures are different to the proposed production figures in the approved budget. The accountants suggest we have no alternative but to reschedule production to maximise contribution based on the best way sales demand can be satisfied. Any threat to customer satisfaction can temporarily be solved by another of our UK plants."

James Grant continued:

"Unfortunately, the labour supply in Department Y is fixed and because of the way KTE has been organised, it takes a long period of training to achieve the skill required. Indeed, management have exacerbated the problem by voluntarily agreeing with the trade unions upon restrictions in the labour supply. We therefore cannot change the Department Y constraint and consequently Departments X and Z may be adversely affected."

It was an uncharacteristically mild intervention by James Grant, and few fully anticipated the implications. However, six months later Ian most certainly did. Redundancies, strikes and industrial strife had destroyed a morale and *esprit de corps* at KTE that had taken many years to build. Abandoning caution, Ian decided to unreservedly let James Grant know his views on the matter, the essence of which was that a company's profits are directly related to the way it treats the workforce, and that people must be treated as individuals and invested with some measure of dignity to obtain their best.

James Grant made no attempt to conceal his look of astonishment, but continued to listen with a mixture of indifference and tolerance. His only reply was that the short-term profit improvement would help people accept the change and that perhaps his accountants could improve their 'people skills'. James Grant left abruptly, leaving Ian contemplating his future. Surprisingly, just over a year later, he was the new personnel director of Toffer, again acting as the buffer between profits and people.

Ian's role in Toffer was varied and interesting; a major part being concerned with the identification, take-over and integration of suitable businesses to enhance Toffer's expansion plans. One such business was Bebe Limited ('Bebe'), a company with a chequered history that in recent years had made a name for itself by concentrating on one product, the Net, and backing it with substantial advertising. James Grant was rather taken with the quality, versatility and reliability of this new product, believing it would round off Toffer's communications activities.

The directors of Bebe soon became involved in talks with Toffer, making the company's financial records freely available for review. While Ian's responsibilities were to investigate the manpower side of Bebe, including the age profile of the directors and executives, service contracts, training facilities and manpower policies, since his outburst at KTE he had tried to develop a wider brief. The accounting team moved fast and investigated every possible figure. Their approach was now predictable, focusing on contribution margins and formatting income statements on a marginal costing basis.

Appendix 2 shows the standard cost card for the Net and Appendix 3 a financial profit statement for the previous year.

At a meeting to discuss the possible acquisition of Bebe, James Grant pondered aloud:

> "The problem is just how accurate are their budgets and forecasts because we know that Bebe's budgetary planning and control systems were not very sophisticated. If we can believe them, this year's sales will match their production capacity of about 12,000 Nets and next year's demand will be even greater, so that they will have to rely on stocks. If so, this is the time to buy them on a price earnings basis."

There was silence, during which various projections prepared by the finance director were studied. James Grant then continued: "My hunch is that the company may only match last year's figures, which would mean that a cash-flow crisis in a year's time would make Bebe ripe for the picking. I have asked Eamon Corr, the financial accountant at Bebe, to e-mail me the latest balance sheet for Bebe (Appendix 4) together with some additional information which will help us arrive a realistic price for the business." James Grant also knew that raising new finance for future acquisitions was an area that he needed to have some answers for when the board of directors convened next week. Toffer is currently financed by a prudent combination of debt and equity, but it looks as though the company will have to find a lot of cash to buy Bebe. The directors generally have an open mind regarding which sources of finance to employ, but two e-mails (Appendix 5) from board members yesterday have given James a problem he could do without. He had already set his mind on making a convertible loan stock issue and firmly believes that Toffer should not increase its dividends for the coming year.

Ian soon lost the thread of the argument. With some apprehension he asked how it could be that there were two results for the previous year and why, if the published accounts were open to doubt, they were accepted by the auditors. All the accountants at the meeting laughed pleasantly and genuinely. "Let's say," said James Grant, "that for decision-making only the marginal or direct cost approach is valid and the IAS 2 hang-up, where profits are anticipated, can lead companies into all sorts of difficulties." James Grant's glance dismissed any further questions and Ian felt it wise to nod in agreement although not understanding for one moment what it all meant. Ian was also uncomfortable with what he perceived as being James Grant's obsession with ensuring that all the directors had appropriate share option plans in place.

Required

Acting as an independent financial consultant, prepare a memorandum to the Board of Toffer that addresses the following issues.

Question 1

Why might the accountants at Toffer concentrate on contribution and marginal costing as the basis of their decision-making?

(4 marks)

Question 2

Why would the accountants prefer marginal costing to absorption costing?

(4 marks)

Question 3

By what means might the accountants analyse costs into their fixed and variable components for the purpose of identifying contribution?

(4 marks)

Question 4

From Appendix 1, calculate the contribution per hour of the Department Y constraint.

(4 marks)

Question 5

Prepare a new budget for KTE based on the most profitable way sales demand can be satisfied, and calculate the extra profit this would yield.

(8 marks)

Question 6

Assuming that each employee of KTE contributes 1,920 hours of work per annum, how many redundancies in Departments X and Z could arise if the new budget was adhered to strictly?

(6 marks)

Question 7

Using Appendix 2 and Appendix 3, prepare a profit statement for Bebe under marginal costing principles.

(5 marks)

Question 8

Assuming this year's sales of Nets match the production capacity of 12,000 units:

(a) prepare a financial statement using absorption costing principles; and
(b) prepare a financial statement using marginal costing principles.

(10 marks)

Question 9

Assuming that demand for Nets next year did increase so that both production of 12,000 and stocks of 4,000 Nets were sold:

(a) prepare a financial statement using absorption costing principles; and
(b) prepare a financial statement using marginal costing principles.

(10 marks)

Question 10

Using the information in Appendix 4, prepare four alternative values for Bebe that a perspective purchaser might use.

(9 marks)

Question 11

Critcally evaluate the valuation methods used above and recommend a price which Toffer should pay for Bebe.

(7 marks)

Question 12

Advise the board of directors on strategies for enhancing the value for the combined company following the acquisition.

(6 marks)

Question 13

In peparation for the board meeting next week, discuss the options available for raising finance for future acquisitions.

(8 marks)

Question 14

Advise on the factors the board should consider before finalising a dividend policy for Toffer.

(8 marks)

Question 15

Outline the importance and limitations of ESOPs (executive share option plans) to the achievement of goal congruence within Toffer.

(7 marks)

Total 100 marks

Appendix 1: KTE's Original Budget

	Alpha € Unit	Beta € Unit	Gamma € Unit
Selling price	620	620	940
Direct materials	99	252	162
Direct labour:			
• Department X	(30 hrs × €9) 270	(15 hrs × €9) 135	(32 hrs × €9) 288
• Department Y	(6 hrs × €12) 72	(8 hrs × €12) 96	(10 hrs × €12) 120
• Department Z	(15 hrs × €9) 135	(8 hrs × €9) 72	(32 hrs × €9) 288
Prime cost	576	555	858
Variable overhead	14	10	18
Marginal cost	590	565	876
Contribution/unit	30	55	64
Proposed production (units)	5,000	2,000	3,000
Total contribution/product	€150,000	€110,000	€192,000

	€
Total contribution	452,000
Fixed overhead	(152,000)
Budgeted profit	300,000

Appendix 2: Net Standard Cost Card

	€ unit
Selling price	1,000
Direct materials	300
Direct labour	100
Prime cost	400
Variable production overheads	100
Marginal cost	500
Fixed overhead:*	
Production	240
Selling and distribution	100
Total cost	840
Profit/unit	160

*Based on an output of 50 Nets per day for a 48-week working year. Over the anticipated range of sales, selling costs, etc., these costs are, for all meaningful purposes, fixed.

Appendix 3: Bebe's Financial Profit Statement (amended from previous year's accounts)

	No. of Units	€ per Unit	€'000s
Sales	8,000	1,000	8,000
Production costs:	12,000		
Variable		500	6,000
Fixed		240	2,880
		740	8,880
less Closing stock	4,000	740	2,960
Cost of goods sold			5,920
Factory profit			2,080
Selling, distribution & administration costs			1,200
Net profit			880

Note: the published annual accounts report a profit of €867,500. Toffer's accountants have taken out various figures and approximated the remainder in line with the standard, with the result being much easier to interpret.

Appendix 4: Bebe's Balance Sheet (at end of last year)

	€'000	€'000
Non-current Assets		
Land and buildings	10,000	
Goodwill	3,000	
Machinery	2,500	
Vehicles	2,500	
		18,000
Current Assets		
Stocks	2,960	
Trade receivables	1,750	
Cash	500	
		5,210
Total assets		23,210
Current Liabilities		
Trade payables	1,800	
Taxation	500	2,300
		20,910
Non-current Liabilities		
Secured loan		6,000
Net assets		14,910
Equity		
€1 ordinary share capital		5,000
Retained Earnings		9,910
		14,910

Additional information:

1. The profit after tax and interest, but before dividends, over the last five years are:

	€'000
Year 1	955
Year 2	525
Year 3	695
Year 4	555
Last year	607*

   *This is profit of €867,500 after taxation at 30%.

   Bebe's annual dividend over the last three years has been €350,000. The company's strategic plan indicates that the company will seek to grow dividends by 3% over the next four years.

2. A recent valuation by independent valuers indicated the following valuations which have not been reflected in the balance sheet above:

	€'000
Land and buildings	8,500
Machinery	2,000
Vehicles	1,500

3. The average price earnings ratios and dividend yields for three public companies in the same industry as Bebe over the past three years have been:

	Paul plc Div.Yield %	P/E	Brian plc Div.Yield %	P/E	Mary plc Div.Yield %	P/E
Current year	8	16	7	14	6	15
Prior year	7	17	6.5	14	7	13.5
Three years ago	4	16	5	14	5	15
Average	6.3	16.3	6.2	14	6	14.5

Appendix 5: E-mails

From:	P. Director
To:	James Grant
Date:	28 XXXX
Subject:	Sources of Finance for Expansion

Good morning James,

Following on from our telephone conversation yesterday, I do not believe this is a good time for issuing equity. The economic situation is bleak and I do not see it improving in the near future. I have a small share portfolio of my own and I plot the monthly prices for each share on graphs, including my small holding of Toffer shares. I have done this for some years now and I can tell you the patterns clearly show that we are heading for a major downturn in share prices. If we went for equity finance, by the time we could get it organised the bear market would be with us and we would need to issue a much larger number of shares.

From:	Q. Director
To:	James Grant
Date:	28 XXXX
Subject:	Financing Future Acquisitions and Dividends

Dear James,

Firstly, please pass on my congratulations to Ian for spotting the potential of Bebe as a possible acquisition target. Make sure we get a good price, although I hear there are some good valuable assets in that company. I also agree with Ian's observation that there are some highly talented individuals working for the company and we need to put that talent to good use in Toffer. James, as for the board meeting next week, we really must pay attention to our financial gearing. If we get that wrong, our share price will be savaged. Everyone keeps talking about external finance, but I am not sure that it is necessary. We make good profits and have done so for some time; can't we use some of the retained profits for financing our expansion of the business?

    Finally, I know there is a lot of doom and gloom out there regarding the economy, however the important thing, in my view, is to keep dividends stable. Do not forget that some of us have remuneration packages tied into shareholder value and this needs to be taken into account when deciding on our dividend policy.

Case 35
Glenview House Hotel
Margaret Healy and John Doran, University College Cork

Introduction

Glenview House Hotel offers up-market 'Bed-and-Breakfast' style accommodation, as well as running a successful restaurant. However, given the nature of the trade over the past two seasons, and the increasing costs of running and maintaining the house itself, the owners have concluded that a strategic rethink of the future of the business is urgently needed.

Glenview House Hotel

Glenview House is a large country house, almost 200 years old. It is set in mature grounds, which have been partly landscaped. There are also a number of stone outbuildings that once served as stables and barns but have fallen into disuse in recent years. Complete with resident ghost, the property has been in the O'Connor family for a number of generations. Twenty-eight years ago Paul and his wife Collette began trading as Glenview House Hotel, initially attracting mainly Irish tourists, but gradually building their profile and attractiveness to international visitors.

In recent years the majority of business at Glenview House Hotel has come through travel agents and tour operators. However, early indications for the current season are poor, with little advance bookings made. The O'Connors have always enjoyed caring for their guests, believing the 'personal touch' is a key element of any visitor experience. Indeed a significant (but not quantified) proportion of the hotel's revenue comes from repeat business from a large pool of loyal customers who have have become 'almost like family'. Lately, however, customers seem to be more demanding and expectant of ever-increasing levels of service and convenience, but at a lower and lower cost per room, per night. Recently, Collette stated:

"Guests are no longer happy to arrive to a clean, warm, comfortable room. Now they want the towels changed every day and 24-hour room service at the flick of a switch. They demand the standards of a resort hotel – but are less willing to pay the price."

Paul and Collette had been considering exiting the business completely, but their only child, Trixie, who has spent the last two years travelling and working in Asia, has recently expressed a wish to retain the property in the family and to become involved in the business activity 'some day'. For this, and other reasons of their own, the O'Connors are considering the possibility of investing in refurbishment and renewal of the premises, along with expanding the range of services offered to guests. Two options are under consideration: converting the stables area into self-catering accommodation, aimed at the Irish 'stay-at-home' family market; or restoring the stables, as part of a riding holidays initiative. Regardless of which course of action is chosen, the project will be financed from loans raised using the existing Glenview House Hotel premises as collateral. The O'Connors have already entered into detailed discussions with two separate construction firms and are awaiting detailed draft drawings and price quotations before approaching their bank with one of the proposals. An informal discussion with their bank manager at a social function has indicated that he would be supportive of their proposal, although he warned of the likely unprecedented severity of economic conditions over the next few years. Other contacts in the industry with a wide overview have noted that the nature of the market is also likely to change significantly in the next few years.

Proposal for Self-catering Accommodation

Converting the stable area into self-catering accommodation has been proposed by Collette as a means of facilitating family groups whilst not impacting on the existing business model for the hotel. A recent surveyor's report on the existing structure supports the development of 10 three-bedroomed units, with integrated kitchen and living facilities. Laundry facilities will also be incorporated as part of a utility room adjacent to the kitchen area of each unit. Appendix 1 lists the costs involved in this proposal, based on the lower of the initial estimates sought from the construction firms.

Collette is enthusiastic about the potential of the proposal. Having researched similar holiday offerings on the internet, she has projected three possible outcomes for the venture, as shown in the table below. It is proposed to charge €350 per unit, per week in the high season (June, July and August – 13 weeks) and €295 for the remainder of the trading year (35 weeks). Costs of laundry, preparation and cleaning of each unit are estimated at €20 per weekly occupancy. Heating and energy costs are added to the customer bill, on a per usage basis. Collette has made the following estimates of the likelihood of possible occupancy rates over the next few years, based on her experience of the ups and downs of the tourist trade over the last three decades. The couple themselves would handle the check-in and general 'concierge' duties.

	Likelihood of Occurence	Average Occupancy rate	
		High Season	Low Season
Best case scenario	25%	90%	50%
Middle-range	50%	50%	25%
Worst case scenario	25%	25%	15%

Proposal for Riding Holidays Initiative

Whilst Paul agrees that a renewal of the Glenview House Hotel business model is needed, he is not sure that self-catering accommodation is the best option. He has been approached by Sean Farrell, the owner of a local riding stables. In recent months, Sean has also faced declining revenues and is finding it increasingly difficult to sell the concept of a day's riding to potential customers. He is convinced, however, that if he combines his business with that of Glenview House Hotel, together they can offer a tailored package that will appeal to a wide range of people in both the Irish market and abroad. Sean sees the proposal for 'Glenview Riding School' in very straightforward terms:

> "It's simple really! I have the horses and the horse-sense; Glenview House provides the bed and lodgings – putting the two together is in everyone's interests."

Collette is more cautious about the proposal. She is worried that having Sean as a business partner may hinder the success of the project. Despite acknowledging Sean's equine expertise, she is very concerned about his business acumen. Sean has offered to alleviate these concerns by investing €200,000 in the joint venture, in return for which he expects at least one-third ownership.

Under the proposed business venture, Glenview House would provide the location and housing of the horses, with Sean retaining ownership of the horses. The large barn area would be converted into an indoor area for use in foul weather situations. Sean's existing network of trails could be extended to incorporate routes throughout the extensive grounds surrounding Glenview House. Riding equipment, including saddles, bridles and safety helmets, would be purchased as new, although Sean is adamant that his existing stock is still fit for purpose. Appendix 2 details the costs associated with the venture.

Collette is also insistent that guests of the hotel should not be charged the full daily rate for use of the riding school facilities. Whilst Sean has no difficulty with this, he and the O'Connors have yet to come to any agreement regarding what this rate should be. Sean is growing increasingly irate at what he sees as Collette's continued interference in negotiations between himself and Paul. Recently he offered the following opinion:

> "Paul sees the potential in this venture for both of us; he needs to fill the bedrooms and my proposal offers an additional attraction at the hotel. However, all Collette seems concerned about is how fast can Paul get their money back."

A Radical Alternative

A few days after their informal discussion, Liam Folan, bank manager of the branch used by the O'Connors, telephoned with a suggestion. The bank's corporate finance arm was proposing that they could advise Glenview House Hotel on a restructuring of the operation of their current business. This alternative would involve the O'Connors retaining ownership of the estate property but leasing the operation of the hotel to a management group, which would operate the business. Paul and Collette would receive an annual lease payment for 10 years, with the management group having an option to renew the lease for a further 10 years. Consideration of this option would be completely separate from the previous two options, neither of which would remain relevant if the leasing alternative were taken up.

Required

Paul and Collette O'Connor are undecided as to which of the options available to them is the right one to follow in the future development of Glenview House Hotel. They have approached you as an independent financial consultant and, having made all of the above information available to you, they now await your advice and recommendations.

Your report should include consideration of the following matters.

Question 1

Evaluate both of the expansion proposals under consideration for the stables area at Glenview House Hotel. Highlight critical aspects of the outcome(s).

(30 marks)

Question 2

Outline the main principles involved in making relevant costing type decisions.

(10 marks)

Question 3

Explain and advise on alternative approaches to determining the rate at which to charge Glenview House Hotel for the use of the riding school facilities. Identify potential or existing sources of conflict and advise on resolution strategies.

(15 marks)

Question 4

In relation to the leasing of the Glenview House Hotel property to a hotel management company, list and discuss the business and financial issues that should be considered in evaluating such an arrangement.

(45 marks)

Total 100 marks

NOTE: taxation aspects of this case can be ignored.

Appendix 1: Costs of Converting the Stables into Self-catering Accommodation

External Site works	€100,000
Construction	€350,000
Internal fit-out, including furniture	€40,000 per unit
Installation of services	€50,000
Planning fees	€2,000
Laying of playground, including fit-out	€10,000
Surveyor's report – initial feasibility study	€4,000
Architect design fees	7% of total cost of project
Laundry facilities	€100 per unit

Appendix 2: Development of Glenview Riding School

Site works, including development of riding routes	€150,000
Construction of internal arena	€50,000
Refurbishment of existing stables	€40,000
Purchase of riding equipment	€10,000
Planning fees	€2,000

Annual Running Costs (based on 8 horses)

Insurance	€5,000
Staff wages	€90,000
Animal feedstuff	€48,000
Veterinary fees	€10,000
Advertising	€5,000

Net Income (based on Sean's estimates)

Daily rate (public)	€110
Daily rate (hotel guests)	?

Annual Usage (based on Sean's estimates)

Daily users (including hotel guests)	1,800 days riding

Case 36
Delaney's Bakehouse Breads
John Doran and Margaret Healy, University College Cork

Overview of the Company

Delaney's Bakery was established in Macroom over 30 years ago by Annie and Denis Delaney as a small, family-run enterprise whose main objective was to supplement the Delaney family income. About 20 years ago, the bakery survived the bitter bread-based price wars fought by the multiples in the Irish market place. This period saw the departure of many of the old established companies, with only the strongest surviving. Annie puts the continued existence of the business during this period down to their simple outlook of attention to detail and an overriding focus on product quality and value:

> "Our motto is simple: *Putting bread on the table*. This works on all levels – it describes exactly what the customer wants – but also includes our initial motivation for starting up the business … As long as we all remember that – good times always follow bad – then we'll keep our feet firmly on the ground."

Throughout the 1990s expansion in the market place enabled Delaney's to grow its business, opening retail outlets across the Munster region, and justifying the move to a large, newly built baking facility on the outskirts of Cork city. This move was financed mainly through existing resources within the company and did not necessitate the sale of the original bakehouse. Annie and Denis Delaney are now about to retire from the business and have transferred ownership of the bakehouse building to their daughter, Noleen.

The Macroom Bakehouse

The original bakehouse is located in what was once a derelict area of town in Macroom. Noleen Delaney is using the premises as the location for producing a range of speciality breads, under the brandname 'Delaney's Bakehouse Breads'. Noleen is keen to exploit the image of the bakehouse as home to an expanding range of speciality breads and as part of the West Cork region's growing cluster of craft industries. She also does not want to break the link with the Delaney's Bread name, as she believes the reputation of the existing company will help establish the Bakehouse brand in the minds of consumers.

Speciality Bread Production

Noleen Delaney is a trained chef. For the past number of years she has been the well-known 'face' of Delaney's Bakery through her regular weekly 'meal of the week' slot on national television. She also writes a daily food column in one of the national newspapers. Her popularity is such that she is regularly asked to endorse new product offerings from a range of industries and suppliers.

Noleen is interested in using the Bakehouse to produce a range of ready-to-bake speciality breads, leveraging the existing reputation of the Delaney's bakery brand in synergy with her own growing profile as a celebrity food professional. Her major difficulty is in finding an outlet for the output volumes necessary to make the project viable. She has been engaged in informal discussions with the management of a major supermarket chain which is interested in a rolling contract for the supply of three such breads in the annual quantities outlined in Appendix 1. The volumes used in Appendix 1 are based on the perceptions of both Noleen and the supermarket about the market potential of these new product offerings and on limited preliminary in-store tasting tests.

Noleen understands that the supermarket group has identified a widening of its bread range as being a key input to its repositioning against key demographics in the consumer market. The supermarket merchandising manager views the Bakehouse Breads proposal as offering an integrated package that would complement existing product offerings, thus allowing the supermarket chain to offer a bread range equal to, or surpassing, its nearest competitor. However, Noleen is wary about the proposal. Without any financial or business training, the process of negotiating the deal is proving more complex than she envisaged, and as a client she has decided to seek your professional help.

The operating processes for the production of the speciality breads can be summarised into a number of cost pools as follows (more detailed information on each process, its related costs and the most suitable cost driver for each cost pool are available in Appendix 2).

Process/Cost Pool
Set-up (including gathering ingredients)
Mixing
Shaping and proofing
Baking
Packing and delivery

Once part-baked, the breads are then vacuum-packed, ready for final baking on-site in retail premises. Prior to the retail baking stage, the vacuum-packed bread has an average lifespan of two weeks. Whilst Noleen believes it may also be possible to freeze the breads at this point, she is unwilling to investigate this further as she is adamant the quality of the finished products would suffer. There has also been some internal disagreement at the Bakehouse as to the value of the accounting exercise that estimated the pooled costs associated with each activity. It is acknowledged by Noleen (who initiated the exercise) that the budgeted information cannot be treated as definitive. In defense of the estimates she stated: "We have to start somewhere if we are going to launch new product offerings." The bakery has traditionally used direct labour cost to absorb overhead costs into product cost.

The Contract Negotiations

A number of commercial issues requiring consideration have also arisen as part of the contract negotiations. To ensure maximum freshness, the final baking stage for each of the bread products is carried out on the individual supermarket premises. To preserve the image of Delaney's Bakehouse Breads as a quality product, Noleen is adamant that ovens are sourced from the leading market supplier. Whilst the supermarket chain is willing to install these ovens, there is disagreement as to their ownership, with the supermarket suggesting it is willing to provide the space required in each of their shops to Noleen rent-free.

The proposal is to initially locate the in-store bakeries in 20 individual store premises for a two-year trial period. The ovens and related equipment will cost €10,500 per store. The average expected product inventory per store (valued at cost) will be €1,500. In addition, product held in storage ahead of on-site baking would remain the property of Noleen, until converted into finished goods for re-sale. If the equipment is to be supermarket-owned, the store negotiating team is pressing that it would also take ownership of the branding of the end product. It would also pay for promotional activities in that case. The supermarket chain is also demanding a price rebate of 10% if it bears the cost of the in-store ovens (versus 2.5% if they remain the property of Noleen). The supermarket chain would also seek 60 days credit instead of 30 days if the supermarket owners bore the capital cost of the ovens. Noleen's cost of capital is 8%. The supermarket chain is unwilling to commit at this stage to either an extension or even continuation of the arrangement after the initial two-year trial period. Issues concerning the timing and frequency of product deliveries are also outstanding.

Noleen is unsure as to the correct course of action to take in the contract negotiations for the sale of her speciality breads. She has approached you, as an independent consultant, to write a report to inform her deliberations. In particular, your report should address the following points.

Required

Question 1

With regard to the proposal to expand the range of speciality breads, provide a calculation of the budgeted production cost per loaf of each of the three main lines of bread under both the proposed activity-based costing basis and under the absorption basis currently used by the firm.

(25 marks)

Question 2

Comment on the outcome of the costing exercise and its implications for the commercial viability of the proposed initiative into pre-baked speciality breads, providing any other calculations you consider necessary. Outline the business options that may be open to the bakery to deal with the issues arising.

(15 marks)

Question 3

In light of the uncertainty on the cost-effectiveness of using more resources in the area of product cost analysis, outline options open to the firm in cost accounting and the relative merits of each option.

(15 marks)

Question 4

In light of the ongoing discussions regarding the structuring of the supermarket contract, evaluate the options related to the ownership of the in-store ovens based only on the information provided. In addition, identify for the client any omissions or issues which, in your opinion, are not addressed adequately in the information supplied.

(45 marks)

Total 100 marks

Appendix 1: Speciality Breads—Estimates of Costing and Production Information

	Harvest Pan	Sultana Loaf	Bagel Loaf
Projected units of output (loaves)	8,000,000	600,000	4,000,000
Production batch size (average)	100	15	50
Sales order batch size (average)	50	15	50
Direct material cost – per loaf	€0.05	€0.09	€0.06
Direct labour cost – per loaf	€0.03	€0.04	€0.03
Weight of materials – grams per loaf	400	450	300
Baking time required – minutes per batch	40	50	25
Proposed selling prices – per loaf	€0.20	€0.30	€0.25

Appendix 2: Expected Overhead Costs

The expected overhead costs associated with the level of activities described in Appendix 1 are as shown below.

Cost Pool	Cost Driver	Budgeted Cost (€)
Set-up (inc. gathering ingredients)	No. of production runs	440,000
Mixing	Weight of materials	122,000
Shaping and proofing	No. of loaves	80,000
Baking	Time required	255,000
Packing and delivery	No. of sales orders	150,000

Case 37

Jenson Car Components

Noel Hyndman and Danielle McMahon,
Queen's University Belfast

The Company and its Products

Located in an industrial estate on the edge of Ballymena, Jenson Car Components Limited (Jenson) was established 30 years ago by Eddie Jenson and for the past 20 years has been managed by Eddie's son, David. Originally the company produced specialist brake discs for high-performing sports cars and it quickly became a leading supplier in the UK and Ireland in this niche market. Since then, as demand has increased and overseas markets have opened, the company has diversified into the production of cam shaft kits and, latterly, catalytic converters for the sports car market. This has required substantial expansion and investment in expensive, largely automated production processes, particularly with the recent addition of catalytic converters to the company's product range. At the same time competition has increased, chiefly from overseas producers, and margins have been somewhat squeezed. Within Jenson, there are three major producing divisions (brake discs, cam shaft kits and catalytic converters) relating to the three product markets that the company services. Company reporting to board level is largely based on product profitability statements (on a total and per unit basis). These are produced quarterly and are reviewed at board level at each of the company's board meetings.

Jenson is regarded as a high-quality producer and its products have achieved particular brand recognition. Consequently, the company has been able to achieve premium prices for its products in the sports car market. Its pricing policy has been to set prices so that the company achieves a 40% gross margin on selling price. This should allow adequate margin to cover all selling, distribution and administration overheads and provide an adequate net margin. Given that its products are aimed exclusively at the sports car market, the company uses a single price within each of the three product markets and this is viewed by management as being appropriate given the similar production demands of each product within these groupings. In addition, it simplifies marketing and invoicing. Each of the product groupings uses production processes common to all products as well as some specialised facilities that are unique to each individual product. The three product groupings (and their individual specialised facilities) are as follows.

Brake Discs

The specialised brake disc facility includes specialised equipment, such as a modern ferrous foundry, electrical autopour furnaces with laser pour systems and automated fettling machines. Full process control is maintained throughout the process with innovative measuring systems. While the brake disc manufacturing facility is fairly mechanised, it relies on highly skilled operators and over 70% of Jenson's production staff are employed in this facility. It is anticipated that sales of brake discs for the current year will be €24 million.

Cam Shaft Kits

The specialised cam shaft facility consists of three four-axis lathes which work on bought-in and in-house-produced aluminium castings and machined components. An electric servo motor is used to vary the valve timings required to very precise levels of accuracy. Sequential automatic hydraulic clamping and unclamping processes are used and changes to the machines are facilitated by the use of sophisticated linked software. Quality inspections take place throughout the process, with a final inspection being carried out using a dedicated 44-channel measuring station that tests critical dimensions. Budgeted cam shaft kit sales for the year are €10 million.

Catalytic Converters

Catalytic converter production was seen as a way of expanding into the very high price end of the component market and, given high failure rates on original equipment fitted to new vehicles, provided the potential for significant sales volume in the long term. This specialised facility, the most recent and most modern in Jenson, was set up only two years ago and uses technologically advanced catalytic converter spinning equipment. This process is extremely automated, requires many machine set-ups and individual parts/materials, and quality inspections take place throughout the process. The very expensive and sensitive raw material used requires very careful handling. Sales of catalytic converters have grown substantially over the last two years and are budgeted to reach €6 million this year. Significant future growth is anticipated as Jenson enhances its presence and reputation in the catalytic converter market.

Product Profitability

It is early July and David Jenson, the managing director of Jenson, is studying the product profitability statements for the first six months of the year aboard the Greencastle ferry. He is concerned that the company is losing margin in one of its key market segments (brake discs), even though he knows it has reduced prices in this segment well below Jenson's normal selling price. He is particularly concerned about what is going on in the market and whether the pricing policy that Jenson is following is appropriate. By the time he drives off the ferry, in his shining 1956 Jaguar XK140 roadster, he decides to e-mail both Lucy Green (the chief accountant at Jenson) and Joe McAllister (the sales director) outlining his concerns.

Some detail (at product level) from the product profitability statements that David Jenson has studied is reproduced in Appendix 1. The company is not experiencing any significant cost variances. Previous discussions at board level have noted that there has been considerable price pressure in the brake disc market, with a range of Chinese discs being available at lower prices than Jenson's target selling price. Joe McAllister decided that prices would have to be lowered to match the competition and maintain market share. This action is reflected in Appendix 1. The situation in the catalytic converter market is the reverse of what is happening in the brake disc market. Joe McAllister had noted that the prices of competing catalytic converters were considerably higher than Jenson's target prices and very early in the year decided to raise prices by over 20%. Amazingly, even with this price increase, sales of catalytic converters have been well above budget. David Jenson ponders on these issues and wonders whether it is time to change the production and sales focus of Jenson; perhaps even exiting the brake disc market.

As the sun sets over Redcastle, he reflects on a recent conversation he had with Lucy Green. She highlighted that the present cost allocation system in the company tracks direct costs (direct material and direct labour) to products, and then allocates production overhead to products based on a direct labour hour basis. This was the system first developed 30 years ago when the company was established (at a time when production was more labour-intensive and direct labour was the dominant cost), and as new products have been added the company has continued to use such a system (more detailed information regarding the calculation of the overhead absorption rate for the current year is provided in Appendix 2). Lucy had queried whether, given the expansion of the company into other markets and the significant variation in the nature of production in producing for each market, the existing costing system is giving appropriate profitability signals. Indeed, she has also questioned the wisdom of establishing prices on a cost-plus basis when the cost information may be problematical. Some months ago she had suggested investigating the possibility of developing an activity-based costing (ABC) system and had provided some rough early workings, using the production overhead budget and the production volume budget for the current year, on tracking costs to appropriate cost pools and developing suitable cost drivers. A summary of these are produced in Appendix 3. After receiving a note from Lucy regarding this, and on being informed that the switch to ABC may be disruptive and costly, David Jenson decided to take no further action. He now wonders whether he was right.

Possible New Product

Another issue that has come to the fore at recent board meetings, and one that is again on the agenda for the forthcoming meeting, is the possibility of expanding the product range by producing oil pumps for the sports car market. It is anticipated that the direct costs of producing an oil pump for high-performing sports cars would be approximately €70 per unit for material and €60 per unit for labour (four hours at €15). In a previous conversation, Joe McAllister, on the basis of his experience with catalytic converters, had suggested that Jenson attempts to establish a likely competitive price as a basis for making a decision regarding entry to this market and, off-the-cuff, thought that the market would take a price of €450 per unit. On being told by David Jenson of Joe's views, Lucy Green commented that this approach is akin to target costing and, given her already expressed concerns as to costing, pricing and evaluating profitability of products, is supportive of such a method in this one-off case. However, she expressed concerns as to the present underlying costing system as the foundation for such an approach.

Possible Acquisition

Putting his foot down just outside Ballyliffin, David remembered a conversation he had had a number of weeks ago with Graham Stewart, a fellow Jaguar enthusiast and majority shareholder in Stewart Ltd. Graham had been a grumpy old man for as long as David could remember, but with the onset of his sixties he was getting particularly fed-up with the demands of running his business. He had set up Stewart Ltd 20 years earlier to build and service kit cars, but over the last decade had diversified into some component production, particularly oil pumps and crankshafts, and building and servicing kit cars was now a much smaller part of his business activities. Many of his staff had been employed in Stewart Ltd for the past two decades, and as far as David was concerned the quality of the products was top notch: his beloved XK140 was currently sporting a Stewart Ltd oil pump, as were the cars of many enthusiasts he knew. If he could buy at the right price, maybe Stewart Ltd was an easy route into the oil pump market. (Information regarding Stewart Ltd, including the latest financial statements, is provided in Appendix 4.)

Involvement of Consultant with These Issues

As darkness falls over the Inishowen peninsula, and David is tucked up and well fed in Fahan, he mulls over these three key issues, all of which will be discussed at the impending meeting: product profitability; adding oil pumps to the product range; and the potential to acquire Stewart Ltd. Given that David Jenson wants to be as prepared as possible for the important discussions that will take place, as he drifts off to sleep he decides that he will ask Nicola Bradley, an independent consultant and good friend, to look at these matters.

Required

As Nicola Bradley, draft a report to David Jenson in order to provide him with some perspective on the above issues. To help you in this matter he has provided all the material that forms part of this case study. David Jenson requests that your report should include the following.

Question 1

With respect to the product profitability report:

(a) A calculation, utilising the information contained in Appendices 1, 2 and 3, of the costs of the three products emanating from an ABC system (using Lucy Green's early ABC workings information).

(14 marks)

(b) An explanation of the reasons for any significant differences in product costs that arise between the current costing system and the ABC system.

(8 marks)

(c) On the basis of your analysis, comments on the product profitability report and its strategic significance (he would particularly welcome observations relating to product pricing and product emphasis).

(12 marks)

Question 2

Issues to be considered by Jenson in a decision on whether or not the present costing system should be changed to one utilising ABC.

(6 marks)

Question 3

With respect to the possible use of target costing:

(a) A calculation of the target cost of an oil pump utilising Jenson's present costing system.

(4 marks)

(b) A brief commentary on why Lucy Green may have concerns regarding this calculation.

(4 marks)

(c) Some views on the advantages of target costing compared to the existing costing and pricing system as a basis for informing pricing and production decisions.

(8 marks)

Question 4

With respect to the potential acquisition of Stewart Ltd:

(a) An estimated valuation of Stewart Ltd using a net assets based method and an earnings based method. Briefly outline the assumptions and limitations of each method used.

(14 marks)

(b) A calculation of an appropriate discount factor for future expected cash-flows approximated by the adjusted cost of equity of Pepper's Parts Ltd (see Appendix 4) as calculated using the Capital Asset Pricing Model.

(6 marks)

(c) A calculation of the discounted payback period of the investment in Stewart Ltd using future cash-flows based on your valuation in part (a) and the discount factor calculated in part (b).

(6 marks)

(d) A commentary on the qualitative factors which should be considered by Jenson in making an offer to Stewart Ltd.

(10 marks)

(e) Any issues which should be addressed in due diligence to be carried out on Stewart Ltd.

(8 marks)

Total 100 marks

Appendix 1: Abstract from Product Profitability Analysis

Actual and Standard Margins Per Unit/Sales Volume Variances – Six Months January – June

	Brake Discs	Cam Shaft Kits	Catalytic Converters
Standard unit cost:			
Direct material	€27	€33	€510
Direct labour	€75	€45	€30
Overhead (€30 per direct labour hour)	€150	€90	€60
	€252	**€168**	**€600**
Budgeted selling price	€420	€280	€1,000
Budgeted margin %	40%	40%	40%
Year to date:			
Actual selling price	€380	€286	€1,200
Actual margin %*	34%	41%	50%
Sales volume variance as % of budgeted sales	5% A	1% A	25% F

*Actual margin is actual selling price minus standard cost.

Appendix 2: Overhead Absorption Rate for Current Year

	Brake Discs	Cam Shaft Kits	Catalytic Converters	Total
Budgeted production and sales in units	57,143	35,714	6,000	
Direct labour hours per unit	5	3	2	
Total direct labour hours	285,715	107,142	12,000	**404,857**

Production Overhead:

Supervision of direct labour	€900,000
Other labour-related overhead	€738,816
Machine depreciation	€2,400,000
Machine running costs	€700,000
Engineering set-up costs	€1,640,000
Quality inspection costs	€1,566,894
Material receipt and handling costs	€4,200,000
Total	€12,145,710

Overhead absorption rate = $\dfrac{€12,145,710}{404,857}$

= **€30 per direct labour hour**

Appendix 3: Summary of Chief Accountant's Early ABC Workings

Cost Pools and Cost Drivers:

Cost Pool:	Cost Driver:
Supervision of direct labour	No. of direct labour hours
Other labour-related overhead	No. of direct labour hours
Machine depreciation	No. of machine hours
Machine running costs	No. of machine hours
Engineering set-up costs	No. of machine set-ups
Quality inspection costs	No. of quality inspections
Material receipt and handling costs	Value of material used and purchased

Total Consumption of Each Cost Driver by Each Product:

	Brake Discs	Cam Shaft Kits	Catalytic Converters
Direct labour hours	285,715	107,142	12,000
Machine hours	114,286	107,142	60,000
Number of machine set-ups	200	200	500
Number of quality inspections	100	150	300
Value of direct material used	€1,542,861	€1,178,562	€3,060,000

Appendix 4: Further Information on Stewart Ltd

Extract from Financial Statements for Year Ended 31.12.XX

	€000s
Profit before interest and tax	470
Interest	65
Profit before tax	405
Tax	125
Profit after tax	280

	€000s
Intangible assets	
Capitalised R&D expenditure	150
Non-current assets	
Premises (Castle St, Enniskillen)	1,100
Manufacturing Equipment	350
	1,450
Current assets	
Inventory	250
Trade Receivables	150
Cash & Cash equivalents	100
	500

Appendix 4 (continued)

Current liabilities

Bank Overdraft	200
Creditors	450
Taxation	125
	775
	1,325
Ordinary Share Capital (200,000 €1 shares)	200
Revenue Reserves	1,125
	1,325

Other Information

- 45% of the shareholding of Stewart Ltd is held by Graham Stewart, a further 25% by his wife and 15% each by their two children.
- Independent valuation indicates that premises are overvalued by approximately €250,000.
- There may be a possibility of selling off the kit building and servicing division, which would realise approximately €600,000. This division includes €210,000 of net assets and generates approximately €50,000 per annum.
- Some cost synergy would be expected after initial redundancy costs of €120,000. A combined management and administrative function is estimated to save €40,000 per year. In addition, combined marketing and strengthening of the brand, plus some other incidental savings, is expected to lead to profit growth of 8% per annum after year one.
- The price/earnings ratio of a similar company (Pepper's Parts Plc) is 9. There are some differences between Jenson and Pepper's Parts. Pepper's Parts does not have such a strong net asset backing; is less liquid; and has not experienced such stable growth as Jenson over recent years.
- The beta value of Pepper's Parts Plc is 1.4. The risk profile of Pepper's Parts Plc is similar to that of Stewart Ltd as both companies are involved in component production and servicing.
- The current rate on government securities is 4% and the market risk premium is currently 6%.
- The tax rate can be assumed to be 30%.

Case 38
Malvern Limited

**Ciaran Connolly and Martin Kelly,
Queen's University Belfast**

You have just been appointed as manager in the Business Services Division of Healy Financial Consultants. As part of your new role you will be providing support and advice to small and medium businesses on a range of financial issues. One of the most important clients requiring your attention is Malvern Limited.

Background

Malvern Limited, a Belfast-based manufacturing company, was established some 20 years ago by Bill Malvern, a talented and flamboyant engineer, with the proceeds of an attractive early retirement package. Bill worked tirelessly to grow the business and, until his retirement in 2XX0, the company manufactured a range of high-quality products, all of which were designed by Bill. In the 10 years before his retirement, Bill groomed his only son, Philip, to take over the business, but when he did succeed his father in 2XX0, Philip did not have the same enthusiasm as his father and never settled into the role. Consequently, much to the disappointment of Bill, Philip decided to leave the company in late 2XX2. Bill, who was the chairman and major shareholder in Malvern Limited at that time, immediately appointed Robert Malvern, his grandson, to run the company. Robert had always been very close to his grandfather and, despite his young age and impetuous nature, had been involved in a number of successful business ventures prior to joining Malvern Limited, some of which had been partially funded by Bill.

Over the next two years, Robert significantly rationalised the activities of the company, reducing the workforce and eliminating all but one of Malvern Limited's products. Robert purchased Malvern Limited from his grandfather at the end of 2XX4, but he soon became restless and, in order to fund other new business ventures, decided to sell the company to Kate Black. It is now the beginning of May 2XX6 and Robert and Kate have agreed a date of sale of 31 May 2XX6, subject to Kate satisfactorily completing her review of the business.

The Product

Malvern Limited now manufactures a single product for the European haulage industry: a quick-release towing mechanism that has proved very popular with British and Irish hauliers because it aids towing stability and enables easy coupling and de-coupling of loaded trailers. The towing mechanism, which was initially developed by Bill Malvern, has to be manufactured to stringent quality and safety standards. There is potential, however, to modify the mechanism to produce a less flexible but much stronger tow bar for use by the Ministry of Defence (MOD).

The Company's Resources

Malvern Limited is situated on the outskirts of Belfast, with easy access to the main arterial roads in and out of the city. The company owns land, part of which contains the factory and administrative offices and part of which is currently undeveloped. The land was purchased some 15 years ago and is potentially worth much more than its current balance sheet value, depending upon whether approval could be obtained for commercial or residential redevelopment. The factory and administrative offices are large and in a reasonable state of repair, and there is scope to expand production within the existing factory building, if necessary.

Unfortunately, the machinery used in the manufacture of the towing mechanism is old and in need of immediate replacement, at a cost of approximately €130,000. The old machinery could be retained as back-up, since it has no resale value and there is sufficient space to store it.

Apart from Robert, Malvern Limited currently employs four permanent staff, hiring temporary and short-term contract labour when required. Fred, the factory supervisor, has been with the company since he left school and is due to retire in two years' time. He dislikes change and can be difficult to work with. Two of the other four permanent employees are Gary, a young enthusiastic operative who joined the company two years ago, and Tony, the accounts assistant who joined six months ago.

The Company's Systems

Tony is a bright, resourceful employee and since joining Malvern Limited has begun to develop the company's budgeting and reporting systems. Traditionally, little importance has been placed upon the preparation of budgets, management accounts or reports. This largely stems from the hands-on role adopted by Bill when he was involved with the company. Philip had little interest in developing the company's systems, while Robert is inclined to take the view that if he can see the men working diligently in the factory, then business must be fine. At present, production levels tend to be kept at a constant rate, regardless of demand, and purchases of raw materials are made on an ad hoc basis. It is mainly by dint of good luck rather than good management that sufficient raw materials are available, although it has become accepted practice to carry high levels of raw materials and towing mechanisms as there is adequate storage space in the factory.

The Competitive Environment

Malvern Limited is one of only a few British and Irish companies which manufacture the towing mechanism. While there are only three manufacturers of the type of vehicle that uses the company's towing mechanism, these vehicles are purchased by a large number of hauliers throughout Europe. Following a short period of sluggish sales, sales of the towing mechanism have been fairly constant over the last two years.

Future Prospects

Kate is optimistic about the company's prospects, believing that, if the company can keep pace with changes in the industry, demand for the towing mechanism will increase considerably in the medium to long term. Furthermore, having examined the financial information prepared by Tony, Kate is confident that the budgeted balance sheet as at 31 May 2XX6 is a reasonable assessment of the company's assets and liabilities on this date (see Appendix 1). She has negotiated a €30,000 overdraft facility to be available to the company from 1 June 2XX6, the date from which she takes over as owner. However, the bank has stated that any further borrowing by Malvern Limited will have to be supported by appropriate detailed budgeted information. Kate is concerned that as the business expands, the gearing levels will increase and she is unsure as to what balance of short-term and long-term debt would be appropriate for Malvern Limited.

Kate has some accounting experience and, with Tony, has gathered some data (see Appendix 2) from Robert and the company's records to enable budgets to be prepared for the four-month period to 30 September 2XX6.

Credit Terms

All sales are on credit and two months' credit is allowed. All purchases of raw materials are on credit and are paid for one month following delivery. Wages, variable and fixed overheads are paid in the month in which they are incurred.

At a recent Investors in People awards evening, Kate got into a conversation with an old school friend who is running a successful business in London, manufacturing solar panels. He suggested that she should look at the possibility of factoring receivables in order to help cash-flow at the early stages of growing the business. Kate has since contacted a factoring company, which has agreed to take over the administration of Malvern Limited's receivables on a non-recourse basis for an annual fee of 1% of turnover. Kate estimates that monthly sales for the eight months to 31 May 2XX7 will be approximately 115 towing mechanisms per month, with the selling price remaining at €300 per towing mechanism. On 1 October 2XX6 the factor would advance 80% of the book value of receivables as at 30 September 2XX6 at an annual rate of 1% above the company's overdraft rate, which is currently 4%. The factor expects to reduce the average receivables period to 30 days. Kate estimates that this will save an average of €2,000 per year in administration costs.

Purchase of New Machinery

Subject to the sale of the company being agreed, Kate has purchased new machinery at a cost of €130,000, with delivery and installation in June 2XX6 and payment in the following month. On 1 July 2XX6, the company will issue 10% debentures to the value of €150,000, with the €150,000 being credited to the company's bank account on the same date. Debenture interest is paid annually in arrears, with repayment due in June 2X11.

Kate is also seriously considering the purchase of a second machine, the 'Airtow', which she believes will enable Malvern Limited to produce a new specialised tow bar mechanism for the MOD. This will be used primarily by the Royal Air Force. Tony has produced some figures (see Appendix 3), which are based on the company raising funds via a bank loan at a fixed rate of 6% (before tax) per annum in 2XX7. It is envisaged this contract will last five years. Tony has informed Kate that the company has historically assessed investment projects using the accounting rate of return (ARR) approach. Malvern Limited pays taxation at 30% per annum, payable in arrears.

Depreciation June – September 2XX6

Buildings	€500
Machinery (including depreciation on new machinery)	€16,000
Vehicles	€5,500

Required

Prepare a memorandum for Kate Black which addresses the following issues.

Question 1

(a) Prepare the raw materials budget and the finished goods budget for each of the four months from June to September 2XX6 inclusive. Each budget should be expressed in either kilograms or towing mechanisms, as appropriate.

(8 marks)

(b) Prepare the sales revenue budget and production cost budget for each of the four months from June to September 2XX6 inclusive, and calculate the budgeted closing inventory, receivables and payables as at 30 September 2XX6.

(8 marks)

(c) Prepare the cash budget for each of the four months from June to September 2XX6 inclusive. (Ignore taxation.)

(7 marks)

(d) With reference to the cash budget you prepared in (c) above, discuss how cash-flow problems can arise and suggest methods for easing cash shortages.

(4 marks)

Question 2

Kate wishes to use the budget information for monitoring and controlling purposes. Describe how Kate might use:

(a) the budget to monitor and control the company's activities (it should also identify the tasks which Kate might require Tony to undertake in implementing the process); and

(5 marks)

(b) a responsibility accounting approach (it should also highlight some of the problems that she might encounter in doing so).

(5 marks)

Question 3

(a) Evaluate whether Malvern Limited should proceed with the investment in the Airtow machine. (You should justify any assumptions made.)

(14 marks)

(b) Outline the problems in continuing to use the accounting rate of return (ARR) for appraising projects.

(3 marks)

(c) Assuming Malvern Limited was able to lease the Airtow machine for five annual payments of €94,500, recommend whether the company should lease or buy the machine.

(6 marks)

(d) Outline what qualitative factors the company should consider before making a final decision to acquire the Airtow machine.

(5 marks)

Question 4

Prepare a budgeted income statement for the four months to 30 September 2XX6 and a budgeted balance sheet as at 30 September 2XX6. (Ignore taxation and your decision in Question 3.)

(15 marks)

Question 5

(a) Using the information you prepared in Question 4 above, calculate the cash operating cycle (in days) as at 30 September 2XX6. Comment on the significance of the cash operating cycle in relation to working capital management.

(4 marks)

(b) Determine whether Malvern Limited should accept the factor's offer.

(6 marks)

(c) What are the advantages to Malvern Limited of factoring its receivables?

(4 marks)

(d) Discuss the main issues Malvern Limited needs to consider when determining an appropriate mix of long-term and short-term debt.

(6 marks)

Total 100 marks

Appendix 1: Budgeted Balance Sheet of Malvern Limited as at 31 May 2XX6

	€ Cost	€ Accumulated Depreciation	€ Net Book Value
Non-current Assets			
Land and buildings	120,000	(20,000)	100,000
Machinery	50,000	(44,000)	6,000
Vehicles	52,000	(16,000)	36,000
	222,000	(80,000)	142,000
Current Assets			
Inventory of raw materials (100 kgs)	4,000		
Inventory of finished goods (110 towing mechanisms)	12,100		
Trade receivables (April €5,900 and May €13,100)	19,000		
	35,100		
Non-current Liabilities			
Trade payables for raw materials	(3,400)		
Bank overdraft	(17,250)		14,450
			156,450
Equity			
€1 ordinary shares			100,000
Retained earnings			56,450
			156,450

Note: finished goods inventory is valued at marginal cost for budget purposes.

Appendix 2: Estimated Production Data

Selling price per towing mechanism	€300
Materials usage per towing mechanism	1 1/2 kgs
Cost of materials per kg	€40
Production wages and variable overheads per towing mechanism	€70
Fixed overheads per month	€3,500

	June	July	August	September
Sales of towing mechanisms	120	125	115	100
Production of towing mechanisms	110	130	116	90
Purchases of raw materials (kgs)	150	160	150	140

Appendix 3: Airtow Machine Projections for Year Ending 31 May

	2XX7 €	2XX8 €	2XX9 €	2X10 €	2X11 €
Sales	200,000	220,000	290,000	290,000	210,000
Materials	(40,000)	(44,000)	(60,000)	(60,000)	(40,000)
Labour	(50,000)	(56,000)	(60,000)	(60,000)	(50,000)
Other costs	(10,000)	(10,000)	(10,000)	(10,000)	(10,000)
Depreciation	(80,000)	(80,000)	(80,000)	(80,000)	(80,000)
Operating profit	20,000	30,000	80,000	80,000	30,000
Loan interest	(27,000)	(27,000)	(27,000)	(27,000)	(27,000)
Profit before taxation	(7,000)	3,000	53,000	53,000	3,000

Tony believes that because the average pre-tax profit from the Airtow is projected to be €21,000 and the average investment is €250,000, this represents a return greater than the 6% cost of finance.

Tony has also gathered the following additional information in relation to the project.

(i) The Airtow will cost €450,000. It will be sold for an estimated €50,000 on 31 May 2X11. Unlike the current machine, the Airtow will attract capital allowances at the rate of 25% on the reducing balance method.
(ii) Labour will be employed specifically for work on this project and will be paid only for the hours they work.
(iii) 'Other costs' in the schedule represent a share of Malvern's general administration costs.
(iv) Incremental fixed production overheads of €1,000 per annum have been excluded from the above schedule.
(v) It is estimated that the nominal expected return required for this type of project would be in the region of 10% (after tax).
(vi) The working capital requirement for this project will represent around 10% of annual sales. This needs to be in place by the beginning of the year concerned, and it will be released at the end of the project.
(vii) Tony has forecast the following inflation rates:

Selling price	4% per year
Labour costs	2% per year

Case 39

Bolt Industries

Noel Hyndman and Danielle McMahon,
Queen's University Belfast

The Company

You (Sonia O'Hare) have recently been appointed finance director of Bolt Industries, a privately owned, family-operated trailer manufacturer. The company was founded 20 years ago by the eccentric, yet brilliant, Crawford Bell, who still maintains a controlling interest, is chairman of the board of directors and was responsible for your appointment. However, nowadays Crawford only fulfils a part-time role and spends considerable time away from the company on his various outside interests (which include motor cycling on his Harley Davidson, playing hockey as a demon forward in the fifths at Downpatrick Hockey Club, and working in the Ukraine helping to build houses for disadvantaged communities with Habitat for Humanity).

As for the company he established, Bolt Industries designs and manufactures dry freight vans, flatbed trailers, refrigerated vans and curtain-sided trailers. It is the largest producer of refrigerated vans, and the third-largest trailer manufacturer, in Ireland. This position is a result of management's focus on providing innovative solutions to customer problems. It has invested heavily in research and development to ensure that its products are at the leading edge of available technology.

Budgeting and Standard Costing System

Bolt Industries operates linked standard costing and budgetary control systems. Management accounts, which are reviewed at monthly board meetings, are produced from the system, and these analyse variances by cost type for each major product. The budgeting cycle begins two months before the commencement of the financial year and the completed budget is normally submitted to the board of directors by the third week in December, when some final 'tweaking' may occur. Traditionally, the budget has been developed by three key members of staff (the finance director, sales director and production director). A number of meetings between the three directors are arranged for November and December, where various scenarios are developed and budget iterations made. The key information for budget preparation has tended to be the sales forecast, and once sales figures for each product line are agreed, the production director and finance director take responsibility for the completion of the other budgets.

Establishing an appropriate sales budget has been problematical in the past. Budgeted volumes for products and budgeted sales prices have been difficult to establish with any degree of accuracy. The market for many of the company's products has become quite competitive, with imported trailers from Eastern Europe being increasingly available at very keen prices (although quality and service with respect to these is often much lower than that with Bolt's products). In addition, establishing an appropriate product and price focus in the budgeting process has been difficult given the absence of any systematic strategic planning procedures within the company. Rolling strategic planning was discontinued several years ago because the external environment was so difficult to predict, particularly in the areas of emerging technology, health and safety issues, and competitive pressures. Since then it has been left to the sales director to come up with sales estimates and target prices at budgeting time. This he does through personal judgment, particularly relying on previous sales trends over the last few years to influence such judgment.

Sales budgets provide an important target for sales staff, with the achievement of these being linked to annual bonus payments. The sales budget is profiled on a monthly basis and broken down by product and by sales representative. While detailed information is produced each month comparing actual sales against budget (by product and by sales representative), annual bonuses are awarded to the entire sales team (including the sales director) on the basis of total annual sales against total annual sales budget at the end of the year. The argument for using a team-based bonus is that the sales team should be rewarded collectively for their effort and this approach encourages team spirit and co-operative effort. It is interesting to note that over the last few years, when sales have increased quite significantly (and the market for trailers has been buoyant), the increase in the sales budget has been quite modest. Sales budgets have been viewed throughout the company as being quite 'soft', although the sales director argues that this provides an essential ingredient to increase motivation and points to the sales growth as evidence of this. The net result of this is that substantial bonuses have been achieved by the sales team.

Once the sales budget has been finalised, production, selling and administration budgets are prepared. These are then introduced into the overall budgeting framework to produce a budgeted income statement, balance sheet and cash-flow forecast. Over the last number of years, this has produced a satisfactory level of budgeted net profit and positive cash-flow and although variances arise, the company has enjoyed acceptable profits and a comfortable cash position. However, it is thought that, given recent upward pressure on international interest rates, belt-tightening may soon be required. Generally, budgets for non-production overheads have not received much attention in the budgeting process, largely being increased in line with the sales budget. However, given anticipated future pressures, it is proposed that in the incoming year budgets for advertising and training be reduced by 15%, while investment in research and development be reduced by 25%.

Many of the production costs used in budget preparation flow from the standard costing system, which was established some years ago. Features of the system include:

- quantities of material and labour for all products were set three years ago and although design and production processes have been modified slightly, the unit quantities have not been changed;
- prices for the materials and rates for labour were set at the same time (three years ago) and have been increased each year in line with the retail price index;
- variances are reported in the management accounting package that is used to report to board members within a few days of the month end, with the cost centre managers receiving the information several days later. In reality, few cost centre managers pay particular attention to variances, although some of the figures are quite substantial.

Possible Expansion

The production director is keen to expand the company's product range and has been encouraging the strategic acquisition of a forklift truck manufacturer to augment its product offering. Many of Bolt's existing customers use forklift trucks in their businesses. Having researched the types of forklift used by Bolt's existing customers, the production director believes that a relatively small, light, electric forklift with a narrow chassis would be particularly attractive (given that for many of Bolt's customers space is at a premium and forklift trucks are not used continuously throughout the working day).

Bolt has identified two possible acquisition candidates (both in North America): Boucher Forklifts (based in Ottawa, in Canada); and Jackson Engineering (based in Tallahassee, in Florida). These companies are both relatively young and have invested heavily in new technology in the exact area of forklift truck manufacturing in which Bolt is interested (although, to date, neither company has been profitable). In terms of market, to date both companies have targeted North America as their sole sales focus. Boucher Forklifts produces the Carleton forklift, which sells at C$14,000. Jackson Engineering produces the Wakulla forklift, a slightly lighter truck, with fewer standard features. It sells for US$11,250. The current exchange rates for the Canadian and US dollars are: €1 = C$1.4; and €1 = US$1.25.

While Bolt does not, at present, sell forklift trucks to its existing customers, the production director believes that such a product would complement its existing sales and, in the not too distant future, enhance profitability with the current customer base.

Other information relating to the possible acquisitions is as follows.

- Budgeted production, selling and administration costs associated with the Carleton (Boucher Forklifts) and the Wakulla (Jackson Engineering) for next year are presented in Appendix 1. These figures have been prepared by a team from Bolt

after discussions with the acquisition targets. In addition, they take into account efficiency savings from further investment by Bolt in new technology of C$20 million (Boucher Forklifts–Carleton) and US$25 million (Jackson Engineering–Wakulla) that is deemed necessary and would be invested immediately should either company be acquired.
- Budgeted sales volumes for next year are presented in Appendix 2. Estimating sales volumes is problematical for each of the products, particularly given the relative youth of both acquisition targets and their underdeveloped customer base. As a consequence, the management of each company has, after discussions with Bolt, estimated a range of possible sales volumes and their associated probabilities. Jackson Engineering is located near a number of potential customers in Florida and has already secured some orders for next year, and is fairly confident of others. The situation regarding Boucher Forklifts is less certain.
- At present, negotiations regarding acquisition are at a fairly advanced stage and Bolt's team believes that Boucher Forklifts could be acquired for about C$140 million, whereas Jackson Engineering would cost US$80 million.
- It is likely that, should either company be acquired, the management team would remain for some time.

Given that the purchase price will be denominated in either US or Canadian dollars, Crawford Bell met with Bolt's bank manager to discuss possible hedging strategies. However, Crawford has expressed concern that he has not been involved in such a transaction before and would like more information on what the strategies suggested by the bank manager would mean for Bolt. The bank manager has provided some prices and other information (available at Appendix 3) and has outlined four possible approaches: enter into a forward contract now to purchase the currency in six months time; enter into a money market hedge now; enter into an option now to purchase the currency in six months time; do nothing now but purchase currency at the spot rate in six months time.

Bolt does not have sufficient reserves to purchase either company outright and as Crawford is reluctant to dilute control by offering share capital, it is proposed to finance the acquisition through borrowing. With a holiday home in Florida, Crawford is aware that lending rates in North America are commonly lower than in the UK and Ireland and he suggests it may be beneficial to finance the acquisition by borrowing in either the USA or Canada.

Request for Your Views

As the most recent senior appointment to Bolt Industries, and therefore a person who would be well placed to provide a bit of objectivity, Crawford Bell is keen to have your views on what should be done in the company. Although somewhat detached from day-to-day management issues, he still wants the company to make decisions that will result in a healthy and prosperous future for the company and its employees. In appointing you to the position of financial director, he saw someone with business acumen and integrity who reflected his views on what a company should be about. Now, with the sun setting on the beautiful Zbruch River, Crawford laid his last brick for the day in the wall of a new house in Volochisk, Ukraine, and glanced across the water to Podvolochisk in the distance as he prepared to turn in for the night. He went to his bed content, knowing that at home you would be looking after the best interests of Bolt Industries, and he looked forward to his return from the Ukraine in two weeks time and an analysis from you on what direction the company should take.

Required

As Sonia O'Hare (the financial director of Bolt Industries), draft an internal memorandum to Crawford Bell dealing with the following issues.

Question 1

With respect to the budgeting and standard costing system (including the bonus system for sales staff), identify any possible weaknesses of the current system, explain the possible consequences of these weaknesses and make recommendations for improvement. Given that Crawford Bell likes focus and detests information overload, he asks that a maximum of eight major weaknesses be identified and the weaknesses, consequences and recommendations be presented succinctly in tabular format.

(32 marks)

Question 2

With respect to the possible acquisition of a forklift truck manufacturer and assuming the current rate of exchange continues to hold:

(a) Calculate the expected profitability of both the Boucher and the Jackson proposals, indicating also the range of possible profit outcomes, and comment on these figures.

(12 marks)

(b) Calculate return on investment and payback for the two options, clearly stating any assumptions that you make. Comment briefly on these figures.

(6 marks)

(c) Calculate the breakeven sales volume and sales value figures for Boucher and Jackson. Comment briefly on these calculations.

(6 marks)

(d) Based on the available information, suggest which, or whether either, of the proposals is attractive to Bolt Industries. The evaluation should draw on the above calculations, together with any relevant qualitative and strategic issues.

(12 marks)

Question 3

With respect to financing the acquisition of either Boucher or Jackson:

(a) Assuming that the acquisition takes place in six months time, calculate the outcome of the hedging strategies suggested by the bank manager. Based on your calculations and other factors you believe to be appropriate, recommend which strategy is optimal for the acquisition of Boucher or Jackson.

(20 marks)

(b) Comment on Crawford Bell's suggestion that it may be beneficial to finance the acquisition by means of a loan denominated in US or Canadian dollars.
(Calculations are not required.)

(12 marks)

Total 100 marks

Appendix 1: Budgeted Production, Selling and Administration Costs for Next Year

	Boucher Forklifts Carleton C$	Jackson Engineering Wakulla US$
Variable costs (per unit):		
Production	8,500	7,000
Selling	1,260	625
Fixed costs (total):	C$ (million)	US$ (million)
Production	27.8	25.8
Selling	7.2	3
Administration	10.4	7.1

Appendix 2: Budgeted Sales Volumes for Next Year

Boucher Forklifts – Carleton		Jackson Engineering – Wakulla	
Sales volume	Probability	Sales Volume	Probability
10,000	0.05	10,000	0.05
12,000	0.15	12,000	0.10
14,000	0.20	14,000	0.40
16,000	0.25	16,000	0.40
18,000	0.35	18,000	0.05

Appendix 3: Exchange and Interest Rates

	Canadian Dollar	US Dollar	
Current Spot Rate (buy)	1.4	1.25	
Six-month Forward Rate (buy)	0.08 premium	0.1 discount	
Estimated Spot Rate in six months (buy)	1.2	1.42	

	Canada	USA	UK/Ireland
Interest Rate – Borrowing	5%	6%	9%
Interest Rate – Deposit	3%	3%	4%

In addition, it is possible to purchase six-month buy options in both currencies.
Canadian Dollar: €1: C$1.29 at a premium of €200 per C$ 200,000.
US Dollar: €1: US$1.38 at a premium of €400 per US$ 500,000.

Case 40
Drumview Limited
**Ciaran Connolly and Martin Kelly,
Queen's University Belfast**

You are a recently qualified chartered accountant and have been appointed to work as an interim manager with Drumview Limited. Your contract is for three months and you are now into your fifth week with the company. You have gathered a considerable amount of information on the background, products, management accounting system, new contracts, costings and capital structure of the company. You have been asked to prepare a report for Christopher, the managing director of Drumview Limited, for presentation to the Board at the end of April 2XX6. Drumview Limited prepares financial statements to 31 December each year.

Background

Believing that there was a market for providing good quality wooden garden and patio furniture, two sisters, Claire and Emer Grant, established Drumview Limited some 15 years ago. After a few early teething problems, the company experienced moderate growth and, by 2XX0, Drumview Limited had developed a reputation for producing products that were above average in quality and price, but not necessarily 'top of the line'. In 2XX5 the company was refinanced with the help of a local venture capital group, which now owns 20% of the one million shares in issue.

Claire and Emer retired from the day-to-day running of the company in 2XX5, with Claire's son, Christopher, assuming responsibility for the daily management of the firm. Having worked in the company since he was a teenager, Christopher had a sound understanding of the various aspects of the business and he approached his new role with great enthusiasm and high hopes for the future. The venture capital company welcomed the appointment of Christopher and believed that he had the leadership qualities to take the business forward. He quickly established a system of standard marginal costing and budgeting, and agreed with the management accountant that stock was to be valued at standard marginal cost for internal reporting purposes. In addition, he introduced regular management team meetings in an effort to encourage shared aims and objectives by improving information flows. Recently, a rival competitor offered Christopher €1.4 million for the business, which got him thinking about the long-term objectives for the company. Christopher has also gained the support of the venture capitalist in taking forward a possible acquisition opportunity. He recently attended a Finance for Non-Financial Managers course and remembers having real difficulties understanding how the investment, financing and dividend decisions were interrelated.

The six members of the management team are:

1. The managing director of the company, Christopher;
2. The management accountant;
3. The buying manager;
4. The production manager;
5. The sales manager; and
6. The financial accountant.

One of the key matters for discussion at the quarterly management meetings are any variances arising between actual results and budgeted results, so that any problems can be identified as early as possible and new ideas can be explored. However, after an initial burst of enthusiasm and spirit of co-operation between the other members of the management team, Christopher is now beginning to become concerned that in recent meetings the various managers seem to have become more defensive about their own positions and are not considering the company as a whole.

Products

One of the products that Drumview Limited currently produces is an eight-seater patio table and chairs. The company produces this patio table and chairs to two specifications aiming at different markets: a standard untreated hardwood version, which is sold through a catalogue; and a deluxe pre-treated pine version, which is sold through independent garden centres. Production and sales of the eight-seater patio table and chairs have shown consistent growth over the past few years, and the deluxe version has become very popular in recent times. The deluxe version is currently one of the company's best-selling and most profitable products and Christopher is keen to maintain market share for this product.

Production Process

Most of the company's products are made from bought-in components that are assembled by the production department. A specialised wood-carving machine is used to make special patterns in the tables and chairs. The patio table and chairs are made almost entirely from wood, except that the chairs have a fabric seat and back. The production processes are the same for both versions of the patio table and chairs, with the two products being distinguished by the type and quality of wood used. Untreated hardwood is used for the standard catalogue version, while pre-treated pine is used for the deluxe version. Both products use the same type of fabric for the seat and back of the chairs. Drumview Limited has tried to build its reputation on developing strong community relationships, and the company has a policy of using local suppliers wherever possible. Currently all purchases of hardwood, pine and fabric are sourced locally.

Quarterly Reporting

Christopher, along with the management accountant, introduced a system of standard marginal costing so that budgets could be prepared and variance analysis readily carried out. At the start of each budget period, the management accountant sends a memo to each of the three departmental managers (buying, production and selling) detailing the planning parameters for the period. Each departmental manager then responds with his/her outline proposals. This is followed by a period of negotiation, after which the finally agreed departmental budgets are circulated to Christopher and each of the departmental managers. Christopher also receives a copy of the full master budget.

Progress against budget is discussed at the quarterly management meetings. In preparation for these meetings, the management accountant compares the actual results for the period with the planned budget and produces a variance analysis statement. Departmental managers receive details of the variances relating to their own departments and are invited to provide explanations at the management meeting. A full copy of the variance report is sent to Christopher, who also attends the quarter-end meetings. At recent meetings, the management accountant has begun to feel that each departmental manager holds him responsible for their shortcomings and is anxious to ensure that no blame is placed on the accounting role.

The Buying Manager

The buying manager recently warned the management accountant that the price of both hardwood and pine was due to rise in the current period. However, the management accountant did not take any account of this when setting the standard for the current period. Indeed, the buying manager believes that he has done very well to achieve the price that he has. Furthermore, the buying manager has found a new supplier for the untreated hardwood at a cheaper rate than the old supplier, but he had to make a bulk purchase to achieve this lower price. In addition, a new supplier for the fabric has also been found and the fabric has been purchased at a cheaper rate of €6.00 per chair; but as this lower price was only available for a short time, a bulk purchase had to be made.

The Production Manager

The production manager warned the management accountant that the time set for producing the eight-seater patio table and chairs was too tight, stating 'you cannot afford to make mistakes, and the men take great care handling and cutting the materials. The untreated hardwood that was purchased did not handle very well.' The production manager also told the management accountant that the increase in work rates that had originally been budgeted for was unlikely to be sufficient as the skilled labour did not like having to pack the table and chairs and therefore took longer over this, also wasting packaging. The production manager suggested that unskilled labour be hired for this purpose. He has also observed that the main wood-cutting machine was causing problems and there had been a recent increase in wastage and downtime.

The storeman has complained about the recent bulk purchases, as he was unaware of their arrival and the storeroom is so full that it is difficult to move around safely. Furthermore, the storeman had to work overtime in order to reorganise the storeroom. He was particularly frustrated as this recent incident occurred shortly after the buying department's bulk-buy of packaging materials.

The Sales Manager

During the period under review, industry prices as a whole increased. The policy of the sales department is to keep the price of the standard hardwood model slightly below that of the competition, largely because a new producer had just entered the market. In contrast, the price of the deluxe model was set higher than that of competitors in order to try and distinguish it from the rest.

The Management Accountant

The management accountant produced the budget from information given to him by the various departmental managers at the start of the period. He has a vague recollection that the buying manager phoned him to moan about prices, but is confident that nothing specific was mentioned or agreed. Budgeted and standard cost information (Appendix 1) and actual results for the quarter (Appendix 2) is provided.

The Financial Accountant

Due to problems identified with the current wood-carving machine, a contract has been placed with an American company to purchase a new machine for $0.5 million. This is the first time that Drumview Limited has entered into a contract with an overseas supplier. The delivery will take six months, with payment due on delivery. Details of the exchange rates are provided in Appendix 3. A columnist for the *Financial Times* is predicting that the $/€ spot rate in six months time may move to 1.22–1.25.

The financial accountant has simultaneously negotiated the sale of the old carving machine to a dealer in Switzerland. The dealer will take delivery of the machine in six months time and has agreed to pay SFr 0.2 million (Swiss francs) at that time. Christopher has suggested that a forward contract might be employed to reduce the transaction risk involved in the purchase of the new machine.

Expansion

Christopher is keen to expand the business further and has identified an opportunity to take over a small supplier of pine wood. The acquisition will probably be financed by a bank loan. Christopher is unsure what cost of capital should be used to appraise the acquisition. One of the partners in the venture capital company has suggested that the company's weighted average cost of capital should be used, but Christopher is adamant that this is too theoretical and unnecessary for a private company such as Drumview Limited. The financial accountant has gathered some information regarding the capital structure of the firm, which is presented in Appendix 4.

Required

Prepare a report for presentation to the Board of Directors that addresses the following issues.

Question 1

(a) Prepare a variance analysis statement that reconciles the budgeted profit figure to the actual profit figure for the quarter.

(22 marks)

(b) Suggest possible causes for the variances calculated.

(9 marks)

Question 2

(a) Describe the external and internal factors which you consider would have an important influence on the profitability of Drumview Limited.

(9 marks)

(b) Discuss the information that the management accountant would need in order to take account of the factors that you have described in Question 2(a) above. From what sources would he be able to obtain such information in his role as management accountant of Drumview Limited?

(9 marks)

Question 3

(a) Calculate the current price of the new machine based on the prevailing spot rate and advise the financial accountant how the exchange risk exposure for Drumview Limited could be hedged using a forward contract.

(5 marks)

(b) Advise the financial accountant on how a money market hedge could be employed to reduce the risk involved in selling the old machine.

(6 marks)

(c) Briefly explain the implications of using futures contracts or currency options in hedging foreign exchange risk.

(3 marks)

(d) Describe the procedure to be followed by the management accountant in formulating the budget for Drumview Limited, and discuss whether he should revise the budgets which have already been established.

(8 marks)

Question 4

(a) Calculate the weighted average cost of capital (WACC) for Drumview Limited.

(12 marks)

(b) Critically evaluate the use of the dividend valuation model (DVM) to calculate the cost of equity.

(5 marks)

(c) Comment on the use of the weighted average cost of capital (WACC) as a discount rate to appraise the potential acquisition of the supplier.

(5 marks)

(d) Explain how the investment, financing and dividend decisions within Drumview Limited are interrelated.

(7 marks)

Total 100 marks

Appendix 1: Budgeted Sales, Production and Standard Cost Information for the Eight-Seater Patio Table and Chairs for the Quarter to 31 March 2XX6

	Standard	Deluxe
Sales price	€150	€400
Sales units	1,300	1,500
Production units	1,300	1,500

There are no stocks held at the beginning of the period.

Standard costs per unit:

Untreated Hardwood Table and Chairs — €

Untreated hardwood (0.5 pallet @ €60 per pallet)	30
Fabric (1 sheet)	10
Labour (3 hours @ €8 per hour)	24
Packaging (1 roll @ €15 per roll)	15
Variable overheads	18
Total variable cost	97

Pre-treated Pine Table and Chairs — €

Pine (9 metres @ €10 per metre)	90
Fabric (1 sheet)	10
Labour (5 hours @ €8 per hour)	40
Packaging (1 roll @ €15 per roll)	15
Variable overheads	30
Total variable cost	185

Additional Information:
Variable costs are charged on a labour hour basis.
Fixed costs for the quarter are expected to be €70,000.

Appendix 2: Actual Results for the Quarter to 31 March 2XX6

	Standard	Deluxe
Sales price	€140	€420
Sales units	1,000	1,700
Production units	1,000	1,700

Raw materials used:

Hardwood – 700 pallets @ €56 per pallet

Pine – 15,500 metres @ €13 per metre

Fabric – 2,700 sheets @ €6 per sheet

Packaging – 2,800 rolls @ €15.20 per roll

Labour – 12,000 hours @ €10 per hour

Variable overhead costs for the quarter – €72,000

Fixed costs for the quarter – €80,000

Appendix 3: Foreign Currency Exchange and Interest Rates

Exchange Rates:

	($/€)	(SFr/€)
Spot	1.32 – 1.35	1.52 – 1.56
Six months discount	0.02 – 0.03	0.015 - 0.020

Interest Rates:

USA six months	1.5%
Switzerland six months	2%
Euro Zone six months	2.5%

Appendix 4: Drumview Limited – Capital Structure Information

Dividends over the last five years are as follows:

	€'000
2XX1	90
2XX2	100
2XX3	120
2XX4	130
2XX5	132 (Just paid)

Bank Overdraft:

This has varied between €50,000 and €150,000 and has a current interest rate of 6% per annum.

Redeemable Loan Stock:

€800,000 of 9% loan stock was issued at par to the venture capital group. It will be redeemed at a 2% premium in five years. The stock is unquoted, but the financial accountant suggests that it should be treated as risk-free, with a pre-tax return of 6% per annum. Drumview pays corporation tax at 30% per annum.

Case 41
Ravenhill Group Limited
Noel Hyndman, Queen's University Belfast

The Company

Ravenhill Group Limited (Ravenhill), with its headquarters in east Belfast, has developed into a major player in the design and manufacture of mobile screening, washing and recycling equipment for the quarry, mining and recycling industries. It commenced business in 1972 as a local manufacturing company serving a number of small quarries in Northern Ireland, but grew by a series of acquisitions over an extended period of time. It now has four divisions (the original company plus three divisions that were acquired when operating as separate manufacturing companies), each with a particular product focus.

Antrim Division

This division concentrates on producing dry screening machinery mainly for use in mining and gravel quarries.

Ballymena Division

This division typically serves similar customers to Antrim Division, but provides highly specialised equipment facilitating the industrial washing of mined or quarried material. This equipment removes particles of sand and soil, which can then be bagged and sold as a valuable end product in the agricultural and horticultural sectors.

Carryduff Division

This division produces industrial recycling equipment that can be used by organisations (mainly local government agencies and private recycling companies) to reduce the amount of demolition, household and commercial waste sent to landfill sites. These machines screen waste by size and weight, and valuable products can be recovered, resold and reused.

Downpatrick Division

This division produces specialised parts which are used by the other divisions in their manufacturing processes and which are sold directly to customers of the other divisions who need replacement parts.

The Issues

You (Celia Wright, the managing director of Ravenhill) have had much to occupy your mind lately. While the company has been very successful in recent years in terms of profit and return on investment, you have been somewhat concerned about the actions of individual heads of division and the manner in which they are evaluated and rewarded. As you participate in your twice-weekly spin class at the local university gymnasium (a necessary engagement to deal with the increasing stress of the job), you contemplate whether the way in which decisions are made and divisions and managers rewarded is really in the best long-term interests of Ravenhill. As Freddie, the rather muscular young man leading the class (and a person for whom you have somewhat of a soft spot) shouts to the spinners to crank up the tension, and as Snow Patrol's latest single blasts through the sound system, your mind wanders to three issues that have caught your attention of late (and which will be discussed at a forthcoming board meeting of Ravenhill). These are outlined below.

Investment Decisions within the Divisions

Ravenhill prides itself on encouraging divisional autonomy among the divisional directors. Managers have a fair degree of freedom to make a range of decisions, including investment decisions. Performance evaluation of divisions is largely based on return on investment and managers and staff within the divisions have a remuneration package with a performance bonus related to return on investment. In the early stages of the budget preparation for the coming year the following draft projections for the divisions have been produced.

Division	Sales €000s	Profit €000s	Investment base €000s
Antrim	€3,000	€400	€2,000
Ballymena	€2,400	€200	€1,500
Carryduff	€3,200	€920	€4,100
Downpatrick	€1,500	€320	€1,100

Subsequent to the production of these figures, a number of new projects are being considered by divisional management for the coming year.

Antrim Division: Antrim can invest €300,000 in new capital equipment (with an estimated life of 10 years) that is expected to generate sales of €350,000 in year one and €450,000 per annum thereafter. Additional working capital of €100,000 is also required on the project. Net profit margin on sales (before depreciation) will be 35%.

Ballymena Division: Ballymena can expand into a new sales area. This will require additional working capital of €100,000 and three new delivery vans (each costing €50,000). Vehicles are expected to have an economic life of four years. Sales of €400,000 are expected in year one (at a net profit margin of 20% before depreciation) and in all subsequent years.

Carryduff Division: Carryduff is considering investment in an environmentally-friendly addition to its power-generation facility in the division. The annual power cost is forecast for the coming year at €200,000, but could be reduced to €160,000 if this new investment is made. The cost of this equipment is €300,000 and it has an estimated useful economic life of 15 years.

Downpatrick Division: Downpatrick has the opportunity to open a new service facility for its customers. This will require capital investment of €300,000 (buildings €200,000, estimated useful life 20 years; machinery €100,000, estimated useful life 10 years) and working capital of €100,000. Additional sales of €300,000 are expected in year one and €400,000 per annum thereafter. A net profit margin of 30% before depreciation is expected.

Notes regarding calculation of return on investment:

- fixed assets are included at opening book value;
- all capital assets are depreciated on a straight-line basis assuming no residual value;
- investment in working capital is assumed to be a continuing investment until a project is complete.

Wider Performance Measurement Framework

You have become increasingly concerned about the company's current performance management system, which focuses solely on return on investment as a basis for judging divisional performance. After a recent presentation you attended regarding the importance of having a multi-dimensional measurement framework as a basis for supporting effective long-term focus in decision-making, you are somewhat of the opinion that the current measurement system needs changing. This presentation stressed the need for non-financial measures of performance. In particular, you realise that key factors in the success of the company have been related to 'keeping customers happy' and efficiency, innovation and quality in the production department. In addition, even when considering financial performance you are aware of potential drawbacks of using return on investment in decision-making situations and wonder whether residual income (or economic value added) would be better.

Replacement Cycle of Vans

At a recent monthly divisional managers' meeting, the issue of how long delivery vans should be kept before replacement has been aired. Each of the divisions owns and maintains a range of such vans. Until now there has been no central guidance to managers regarding this and each divisional manager has developed his/her own policy. Two of the divisions have a rule of thumb that vans should be replaced periodically at set intervals (one of the divisions replaces every two years, the other every three years) on the basis that annual mileage is relatively high and as vans age the maintenance and running costs increase. The other two divisions replace only when existing vans are no longer roadworthy. While recognising that older vans have higher maintenance and running costs, they are of the view that, given the high acquisition costs, it is cheaper to 'run the vans into the ground' (as the manager of the Ballymena Division commented – a man known for his frugal ways).

To get some perspective on this, Celia Wright has asked one of her staff to analyse, on the basis of the records held by the divisions, the costs relating to differing replacement cycles. For comparability purposes it has been decided to look at the records relating to a Renault Trafic van, a vehicle used in all of the divisions. On conducting the exercise, it has been found that the average annual mileage of such a van in each of the divisions is relatively similar. Information relating to the various replacement cycles is shown in Appendix 1. Ravenhill has estimated that its cost of capital is 8%.

The Task

At the end of next month you (Celia Wright), as managing director of Ravenhill, will provide the board with an analysis of these issues. As the spin class ends, and as you warm down to a slow one from Take That, your mind turns to the task ahead for the rest of the evening – to commence preparing a briefing note relating to these issues for the forthcoming meeting. Freddie calls you to stretch your hamstrings as a finale. You dismount your bike, collect your things and brace yourself for the evening's work. As you exit, you catch Freddie's eye. You think lightly: 'It is a truth universally acknowledged that a spin trainer in possession of a good bike must be in want of a wife' (or something like that; words familiar from your undergraduate English studies). But no time for that now; the briefing note awaits!

Required

As Celia Wright (the managing director), draft the briefing paper for the next board meeting. This should include the following issues.

Question 1

With respect to the investment decisions within the divisions:

(a) Calculations of the expected return on investment for each division (ignoring the new projects).

(4 marks)

(b) Calculations of the return on investment for each of the new projects (in both years one and two).

(16 marks)

(c) A discussion of whether the divisional managers are likely to accept or reject these projects.

(12 marks)

(d) Comments on the impact of this for the company as a whole.

(6 marks)

Question 2

With respect to the performance evaluation system currently used:

(a) A summary of the arguments for and against replacing the return on investment measurement with residual income. You should also show how this would impact on the decision regarding the new project in the Carryduff Division (years one and two only). Comment on the residual income numbers calculated.

(12 marks)

(b) A calculation of the net present value of the new project in the Carryduff Division. Comment on the figure calculated.

(6 marks)

(c) Outline two disadvantages of Ravenhill's present performance measurement system.

(4 marks)

(d) In respect of sales and production, suggest, giving reasons, two specific non-financial measures (one for each area) that might be useful to Ravenhill in divisional performance evaluation.

(12 marks)

Question 3

With respect to the replacement cycle of vans:

(a) Based on the information included in Appendix 1, a calculation of the optimal replacement cycle for vans.

(20 marks)

(b) An outline of four qualitative factors that might impact on the decision.

(8 marks)

Total 100 marks

Appendix 1: Acquisition and Running Costs Relating to Various Replacement Cycles for a Trafic Van

Time (Year)	0	1	2	3	4	5
Outlay (€)	15,000					
Operating costs (€)		4,100	4,300	4,700	5,200	5,800
Maintenance (€)			1,500	1,800	2,000	4,000
Value if sold (€)		8,400	6,000	3,500	2,000	300

Case 42

The Killyleagh Cycle Company

Noel Hyndman and Danielle McMahon,
Queen's University Belfast

Overview of the Company

The Killyleagh Cycle Company (KCC), a company set up in 1996 and located near Strangford Lough, manufactures and sells a range of cycles targeted at particular specialised segments of the market. The company is a division of the Down Industries Group (DIG) and central management of DIG has embraced decentralisation as a means of empowering local managers, controlling costs and improving profitability. Each of the divisions of DIG is judged independently on the basis of its return on investment, against a target of 15% (an approximation of DIG's cost of capital, detailed information relating to DIG's financial structure and the costs of various elements of financing is provided in Appendix 1). Within KCC, each of the range of cycles is manufactured in separate departments, and controls and evaluations are made at this level to ensure that, overall, the 15% target is achieved.

Given the growing leisure market, and the particular expertise and reputation that KCC has developed, turnover has risen rapidly with considerable sales growth in the UK and Ireland (KCC's main markets). While all of KCC's sales are to external customers, there is an element of interdivisional trading within the DIG, with KCC purchasing several parts and components from other DIG divisions. Two of KCC's products are:

- The Tollymore Tourer (TT) – a durable, value-for-money product for general road use by the occasional cyclist. The aluminium alloy cycle frame for this product is provided by another division of DIG (Eglinton Engineering and Electrical (EEE)). Although the TT is viewed favourably by customers, on a price basis it has come under pressure from imported cycles.
- The Donard Trekker (DT) – a high-specification, lightweight, carbon fibre-framed cycle targeted at the growing number of serious mountain bikers. It is a

high quality, high price product with few obvious rivals. It enjoys a particularly loyal following from local enthusiasts and by many mountain bike aficionados across the UK and Ireland.

Brian Thompson, KCC's chief executive and a keen cyclist himself, has been troubled by a number of matters surrounding the production and sales of the two products described above (the TT and the DT). These are outlined below.

The Tollymore Tourer (TT) Department

The TT is produced within KCC utilising a cycle frame provided by Eglinton Engineering and Electrical (EEE), another division of the DIG; KCC does not have the authority to purchase the frame from any other source. Each TT requires a cycle frame from EEE and KCC pays EEE €80 per unit (delivered). Brian Thompson has consistently complained that the transfer price that KCC has to pay for the frame is too high and undermines the ability of KCC to achieve the target return on investment. In discussions with the central management of DIG and with David Dunlop, the chief executive of EEE, it has emerged that:

- although EEE sells the cycle frame on the external market at €80, the department in EEE making the cycle frame is operating considerably below capacity. External sales (excluding transfers to KCC) are budgeted at 50,000 units next year;
- EEE's costs relating to the production of the cycle frame are: variable €40 per unit; fixed costs €1,500,000 per annum;
- investment in EEE that is related to the production of the cycle frame is about €3,500,000.

Brian Thompson has produced a budget for the Tollymore Tourer department of KCC for the next year and a summary of this is shown in Appendix 2.

KCC has a more modern plant in its Tollymore Tourer department than the average in EEE and Brian Thompson has expressed concern over the comparatively low return on investment in the Tollymore Tourer department of KCC (which has resulted in a reduced overall return on investment for KCC). The fixed assets of all divisions within DIG are valued on the basis of net book value based on the historic cost.

DIG has a policy of interdivisional transfers being made at market price. Brian Thompson complains about this and, on reflecting on the situation with respect to the TT, comments, "It's bad enough having my investment in fixed assets valued at recent (very high) acquisition costs, but having to pay such high prices for EEE's products is grossly unfair." Thompson is particularly sensitive to these issues as he is paid a bonus on his ability to surpass the target return on investment for KCC. The higher the return on investment, the bigger the bonus. At present he is considering action to improve the return on investment through cost-cutting. One option is to reduce research and development expenditure in the coming year by €100,000. This could be achieved by postponing a programme aimed at improving the quality and reducing the cost (through efficiency savings) of the TT. A second option would be to reduce staff training in the Tollymore Tourer department to a level below its present budget. This would save €50,000. Both of these fixed-cost expenditures are included in the budgeted fixed costs of €500,000.

The Donard Trekker (DT) Department

The DT is largely made within KCC. It is produced to a very high specification, with its frame manufactured using reinforced carbon fibre in order to reduce weight without sacrificing strength: the frame is a critical aspect of the DT and one that gives it competitive advantage over its rivals. At present one standard model is produced, although plans have been developed to add new models to suit more specific segments of the mountain bike market. The DT is priced at €1,600.

Manufacturing consists basically of three processes: production of the carbon fibre frame, assembly and finishing. The revolutionary manufacturing process related to the production of the carbon fibre frame has been developed within KCC and is highly labour intensive. In the first process, all ingredients to make the carbon fibre frame are mixed before individual layers are spun and bonded using extra-strength epoxy resin. Given the detailed specification, high level of precision required in preparing the carbon fibre mix, sophistication of the process and strict time requirements to produce and bond each layer of carbon fibre, frames have to be produced individually. Assembly includes hand additions to the frame, for example trekker wheels and gears, shock absorbers, sports pedals, disc brakes and a safety seat. Finishing consists of quality control checks and the packing of the cycle for dispatch.

To help control the process and also provide data to evaluate performance, several months ago the Donard Trekker department developed a standard cost system with respect to the production of the carbon fibre frame as a pilot study. Ronnie Hurst, the production supervisor, and Katy Little, KCC's accountant, agreed a standard cost for each carbon fibre cycle frame after lengthy consultation. However, after reviewing the actual performance relating to the production of the carbon fibre frames over several recent periods, Katy Little expressed her disappointment about the apparent lack of attention being paid to the standard costs and continuing unfavourable variances. Data relating to the standard cost of a carbon fibre cycle frame and the most recent month's actual results are provided in Appendix 3.

Before proceeding with further analysis, Little called Hurst to arrange a discussion of variances. She also told Brian Thompson: "Maybe we should look into an automated moulding operation. Although I haven't finished my analysis, it looks like there will be unfavourable variances again. Hurst insists that the standards are reasonable, then never meets them!"

Thompson seemed disturbed and answered, "Well, some variances are inevitable. Why don't you analyse them in some meaningful manner and discuss your ideas for automating the process with Hurst, who is an expert in carbon fibre production and whose opinion I respect." He continued, "While I am convinced that cost control is beneficial, it has not been the basis for our success in the past: that was driven by being innovative, responding to customers' needs and producing high-quality products. I am somewhat concerned that when we have sorted out this standard costing system (and I am convinced we will), we might have too much focus on costs and too little focus on other factors that really bring us success."

Required

Brian Thompson has approached DIG's central management expressing concern about the above issues. Following a forthright discussion between Thompson and DIG's central management, where all of the above facts, figures and opinions were aired, the central management of the DIG has asked you, as an independent consultant, to write a report in order to provide them with some objective views on the above and other related matters. This will help them in their deliberations. In particular, your report should include the following.

Question 1

With respect to the Tollymore Tourer department:

(a) A calculation, utilising the existing transfer pricing system, of the budgeted rates of return by the Tollymore Tourer department and that part of Eglinton Engineering and Electrical producing aluminium alloy cycle frames, and a commentary on these figures.

(14 marks)

(b) A discussion of the suggestion that, as presently calculated, these rates of return figures may be misleading. On the basis of this, make recommendations as to changes in the transfer pricing system that you feel are appropriate. If your recommendations include a change in the transfer pricing system, calculate the impact of this change on the rates of return as calculated above (assuming no change in the investment base).

(16 marks)

Question 2

With respect to the Donard Trekker department:

(a) Calculations of material, labour and overhead variances relating to the production of carbon fibre frames for the month (to the extent that they can be calculated from the information supplied). Mix variances should not be calculated.

(16 marks)

(b) An outline of the possible reasons for the variances and of questions DIG group central management may ask Brian Thompson.

(8 marks)

Question 3

With respect to the 15% performance target set by DIG:

(a) A calculation of the weighted average cost of capital for DIG using the dividend growth model to calculate the cost of equity (the information contained in Appendix 1 should be used for this).

(22 marks)

(b) An outline of the limitations of using the weighted average cost of capital method.

(4 marks)

(c) A comparison of your answer in (a) above to the target that the company presently uses, in particular commenting on whether it is appropriate to continue using the 15% target.

(8 marks)

Question 4

Comment, including specific suggestions, if appropriate, on the advisability of expanding the performance measurement system to incorporate non-financial measures in the evaluation of DIG.

(12 marks)

Total 100 marks

Appendix 1: Information on Down Industries Group's Financial Structure

1. DIG has issued ordinary share capital of 1,000,000 €1 shares, presently trading at 250p per share (cum. div.).
2. DIG has declared a dividend of €250,000 for the year just ended. Over the past four years, dividends have increased year on year by an average of 4%, reflecting year-on-year increases in profitability.
3. DIG has also issued €1,500,000 of 8% preference shares, currently priced at €120 per cent, before dividend payment.
4. €1,000,000 has been issued in 12% irredeemable debenture stock and interest is due. The debenture stock has a current price of €95 per cent.
5. Net assets of the company are €6.4 million, including an overdraft of €300,000, however no other bank loans are held.
6. Tax is expected to remain at the current rate of 30% for the foreseeable future.

Appendix 2: Summary of KCC's Budget for the Tollymore Tourer for Next Year

	Tollymore Tourer Department (KCC)
Selling price per cycle	€120
Variable costs:	€
Direct material	10
Cycle frame from EEE	80
Direct labour	5
Variable overhead	5
Total variable costs per unit	100
Fixed costs per annum	€500,000
Demand at current selling prices	35,000 units
Maximum capacity	50,000 units
Investment in Tollymore Tourer department	€4,000,000

Appendix 3: Standard Costs and Actual Costs for the Production of a Carbon Fibre Frame

Standard Cost for a Frame:

Materials	Material A	12 square metres	@ €13.50	=	€162.00
	Material B	4 kgs.	@ €25.00	=	€100.00
Direct labour	Grade X	0.5 hr.	@ €13.50	=	€6.75
	Grade Y	1.0 hr.	@ €13.50	=	€13.50
Indirect costs	Absorb at €16.20 per frame*		@ €16.20	=	€16.20
		Total cost to produce a carbon fibre frame			**€298.45**

*The normal volume of operations for overhead derivation purposes was assumed to be 450 frames per month.

The estimated monthly indirect cost equation was:
Budget = €6.48 * frames + €4,374.

Actual Costs (Most Recent Month) for Production of 430 Frames:

Materials:

Purchased	6,000 sq. m Material A @ €12.50 per metre
	2,000 kgs. Material B @ €26.70 per kg.
Used	5,400 sq. m Material A
	1,900 kgs. Material B
Direct labour:	Grade X 210 hrs. @ €14.06 per hr.
	Grade Y 480 hrs. @ €13.50 per hr.
Overhead:	Incurred €7,425

Case 43
AerThomond plc

Antoinette Flynn and Mairead Tracey, University of Limerick

Overview of the Company

AerThomond (AT) plc is a well-established airline based in the mid-west of Ireland, with a low fares charter to Western Europe and North America. This airline was founded 20 years ago and has grown to become one of the largest airlines serving Europe, carrying 15 million passengers per annum to 28 cities across Western Europe and North America. The airline has weathered the downturn in the industry with limited cutbacks and redundancies. The management of the airline attributes its success to its continued dedication to high-quality customer service, delivered with a '*céad míle fáilte*' welcome on a budget fare! Industry analysts have keenly noted that the company's commitment to a stable work environment for all employees is a vital ingredient to the company's year-on-year success. Indeed, according to the company's website, its employees are afforded "*the same value, respect, and caring attitude within AerThomond that is shown to every AerThomond customer.*"

However, over the last year, AT has experienced a squeeze on its profit margins due to increased competition from other low-fare airlines (Ryanair and SkyEurope Airlines specifically) and a general fall in demand due to a global downturn. The recently appointed chief executive officer (CEO), Siobhan O'Brien, noted that AT share price has fallen over the past year by nearly a quarter and attributes that drop to increased competition in a more challenging market. The board of directors has decided that the company needs to cut uncompetitive routes and expand aggressively into Eastern Europe and the Balkans to remain viable in this industry.

This new strategic direction would require ordering at least 24 new B737-800 aircraft from Boeing, with delivery dates of 2X10 to 2X16. The goal is to grow the company to over 28 million passengers a year, flying to 40 cities in total, while providing a reliable and fun service for customers and employees alike. As part of this long-term course of action, the board of directors has decided initially to purchase five short-haul aircraft at a total cost of €15 million. In March 2XX9, the management team of AT met to discuss in more depth the proposal to purchase or lease five short-haul aircraft. There was general enthusiasm for this new strategic direction and the new aircraft were expected to generate an annual after-tax cash-flow of €3 million for 15 years.

AT Management Meeting

The initial focus of the meeting was to decide whether AT should borrow to finance the purchase of the aircraft or lease the aircraft. AT had €10 million in cash and marketable securities (see Appendix 1), but Donogh Moloney, the chief financial officer (CFO), pointed out that the company needed at least €10 million in cash to meet normal outflow and as a contingency reserve per annum. This meant that in the event of purchasing the aircraft, there would be a cash deficiency of €15 million, which the firm could cover by additional borrowing. The latest debt market information indicates that the current yield on AT debt is 5.71%. Irrespective of whether the company purchases or leases the aircraft, AT will have to lease an additional hangar at a cost of €108,000 per annum and employ eight additional crew and 10 maintenance staff at an annual cost of €450,000.

Prior to this meeting, Donogh had been in negotiations with various aircraft leasing companies and today he presented the best deal to the management group. GlobeAer plc was offering five new B737-800 aircraft for €4 million rental paid in advance annually, over five years. While Donogh agreed that €20 million did seem excessive, the staged nature of the lease agreement and the relatively small annual payments were very attractive, especially now that availability of finance is restricted. He was convinced that once the capital allowances were incorporated into the decision process, the lease deal would prove worthy. AT's capital allowances policy is applied on a straight-line basis, disregarding any residual value.

Siobhan swiftly pointed out that while she respected Donogh's expertise and opinion, the fact remained that Donogh had yet to present evidence to support his stance and therefore other financing options should not be ruled out at this initial stage. Donogh nodded in agreement, but was secretly confident that the €25,000 consultancy fee the company paid to cover the cost of negotiating and securing the lease deal would not be in vain. In addition to this fee, Donogh incurred travel and entertainment costs to the tune of €14,500 when he twice visited GlobeAer plc headquarters in Australia, to discuss the lease deal.

Recovering quickly, Donogh agreed with Siobhan and promised to have those figures to her before the end of the week. He stressed that while borrowing to purchase the aircraft is an option, the airline industry was subject to wide swings in profits and the firm should be careful to avoid the risk of excessive borrowing. He estimated that the current total debt to capital employed ratio was about 52% and that a further debt issue would raise the ratio to 55%, which is above the industry target debt ratio of 52%. He surprised the group by suggesting a stock issue in lieu of additional gearing. According to Donogh, the only downside of an issue was that investors might jump to the conclusion that AT management believed the stock was overpriced. Indeed, the CFO has calculated that the AT share price (ex-dividend) would be expected to fall by 10% after this share issue. Donogh had some concerns that a stock issue announcement might prompt an unjustified sell-off by investors.

To avoid this pitfall, he recommended that the company explain carefully to the shareholders the reasons for the issue. In order to increase the demand for the stock issue, Donogh suggested that the board should recommend an increase in dividend payment, bearing in mind that the current growth in dividends year on year is a steady 7.5%. According to Donogh, this dividend increase would provide a tangible signal of management's confidence in the future of the company, and would buoy up the issue. While admitting that the arguments were finely balanced and assuming that the lease deal wasn't viable, the CFO recommended an issue of stock rather than increase borrowing. This proposal was made in the context of AT's current equity price of €15.90 a share (cum dividend).

Throughout the CFO's presentation to the board, Siobhan O'Brien had a quizzical look and a permanent frown-line. Donogh was unsure whether this was Siobhan's normal countenance or whether she was signalling her concern. Siobhan was an accountant by profession and had risen through the ranks quickly, on the basis of her decisiveness and strategic thinking. From that perspective, Donogh was wary of her. Without waiting for comments from the board, Siobhan immediately cut across Donogh with her key concerns:

"Basically Donogh, these arguments cut little ice with me." I know that you're the expert on all this, but everything you say flies in the face of common sense. Why should we want to sell more equity when our stock has fallen over the past year? Our stock is currently offering a dividend yield of 6%, which makes AT equity an expensive source of capital. Indeed, if I recall my professional training correctly, equity finance is usually the last resort for companies seeking investment funding, as it is the most expensive source.

"Furthermore, in my opinion, increasing the dividend would simply make it more expensive. I really don't see the point of paying out more money to the stockholders at the same time that we are asking *them* for cash, although I think I understand where you are coming from theoretically. If we increase the dividend, we will need to increase the amount of the stock issue; so we will just be paying the higher dividend out of the shareholders' own pockets. I think that the type of shareholder attracted to AT isn't going to appreciate that tactic. You're also ignoring the question of dilution. It's not playing fair by our existing shareholders if we now issue stock for less than the current market price."

After further discussion and debate, the management meeting ended with a general agreement that the investment of €15 million was both worthwhile in principle and strategically in line with AT's long-term goals. However, there was no agreement about the source of funding and the item was postponed until the next management meeting in a week's time. Siobhan closed the meeting by saying, "Donogh, I don't want to push my views on this – after all, you're the expert. We don't need to make a firm recommendation to the board until next month. In the meantime why don't you get one of your newly recruited accountants to look at the lease deal and the other finance options?"

The AT Finance Team

Donogh was disappointed with the outcome of the management team meeting, but privately agreed that Siobhan had some valid points. Later that day in the executive lounge, Donogh had the opportunity to ask Siobhan to recommend an alternative course of action, which she willingly did:

> "How about this, Donogh? My calculations show that the debt ratio is only 41%, which doesn't sound excessive to me, so borrowing to finance this investment is a reasonable course of action. Given the current yield of 5.71% and with a tax break on the interest on borrowing, our real cost of borrowing is 5%. According to my calculations, that is about 80% of our current dividend yield, an attractive comparison, wouldn't you agree? Based on your figures, we expect to earn an accounting rate of return of 20% on these new aircraft. Obviously, if we can raise money at 5% and then, invest it at 20%, that's a good deal in anyone's language, wouldn't you agree?"

That night, Donogh mulled over Siobhan's comments, but some of her figures didn't gel with his appreciation of this deal and the current gearing status of the company. For instance, his figures showed that the company's current weighted average cost of capital is approximately 9%. Having said all that, Donogh was aware of a distant memory from his college days prompting him to consider the non-financial perspectives when translating corporate strategy into action. The next day Donogh called an emergency meeting of the AT finance department. The issues that Donogh wanted his team to address included an assessment of the lease or buy option, confirmation of the figures already put on the table by Siobhan, a review of the impact of the various sources of finance on the cost of capital and the management of this new strategic direction. Donogh would then be in a position to recommend whether the company should proceed with the investment. He should also be in a position to identify the optimal financing strategy for AT plc. Donogh has set out the following questions to be addressed by his finance team.

Required

Question 1 (read all parts before attempting the question)

(a) You have been commissioned by the CFO to, first, establish the financial viability of the proposed investment in five B737-800 aircraft, given the expected after-tax cash-flows and, secondly, to determine the attractiveness of the lease deal offered by GlobeAer plc. Write a report to Donogh Moloney explaining your recommendation, and support your position with detailed figures.

(i) In preparing your report, calculate the company's current weighted average cost of capital (WACC), assuming a corporation tax rate of 12.5%. Use the WACC figure to assess the attractiveness of the investment proposal.

(10 marks)

(ii) Next, determine whether AT should accept the GlobeAer plc lease deal or purchase the aircraft outright. For comparison purposes, assume that the firm would be able to borrow at its current rate and there is a time lag of 12 months for tax payments.

(14 marks)

(iii) As part of that report, outline the advantages and disadvantages of leasing versus the purchase of assets.

(4 marks)

(b) The board of directors of AerThomond plc has agreed a new strategic direction that has both tangible and intangible elements. They wish to grow the company, to service 28 million passengers a year, flying to 40 cities around the world, while providing a reliable and fun service for customers and employees alike. Given the financial and non-financial nature of these goals, the CFO is aware of the need for a strategic planning and management system that will translate this corporate strategy into action. Consequently, Donogh has assigned you to write a separate report recommending an appropriate system to measure and monitor AT's performance *vis-à-vis* this new strategic departure.

(20 marks)

Question 2 (read all parts before attempting the question)

(a) Using your answer to Question 1, the information gathered from the financial statements of AT and the case study, write another report to the CFO recommending the optimal means of funding this project in order to maximise shareholder wealth. As part of the report, verify the CEO's and CFO's apparently conflicting figures, and calculate the new weighted average cost of capital. You can assume that AT can borrow the investment funds required via a term loan with comparable terms to existing debentures and that the increase in debt has no effect on the cost of equity. Comment on the appropriateness of using a company-wide weighted average cost of capital figure to assess individual projects.

(12 marks)

(b) As part of your report, elaborate on the significance of the following statement from the CEO, Siobhan O'Brien – "Equity finance is usually the last resort for companies seeking investment funding, as it is the most expensive source" – in relation to Miller and Modigliani's (1958) theory of capital structure.

(20 marks)

(c) Finally, in your report, critically discuss the different theoretical arguments that the CFO and the CEO allude to in the following statements (and incorporate this discussion into your final recommendation):

Donogh recommended that: "*This dividend increase would provide a tangible signal of management's confidence in the future of the company and would buoy up the issue.*"

Siobhan argued that: "*If we increase the dividend, we will need to increase the amount of the stock issue; so we will just be paying the higher dividend out of the shareholders' own pockets.*"

(20 marks)

Total 100 marks

Appendix 1: Summary Financial Statements for AerThomond, 31 December 2XX8
(Figures are book values, in millions of Euro)

Extract from Latest Balance Sheet

	€million	€million	€million
Fixed Assets			219.00
Cash and marketable securities		10.00	
Other current assets		56.00	
		66.00	
Current liabilities			
Bank debt	29.00		
Other current liabilities	10.00	39.00	27.00
			246.00
Long-term liabilities			
10% Debenture, due 2X20 (par €1,000)		100.00	
Equity and Reserves			
Ordinary share capital (par €12)	120.00		
Retained earnings	26.00	146.00	246.00

Extract from Profit and Loss Account

	€million
Gross profit	67.50
Depreciation	20.00
Interest	7.50
Pre-tax profit	40.00
Tax	5.00
Net profit	35.00
Dividend	9.00
Retained earnings	26.00

Case 44

Plastic Products

Michelle Carr and Derry Cotter, University College Cork

Overview of the Company

Plastic Products Limited is a large private company. The company has achieved excellent profit performance since incorporation 10 years ago, but in recent years the rate of annual sales growth has not been maintained. The board of directors is currently evaluating how this problem might be addressed.

Two alternative growth strategies are being considered. The first involves internal expansion by identifying capital projects to expand the company's existing sales level. Alternatively, Plastic Products Limited is considering a policy of expansion by means of the acquisition of other smaller companies with an established sales base.

Two alternative cost-management strategies are also being considered. The first involves focusing on continous improvement by introducing a just-in-time (JIT) manufacturing system. On the other hand, Plastic Products Limited is considering replacing its existing absorption costing system with an activity-based costing (ABC) system.

(a) Internal expansion

A number of capital projects are currently being examined. One such project is the proposal to commence production of a new plastic component, codenamed 'the Plastech'. Details are as follows.

- Machinery, costing €400,000, would have to be purchased immediately (i.e. on 31 July 2XX6). This machinery is expected to have a useful life of four years, at which point it is expected to have a residual value of €50,000.
- Capital allowances can be claimed at 20% per annum on a straight-line basis.
- Design costs will total €100,000, of which €70,000 has been paid, and a further €20,000 contracted for and payable at the end of July 2XX7.

- Sales are estimated at 60,000 units per annum for four years. The unit selling price of the Plastech will be €10 per unit.
- The unit contribution margin, before deducting depreciation on new machinery, and before deducting bad debts and discount, is expected to be 50%.
- Fixed overheads will be €150,000 per annum. This includes €30,000 of head office management charges.
- Stocks of the Plastech of 10% of the following year's sales volume are required. It should be assumed that stocks are valued on the basis of unit variable cost.
- Customers will receive three months credit on sales, and bad debts are estimated at 3% of sales. Alternatively, the offer of a cash discount of 2% for payment within one month would reduce bad debts to 1% of total sales. It is expected that 60% of customers would take up the offer of the cash discount.
- Plastic Products Limited will receive one month's credit from its raw material supplier. Raw materials represent 40% of total variable costs.
- Annual interest at 12% will be incurred in financing working capital requirements.
- Initial working capital requirements should be assumed to arise on 31 July 2XX6.
- Should this project be undertaken, an immediate saving of €60,000 redundancy costs would be made, and machinery which would otherwise have had to be scrapped at an immediate cost of €20,000 would now be utilised.

Sources of Finance

Plastic Products Limited has one million issued equity shares, with an estimated market value of €50 per share (ex-div.). Additional equity capital would be issued at a discount of 10% and issue expenses would amount to €3 per share.

Plastic Products Limited has a constant dividend payout ratio of 30% of after-tax profits.

Profits after tax in recent years have been as follows:

2XX1	€1,100,000
2XX2	€1,400,000
2XX3	€900,000
2XX4	€1,500,000
2XX5	€1,850,000

The company also has €15 million of 7% irredeemable preference shares. The estimated market value is €108 per €100 nominal and half a year's dividend is accrued.

Plastic Products Limited also has €10 million of 10% irredeemable debentures. The current market value is €118, including one year's accrued interest.

Leasing

Should Plastic Products Limited decide to proceed with the Plastech project, the machinery required on 31 July can be acquired by outright purchase, or alternatively it can be leased. Four lease instalments of €130,000 would be payable annually in advance. Plastic Products Limited has access to borrowed funds at a rate of 10%. If the new machine is leased, possession of the machine will revert to the lessor at the end of 2XX9.

(b) External Growth

As part of its alternative expansion route of 'growth by acquisition', Plastic Products Limited is currently examining the possible purchase of a small local company. Metal Fasteners Limited was founded in June 2XX1 by George Simpson, who is now considering selling the company, with a view to exploring other interests. A listed company engaged in the same sector of the metal industry had earnings of €10 million for the most recent financial year (forecast earnings for 2XX6 of €15 million). This company's share price was €2 per share when its results were released, and it has 50 million issued equity shares. Its P/E ratio has not changed significantly over the years.

An analysis of its financial position shows that Metal Fasteners Limited has a substantially higher debt equity ratio than the industry norm. This differential largely relates to a long-term loan of €500,000 raised by Metal Fasteners Limited on 1 December 2XX5, at a fixed rate of interest of 10% per annum.

The accounting policies used by Metal Fasteners Limited are typical of the metal industry, but the application of the accounting policies of Plastic Products Limited would increase annual after-tax earnings by €30,000. Should Plastic Products Limited decide to acquire Metal Fasteners Limited, once-off rationalisation costs of €200,000 will be incurred, but annual synergy benefits of €150,000 will be achieved. Plastic Products Limited will also be able to dispose of part of the premises of Metal Fasteners Limited for €480,000. This asset has a net book value of €180,000 and has been depreciated at 2% per annum on a reducing balance basis. The market value of the other land and buildings is €1.3 million.

A summary of financial information relating to Metal Fasteners Limited is outlined in Appendix 1.

(c) A JIT Manufacturing System

Plastic Products Limited is considering a number of cost-management strategies. One strategy is that the company adopts a JIT manufacturing system, which will make the manufacturing process more efficient and effective. It has been decided to assess the potential of the system on two existing product lines: Plasex and Plasent.

The budgeted details for next year are as follows:

	Plasex	Plasent
Direct materials	€126.00	€146.20
Direct labour	€56.00	€64.60
Total direct costs per unit	€182.00	€210.80
Budgeted production	37,500	37,500
No. of production runs	250	250
No. of orders executed	400	400
Machine hours	24,000	40,000

Annual overheads

	Fixed	Variable
Set-ups	€11,330	€3,000 per production run
Materials handling	€16,445	€500 per order executed
Inspection	€19,940	€4,000 per production run
Machining	€62,270	€20 per machine hour
Distribution and warehousing	€10,450	€700 per order executed

The introduction of the JIT system would have the following impact on both fixed and variable costs:

Direct labour	Increase by 10%
Set-ups	Decrease by 15%
Materials handling	Decrease by 15%
Inspection	Decrease by 15%
Machining	Decrease by 7.5%
Distribution and warehousing	Eliminated

(d) An ABC System

As part of its cost-management strategy, Plastic Products Limited is also considering switching to an ABC system. As finance director you are convinced that competitors are selling at prices well below their actual manufacturing costs. One competitor has offered the Plasone product at €10 per unit. This is €6 less than Plastic Products Limited's selling price for that product.

The following information outlines the manufacturing activities and costs associated with the two products for Plastic Products Limited:

	Plasone	Plaster
Sales price per unit	€16.00	€12.00
Sales units	100,000	20,000
Direct materials cost per unit	€1.75	€1.90
Direct labour cost per unit	€2.50	€1.25
Manufacturing overhead cost per unit	€6.35	€3.18

The existing absorption costing system allocates manufacturing overhead costs to products on the basis of direct labour hours. The estimated manufacturing overhead cost is €1,398,000. The following information on manufacturing overhead costs and activities has also been provided.

	Activity Cost Drivers	Activity Cost
Machine set-ups	No. of set-ups	€48,000
Machine depreciation	No. of machine hours	€350,000
Purchasing	No. of purchase orders	€420,000
Engineering	No. of engineering hours	€400,000
Material handling	No. of material moves	€180,000
		€1,398,000

(e) Additional Information

The following information should be assumed to apply in respect of Plastic Products Limited.

(i) The company pays corporation tax at 40%, one year in arrears.
(ii) The accounting year end is 31 July.

The following information should be assumed to apply in respect of Metal Fasteners Limited.

(i) The company pays corporation tax at 40%.
(ii) The company does not have any losses forward.

Required

As finance director of Plastic Products Limited, you are required to prepare a report for the board of directors relating to the company's desire to achieve increased growth in its level of sales and increased focus on cost management. Your report should specifically address the following issues.

Question 1

Internal expansion

In respect of the proposed 'Plastech' project, you are required to undertake the following analysis.

(a) Calculate the payback period, based on the net cash outflow at 31 July 2XX6.

(2 marks)

(b) Calculate the accounting rate of return.

(3 marks)

(c) Calculate Plastic Products Limited's weighted average cost of capital.

(4 marks)

(d) Recommend whether this project should be accepted should the internal expansion route be adopted.

(10 marks)

(e) Measure the extent to which the outcome of the project is sensitive to the level of fixed overheads.

(2 marks)

(f) Evaluate the alternative methods of financing the acquisition of the machinery on 31 July 2XX6.

(4 marks)

Question 2

External expansion

In respect of the proposed acquisition of Metal Fasteners Limited, you are required to prepare the following information.

(a) A valuation of Metal Fasteners Limited using both an assets and an earnings basis.

(10 marks)

(b) A recommendation as to what value would be considered appropriate, and the optimal manner in which the consideration package should be structured.

(4 marks)

(c) An evaluation of the alternative methods of financing the proposed acquisition.

(3 marks)

(d) A discussion of the current dividend policy of Plastic Products Limited in the light of the possible flotation of its shares.

(5 marks)

(e) An examination of the alternatives available to Plastic Products Limited to address the risk of an interest rate increase, should the acquisition of Metal Fasteners Limited be financed by borrowings.

(3 marks)

Question 3

JIT manufacturing system

In respect of the proposal to implement a JIT manufacturing system, you are required to prepare the following information.

(a) Outline the main features of a JIT philosophy.

(4 marks)

(b) Based on budgeted production levels, calculate the total annual savings that would be achieved by introducing the JIT system.

(5 marks)

(c) Assuming that Plastic Products Limited adopts the JIT system, and that the revised variable overhead cost per product remains constant (as per the proposed JIT system budget), calculate the profit-maximising price and output level for each product based on the following information:

(11 marks)

	Plasex		Plasent
Price	Demand	Price	Demand
€200	37,500	€220	37,500
€287	32,500	€280	30,000
€300	25,000	€325	22,500
€325	17,500	€375	17,500

(d) Outline to the management of Plastic Products Limited the conditions necessary for the successful implementation of a JIT manufacturing system.

(5 marks)

Question 4

An ABC system

In respect of the proposal to implement an ABC system you are required to undertake the following analysis.

(a) Calculate the unit product cost for Plasone and Plastor using the absorption costing system.

(4 marks)

(b) Calculate the unit product cost for Plasone and Plastor using an ABC system.

(6 marks)

(c) Comment on any conclusions which may be drawn from (a) and (b) that could have pricing and profit implications for Plastic Products Limited.

(5 marks)

(d) Outline why the existing absorption costing system, which uses direct labour hours, is a poor base for the allocation of overheads.

(7 marks)

(e) Explain why top management support is crucial when attempting to implement an ABC system.

(3 marks)

Total 100 marks

Appendix 1: Balance Sheet of Metal Fasteners Limited at 31 December 2XX5

	€'000	€'000
Fixed assets		
Land and buildings	1,100	
Plant and machinery	950	
Fixtures and fittings	200	
		2,250
Current assets		
Stocks	900	
Debtors	1,300	
Bank	150	
	2,350	
Current liabilities		
Creditors	800	
Taxation	824	
Working capital		726
Net assets		2,976
Financed by:		
Ordinary share capital		100
Revenue reserves		1,376
Ordinary shareholders' funds		1,476
Loans		1,500
		2,976

Income Statement of Metal Fasteners Limited for the Year Ended 31 December 2XX5

	€'000
Turnover	3,900
Cost of sales	(1,600)
Gross profit	2,300
Net operating expenses	(800)
Foreign exchange loss	(50)
Profit on ordinary activities before interest	1,450
Interest	(170)
Profit on ordinary activities before taxation	1,280
Taxation	(500)
Profit for financial year	780
Revenue reserves at 1 January 2XX5	596
Revenue reserves at 31 December 2XX5	1,376

Should Plastic Products Limited proceed with the acquisition of Metal Fasteners Limited, there are different views as to how the purchase should be financed. The Board would prefer to fund the acquisition with further debt, but there has been speculation that the company's bankers would apply restrictive covenants, and that Plastic Products Limited may not have appropriate security for the loan required. There is also concern that a substantial interest rate increase will arise prior to the required funds being drawn down by Plastic Products Limited.

As an alternative the Board is considering a flotation of the company's shares on the Irish Enterprise Exchange. They are reluctant to adopt this latter course of action, however, as Plastic Products Limited uses income decreasing policies (relative to quoted companies in the plastics industry). It is feared that this would result in the company's shares being quoted at a discount.

Case 45

Stationery Products

Michelle Carr and Derry Cotter, University College Cork

Introduction

As his plane circled over Dublin Airport, Peter Crimpson was wondering whether the role of finance director should come with a health warning. It was the third week, and third company, in succession where he was being drafted in as deputy. This time it was in place of John Flood, finance director of Stationery Products, who had come down with a bout of pleurisy. His absence coincided with important decisions which the managing director (MD), Margaret Drumm, believed could not be delayed until his return.

A driver in the arrivals area flashed a card with his name and in no time at all Peter Crimpson was whisked to the company headquarters on the north of the city. There, the receptionist issued a security pass and accompanied him to Margaret Drumm's office, at the end of the corridor.

"Come in Peter", said the MD, looking decidedly relieved to see him.
"John is out sick, I understand."
"That's right. These things always seem to happen at the wrong time. Thanks for coming at such short notice."
"It's my pleasure. Maybe you'd like to fill me in on what's been happening."
"Well, we're at a bit of a crossroads really. On the one hand, Stationery Products is looking at expanding, by investing in a new product, which would be complementary to our existing customised stationery lines. But there's also the possibility that we might be taken over."
"I see. It's certainly a bad time for John to have fallen ill."
"And then, there are risk issues as well. We've started to source our materials from the US. They're competitive, and the quality is really good. But John was concerned about the currency risk."
"Finally, Peter, I'm personally concerned that many of our customary measures of divisional performance are regarded as having a short-term orientation. For

example profit, return on investment and residual income. There's a possibility that some managers may not be behaving ethically when making decisions that are impacting on their division's performance."

"I understand. I'll investigate divisional performance, and perhaps you would consider implementing a balanaced scorecard performance system."

"Yes, of course. John has been discussing the balanced scorecard for some time now, but I have my reservations, I'd appreciate your opinion."

"So you'd like me to report back on each of these issues."

"Yes, Peter, and we're under a bit of pressure as you can see. We're meeting with our potential suitor next week. We need to know what's going on."

"Well, I'll get straight on it then. Let's schedule a meeting for the end of the week."

"Perfect!"

Required

On the assumption that you are filling the role of Peter Crimpson, you are required to draft a report for your forthcoming meeting with Margaret Drumm. You should address the following issues.

Question 1

Proposed Capital Investment

(a) Calculate the weighted average cost of capital (WACC) of Stationery Products (see Appendix 1).

(12 marks)

(b) Recommend whether Stationery Products should proceed with its proposed investment in the new product (see Appendix 2).

(14 marks)

(c) Compute the project's payback period.

(3 marks)

(d) Calculate the project's post-tax accounting rate of return (ARR).

(3 marks)

Question 2

Takeover Bid

Using the information provided in Appendix 3, calculate a valuation range for the equity shares of Stationery Products. (Note: the valuation of Stationery Products should be computed without considering the capital investment project in Question 1. above.)

(12 marks)

Question 3

Risk

In respect of its most recent purchase of materials from a US supplier (see Appendix 4), outline what risk-management techniques are available to Stationery Products.

(6 marks)

Question 4

Divisional Performance

(a) Outline the benefits and limitations of retaining Stationery Products' current divisional structure (see Appendix 5).

(8 marks)

(b) Discuss the potential problems that may result as a consequence of using short-term measures of divisional performance, and offer some suggestions as to how they could be overcome.

(8 marks)

(c) Using the information provided in Appendix 5, evaluate the recent performance of each of the firm's three divisions using the following measures: return on capital employed, residual income and economic value added. Assume that Stationery Products' cost of capital for this exercise is 4%. For the purposes of calculating economic value added, assume that any value creating expenditures incurred by the firm will generate a return for a four-year period only.

(14 marks)

Question 5

Balanced Scorecard

(a) Explain the balanced scorecard and how it could be used by Stationery Products to measure performance.
(b) Provide illustrations of potential scorecard measures.
(c) Explain how the balanced scorecard links strategy formulation to financial outcomes.

(20 marks)

Total 100 marks

Appendix 1: Capital Structure

Stationery Products, which has an accounting year end of 31 July, has the following sources of long-term capital, and pays corporation tax at 12.5%, one year in arrears.

(i) Ordinary Shares

Stationery Products has one million issued equity shares of €1 each. Current market value is €4. The dividend yield is 5%, and the shares will be declared ex-div. one week from now. Dividends have increased by 10% per annum over the last five years.

Stationery Products also has reserves of €2 million, and a share premium account of €0.8 million.

(ii) Preference Shares

Stationery Products has two million issued 10% irredeemable preference shares of €1 each. Current market value is €1.50. The shares are currently trading ex-div., and a half-year's dividend will be paid in two weeks time.

(iii) Debentures

Stationery Products has €3 million of 8% redeemable debentures, whose current market value, ex-interest, is 107%. New debentures would be redeemable in three years at a premium of 6% on par value.

Appendix 2: Proposed Capital Investment

Stationery Products is currently (at 1 August 2XX6) considering an investment in a new product, which is similar to Stationery Products' existing customised stationery range. The investment is expected to involve the following costs and revenues.

(i) An immediate purchase of capital equipment costing €2 million would be required. This equipment is expected to have a residual value in four years of €200,000, and will be depreciated at 25% per annum on a straight-line basis. Capital allowances can be claimed at 15% per annum straight line.

(ii) Sales of the new product will be €2.5 million per annum for four years. Stationery Products earns a contribution of 50% on sales.

(iii) The new product would require that a new stores manager be recruited at a cost of €60,000 per annum. However, there is an 80% probability that a manager who is due to retire would be interested in taking up the position, at an annual salary of €40,000. If he retires, the company will have to make annual contributions of €15,000 to fund his pension.

(iv) The new product will require stock equal to one month's annual sales to be carried. Unit finished goods stock costs 30% of selling price. Stationery Products is currently considering the credit terms that will be offered to customers. Credit of 60 days is being considered, although an alternative of 2% 20 days, net 60 is also under examination. If a cash discount policy is implemented, it is expected that 40% of customers will avail of the discount. It is also expected that bad debts would fall from 2% to 1% of gross sales. Any working capital requirement should be assumed to arise at 1 August 2XX6.

(v) Annual interest costs of €50,000 will be incurred in financing the working capital requirements.
(vi) Annual fixed overheads relating to the new product are estimated at €100,000 and, in addition, there will be allocated annual fixed overheads of €40,000.
(vii) Research and development costs of €200,000 have been incurred, and a further €150,000 has been contracted for.

Appendix 3: Potential Takeover Bid

As Margaret Drumm has explained, there is speculation in the industry that Stationery Products will shortly become the target of a takeover bid. She is anxious to establish what value the shareholders of Stationery Products should put on their company, and has provided the following information:

(i) Income Statement

	€'000
Profit before tax for the year ended 31 July 2XX5	700
Taxation	(100)
Profit after taxation	600

Left-Right plc is in the same industry as Stationery Products. Its share price currently is €5. Left-Right plc has a dividend yield of 5% and a dividend cover ratio of two.

It is generally accepted that the acquisition of Stationery Products would allow the acquirer to significantly reduce its own research and development expenditure, with annual after-tax savings of €300,000.

Properties, currently used by Stationery Products' staff, could be let at a market rental of €100,000 per annum.

An acquiring company, through re-structuring, could achieve annual cost savings, pre-tax, of €200,000. This would involve once-off rationalisation costs of €800,000.

(ii) Balance Sheet

Stationery Products' net assets (total assets less amounts due within five years) in its balance sheet at 31 July 2XX5 amounted to €8.8 million. This includes unamortised goodwill of €1 million. Stationery Products has long-term borrowings (including preference share capital) of €5 million. The following additional information is available:
The net asset figure includes buildings of €600,000 which have a market value of €1 million.

- One of Stationery Products' principal customers defaulted in November 2XX5, after the July accounts had been finalised. The amount owing to Stationery Products at 31 July 2XX5 was €400,000. Inventory, included in the Balance Sheet at €300,000, was produced to the specific requirements of the now insolvent customer. This inventory cannot be sold to any other customer, and disposal costs will amount to €100,000.
- It was 80% probable, at 31 July 2XX5, that Stationery Products would succeed in litigation taken against a supplier. If successful, Stationery Products stood to receive a refund of €250,000. No record of this was made in Stationery Products' balance sheet at 31 July 2XX5. Subsequently, Stationery Products was successful, and the refund has since been received from the supplier.

Appendix 4: Foreign Exchange Risk

On 1 August 2XX6 Stationery Products purchased goods for $500,000, three months credit being received from the US supplier. Stationery Products has a bank overdraft of €1.2 million. It can borrow funds at 2% above base rate, and deposit funds at 2% below base rate.

Exchange Rates

Spot rate 1 August 2XX6   €1 = $1.1311 - $1.1354

Annual Base Interest Rates

€	$
6%	4%

Appendix 5: Divisional Performance

Stationery Products operates on a divisional basis. The company has three divisions; the customised stationery division, the office stationery division and a facilities management division. Each division operates as an investment centre. The following financial information is available.

	Customised Stationery	Office Stationery	Facilities Management
Sales revenue	€4,250,000	€5,625,000	€3,625,000
Direct material costs	€462,000	€490,000	€405,000
Indirect material costs	€112,000	€117,000	€75,000
Direct labour costs	€370,000	€407,000	€312,000
Indirect labour costs	€57,000	€60,000	€65,000
Variable production overhead	€172,000	€200,000	€162,000
Fixed production overhead	€145,000	€250,000	€125,000
Administration costs	€125,000	€95,000	€150,000
Insurance costs	€37,000	€47,000	€57,000
Utilities	€25,000	€32,000	€27,000
Service charge	€9,000	€9,000	€10,000
Capital employed	€7,500,000	€12,500,000	€12,500,000
Depreciation	€112,000	€125,000	€145,000
Professional fees	€225,000	0	€90,000
R&D	€1,250,000	€2,125,000	€500,000
General expenses	€550,000	€765,000	€337,000

Index

absorption costing 33–9, 57, 203–12, 219–23, 227, 231, 281–6
accounting profit 159–64
accounting rate of return 160, 161, 163, 239, 276, 285, 292
accounts receivable management *see* credit control
acquisitions 79–82, 135–7, 149–58, 159–64, 204–8, 228, 245–6, 283
activity-based costing 3–9, 20, 51–8, 59–66, 219–23, 225–33, 281–9
administration costs 8–9, 25, 54–6, 81
advertising 4, 8, 12, 19, 23, 25, 94
  see also marketing
AerThomond plc 273–9
agency 5–6, 7
ARR *see* accounting rate of return
assets
  non-current 29
  rate-sensitive 176–8
  valuations 80, 81
Autoparts SA 79–82

balanced scorecard 16, 18, 22, 51–8, 89–92, 291–6
bank debt 152
Beara Bay Cheese 3–9
benchmarking 36
Blackwater Hotel Group plc 147–8
Bolo's Food Company 197–202
Bolt Industries 243–9
bonds 167, 176, 180–81
bonuses *see* incentive schemes
branding 52, 69, 71, 172, 219–23
breakeven analysis 4–9, 17, 25, 35, 39, 49, 57, 199, 247
budgetary control systems 152, 243–5
budgeting 67–73, 75–8, 97–104, 203–12, 235–42, 243–9, 251–8
  cash budgets 115–20, 121–7, 239
  profit budgets 115–20, 121–7
business plans 3, 8, 23, 197, 200

Calvin plc 129–32
capacity 36, 129, 131
capital
  debt financed 29, 151–2, 153
  equity financed 29, 151–2, 153
  venture capital 197–202
capital allowances 147, 274, 281
capital asset pricing model 153, 155, 183–8, 230
capital investment 83–8, 90, 147, 167, 294–5
capital structure 129–32, 151–2, 153, 165–70, 273–9, 294
CAPM *see* capital asset pricing model
cash budgets 115–20, 121–7, 239
cash surplus 129–32, 160
cashflow 122–5, 237
  see also liquidity
cashflow projections 161, 244
Castlegrove Enterprises 33–9
Chicken Pieces 45–50
Choco Group 93–6
commercial paper 176
company valuation 133–8, 203–12, 225–33, 281–9, 291–6
compensation schemes 79–82
competition 60, 77, 227, 273
concession agreements 68–9
consolidation 135
contribution margin 5, 8, 15, 17, 36, 37, 39, 200, 203, 205, 282
The Corner Café 121–7
corporate bonds 180–81
corporation tax 140, 141
cost allocation 45–50, 227
  see also costings
cost drivers 20, 63, 66, 223, 232, 284
cost of capital 147–8, 149–58, 159–64, 165–70, 221, 251–8, 265–71, 273–9, 281–9, 291–6
cost of debt 29, 153, 167–8, 276
cost of equity 29, 153, 166, 167–8, 274–5

cost of sales 116, 117, 124–5
cost reduction 151
cost-volume-profit see CVP analysis
costings
   absorption 33–9, 57, 203–12, 219–23, 227, 231, 281–6
   activity-based 3–9, 20, 51–8, 59–66, 219–23, 225–33, 281–9
   joint 48
   kaizen 16, 18
   life-cycle 27–31, 41–3, 93–6
   marginal 203–12, 251–2
   process 48, 49
   standard 243–9, 251–2, 267–8
   target 41–3, 51–8, 225–33
   variable 33–9
costs
   administration 8–9, 25, 54–6, 81
   distribution 4, 8, 19–22, 29, 47, 199
   fixed 15, 17, 20, 21, 29, 36–9
   labour 5, 12, 14–15, 24, 37, 53–6, 61, 69–70, 116–17, 122–5, 221
   manufacturing 13, 29, 37, 39
   marketing 5, 12, 19, 29, 54–6, 94, 108, 109, 221
   materials 5, 12, 14–15, 37, 53–6, 61, 116, 117
   product development 12, 35–9
   quality 12–13, 14–17
   research and development 12, 28, 29
   variable 15, 17, 20, 21, 29, 36–9
credit control 85, 86, 108–9, 116–17, 237–8
credit risk 179–82
critical success factors 48
customer service 69
CVP analysis 3–9, 11–18, 19–22, 23–6, 27–31, 36–45–50, 197–202

Darling & Company 133–8
DCF *see* discounted cash flow
debentures 152, 238
debt 29, 117, 118, 151–2, 153, 167–8, 237, 276
decentralisation 265

decision making 3–9, 11–18, 19–22, 33–9, 45–50, 51–8, 59–66, 83–8, 213–17, 219–23
   finance decisions 149–58, 165–70
   investment decisions 193
   under uncertainty 67–73, 75–8, 243–9
defined benefit pension schemes 179–82, 183–8
defined contribution pension schemes 183–8
Delaney's Bakehouse Breads 219–23
depreciation 29, 70, 80, 154, 162, 238
design costs 28, 29
dilution 275
direct labour costs *see* labour costs
direct materials costs *see* materials costs
discounted cash flow 159–64, 166, 230
distribution 4, 8, 19–22, 29, 47, 199
diversification 34, 149–58
dividend policy 129–32, 152, 160, 203–12, 273–9, 282, 286
dividend valuation model 256
divisional performance 79–82, 89–92, 93–6, 97–104, 259–64, 265–71, 291–6
downward spiral effect 36
Drumview Limited 251–8
due diligence 230
DVM *see* dividend valuation model

EasyONline 23–6
e-business 19–22
economic value added 259–64
economies of scale 23, 60
efficiency 99, 267
Elveron Limited 97–104
enterprise resource planning systems 84–8
ERP systems *see* enterprise resource planning systems
equity 29, 151–2, 153, 166–8, 274–5
equity beta 134, 148, 153–4, 155, 162, 166, 168
EVA *see* economic value added

expansion 68, 139–45, 149–58, 159–64, 199, 204–8, 245–6, 281–9
  see also growth
exports 129, 160

factoring 237–8, 240
finance
  sources of 121–7, 165–70, 197–202, 273–9, 281–9
  through debt 29, 117, 118, 151–2, 153
  through equity 29, 151–2, 153
financial evaluation of strategies 107–13
financial planning, personal 189–93
financing decisions 149–58, 165–70
First Financial 175–8
First National 179–82
fixed costs 15, 17, 20, 21, 29, 36–9
flexible working 98
footfall 23, 70–71
forecast error 154, 156
foreign currency swaps 171–4
foreign direct investment 141
foreign exchange risk 139–45, 243–9, 251–8, 291–6

gearing 129–30, 237, 274, 276
  see also leverage ratios
Genting Theme Park 75–8
Glenview House Hotel 213–17
Good Eating Company plc 183–8
gross profit margin see profit margin
growth 71, 79, 97, 107, 110–13, 135, 149–58, 199, 281–9
  see also expansion

hedging strategies 246, 256
Horizons Group 51–8
hurdle rates 153–4, 155, 156

imports 47
incentive schemes 38, 79–82, 100, 101, 104, 244, 260, 266
income statements 33–9
information management 69–70
interest rate risk 175–8, 286

interest rate swaps 171–4
internal rate of return 136, 137, 142, 152–3, 156, 163
investment appraisal 27–31, 129–32, 133–8, 139–45, 147–8, 149–58, 159–64, 219–23, 235–42, 259–64, 273–9, 281–9, 291–6
IXL Limited 83–8

Jenson Car Components 225–33
JIT see just-in-time manufacturing
joint costing 48
just-in-time manufacturing 85–8, 131, 281–9

kaizen costing 16, 18
key performance indicators 48, 69
The Killyleagh Cycle Company 265–71

labour costs 5, 12, 14–15, 24, 37, 53–6, 61, 69–70, 116–17, 122–5, 221
labour standards 99, 101, 104
leasing 213–17, 273–9, 282–3
Lennon Department Store Limited 67–73
leverage ratios 166–7
  see also gearing
liabilities, rate-sensitive 176–8
life-cycle costing 27–31, 41–3, 96
liquidity 107–13, 115–20
  see also cashflow
loan stock 152
location 67–8, 69, 140

Malvern Limited 235–42
management buyouts 135, 136
management information systems 69–70
manufacturing costs 13, 29, 37, 39
marginal costing 203–12, 251–2
market risk premium 162
market share 13–14, 34, 227
marketing 4, 5, 12, 29, 54–6, 108, 109, 221
  see also advertising
materials costs 5, 12, 14–15, 37, 53–6, 61, 116, 117

Mega Meals Limited 171–4
mergers 149–58, 203
Mississippi Inc. 19–22
motivation 99
multidimensional performance
    measurement 273–9

net income 189–93
net present value 29–30, 142, 152,
    156, 161, 163, 172, 263
net worth 189–93
Newtown Manufacturing Limited 59–66
non-current assets 29
non-financial performance measures
    45–50, 259–64, 265–71

optimal pricing 23–6, 281–9
outsourcing 20–22
overheads 4–6, 8–9, 12–13, 14–15, 25,
    36–8, 54–6, 61, 81, 221, 227, 282
    see also costs

packaging 4, 6, 8, 12, 94
payback period evaluation 152, 247,
    285, 292
payroll costs *see* labour costs
Pension Protection Fund 185–6
pensions 179–82, 183–8
performance
    divisional 79–82, 89–92, 93–6,
        97–104, 259–64, 265–71, 291–6
    measurement 38, 75–8, 89–92,
        93–6, 97–104, 259–64,
        265–71, 273–9
    multidimensional 273–9
    non-financial 45–50, 259–64,
        265–71
    targets 59, 60
personal financial planning 189–93
Plastic Products 281–9
portfolio theory 193
The Pottery Company Limited 107–13,
    115–20
price/earnings ratios 151, 154
pricing strategies 23–6, 36, 76, 96, 125,
    225–7, 281–9

process costing 48, 49
product development 12, 27–31, 34–9
product life-cycles 27–31, 41–3
product mix 61, 68–72, 94, 198,
    200, 202
production management 36
profit budgets 115–20, 121–7
profit margin 69–70, 122, 225
profit opportunity rankings 142, 144
profitability 41–3, 61, 70–71, 77, 81,
    160, 161, 163, 226–7, 247
    see also CVP analysis
promotions 8, 34, 221

quality control 12–13, 14–17
quantitative easing 175, 177–8

Ravenhill Group Limited 259–64
regression analysis 13
remuneration 100, 101, 104, 108
replacement cycles 261–2, 263
research and development *see* product
    development
restructuring 98, 134
residual income 89–92, 94–5,
    259–64, 292
retained earnings 151, 153, 159,
    166, 167
return on capital employed 80, 81
return on investment 31, 60, 83–8,
    89–92, 94–5, 247, 259–64,
    265–6, 292
reverse takeovers 150
risk 67–73
    credit risk 179–82
    foreign exchange risk 139–45,
        243–9, 251–8, 291–6
    interest rate risk 175–8, 286
    and return 193
risk exposures 153–4, 155, 175–8
risk free rate 148, 162, 166, 181
risk management 171–4, 175–8,
    179–82
ROCE *see* return on capital employed
ROI *see* return on investment
ROR *see* accounting rate of return

sales monitoring 69–70
sales projections 36, 39
Salmon Spray 159–64
SAP systems 84–8
scenarios 244
sensitivity analysis 23–6, 77, 78, 147–8, 154–5, 159–64
share allocation 150–51
share option plans 206, 208
share prices 134–5
share repurchase 160
space allocation 70–71
Spektrik plc 41–3
standard costing 243–9, 251–2, 267–8
stock control 36, 83–8, 108, 116, 117
storage costs 3, 5
strategic management accounting 75–8
strategic planning 60, 70–72, 244
strategy evaluation 107–13, 135–8, 213–17, 225–33, 281–9
Stationery Products 291–6
Sun Shine Limited 139–45

takeover bids 135–6, 137, 291–2, 295
   see also acquisitions
Tannam plc 149–58
target costing 41–3, 51–8, 225–33

Terra Inc. 11–18
Toffer Group plc 203–12
Top Flite plc 89–92
transfer pricing 93–6, 140, 265–71
treasury bonds 176

uncertainty 67–73, 75–8, 243–9

value addition 48
variable costing 33–9
variable costs 15, 17, 20, 21, 29, 36–9
variance analysis 97–104, 251–8, 265–71
Varsity plc 27–31
VAT 69–70
venture capital 197–202

WACC *see* weighted average cost of capital
Waterlife plc 165–70
weighted average cost of capital 153, 155, 167, 168, 255, 256, 269, 276, 285, 292
working capital management 83, 107–13, 115–20, 121–7, 219–23, 235–42